Seventh
&
Central

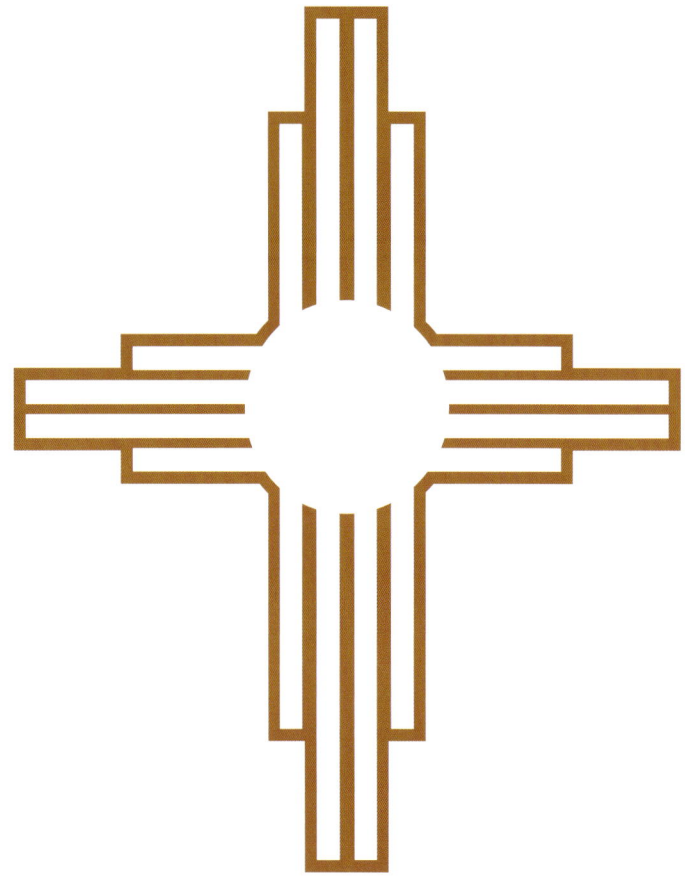

Nathaniel Tetsuro Paolinelli

University of New Mexico Press   Albuquerque

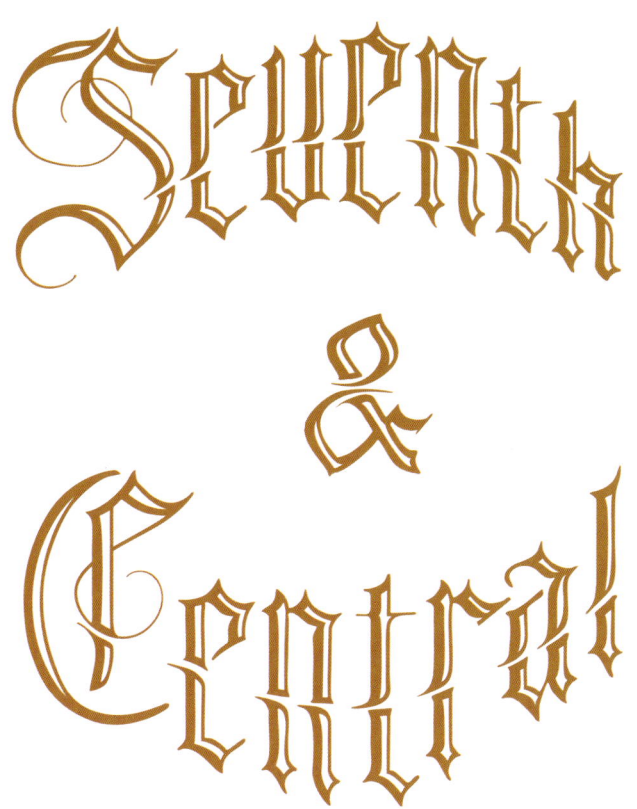

Seventh & Central

LOWRIDERS

© 2026 by Nathaniel Tetsuro Paolinelli
All rights reserved. Published 2026
Printed in China

ISBN 978-0-8263-6924-6 (paper)

Library of Congress Cataloging-in-Publication data is on file with the
Library of Congress.

Founded in 1889, the University of New Mexico sits on the traditional
homelands of the Pueblo of Sandia. The original peoples of New
Mexico—Pueblo, Navajo, and Apache—since time immemorial have deep
connections to the land and have made significant contributions to
the broader community statewide. We honor the land itself and those
who remain stewards of this land throughout the generations and also
acknowledge our committed relationship to Indigenous peoples. We
gratefully recognize our history.

Cover image by Nathaniel Tetsuro Paolinelli
Designed by Isaac Morris

Composed in Brokensript and Halyard.

Seventh
&
Central

Seventh and Central

Sundays are for cruising. If you find yourself in downtown Albuquerque on a Sunday afternoon, you're likely to see lowriders cruising down Central Avenue. It was here that my journey into this world began. In New Mexico, lowrider culture runs deep. It's more than just cars—it's a lifestyle, a community, and an art form. Each vehicle is an artistic expression of its owner, from the finely engraved chrome to the meticulously crafted paint jobs that rival any art gallery. These lowriders aren't just cars; they're vibrant, moving works of art like nothing else on the road.

For many, lowrider culture starts at birth. Newborns go cruising with their parents, growing up immersed in the scene. Though lowriders can be found all over the country and the world, they hold a special place in New Mexico's identity, where the culture dates back to the early days of lowriding. Family and tradition are cornerstones, with generations often cruising together. The generosity in this community is immense. When someone is in need, support flows in naturally, a kindness I rarely see outside of this world. Traditions and customs are passed down, just like the cars themselves, from one generation to the next.

I'm from Albuquerque, and although I didn't grow up in this community, I've been welcomed into its heart. Without this kindness, the photographs I've made wouldn't have been possible. I've always been something of a street photographer, and downtown Albuquerque is where I spend the most time. As I wandered with my camera, I noticed that Sundays brought lowriders out in droves. In 2018 I set out specifically to photograph lowriders. I didn't know anyone in the community at that point, but I soon recognized a familiar face: Steven "Sparky" Gomez. We'd met years earlier at a gas station, and now here he was on Seventh and Central with a vintage trailer turned hot-dog truck. I stopped, had a Sancho Dog, and struck up a conversation with him. He made me feel welcome, and I later brought him a print as a thank you. I visited a few more times after that, though not as often as I'd have liked.

In 2021, Sparky passed away, just as the world was beginning to emerge from the pandemic. It was around that time I dedicated myself more fully to photography. From that point on, I started building connections, making friends, and taking photographs with true intention. The intersection at Seventh Street and Central Avenue became a key spot for me to document lowrider culture. At times the entire intersection would fill with cars and people, creating a thrilling atmosphere that felt like the heart of the community. Over time, changes to the area led the lowriders to move on. But that's the nature of this culture—they've cruised many parts of this town, and when one gathering spot ends, another one opens up. Ultimately it's not about the location; it's about the people and the community that bring it to life.

Initially my focus was on capturing interesting scenes as a photographer. But as I spent more time in this world, I found myself drawn into the culture and history behind the cars, and my relationships with the people I was photographing grew. I realized that this was no longer just about my personal project; it was about documenting a culture that makes New Mexico unique and extraordinary. I've spent quiet moments with Flaco, who taught me the proper way to iron a crease into a pair of pants, and I've even ended up in a music video. From birthday parties to funerals and club initiations, I've been invited into the lives of so many people, and it's all of them who made this book possible.

I feel truly welcomed by this community; they've let me be present in every way with my camera. When I'm making these photographs, I'm not out there on assignment or working on a project. I'm simply spending time with friends, capturing moments and memories, because that's what brings me the most joy in life.

(*following pages*) Steven "Sparky" Gomez, Seventh Street and Central Avenvue, Downtown Albuquerque, 2018.

Portrait of Jose's Daughter, Albuquerque, 2023.

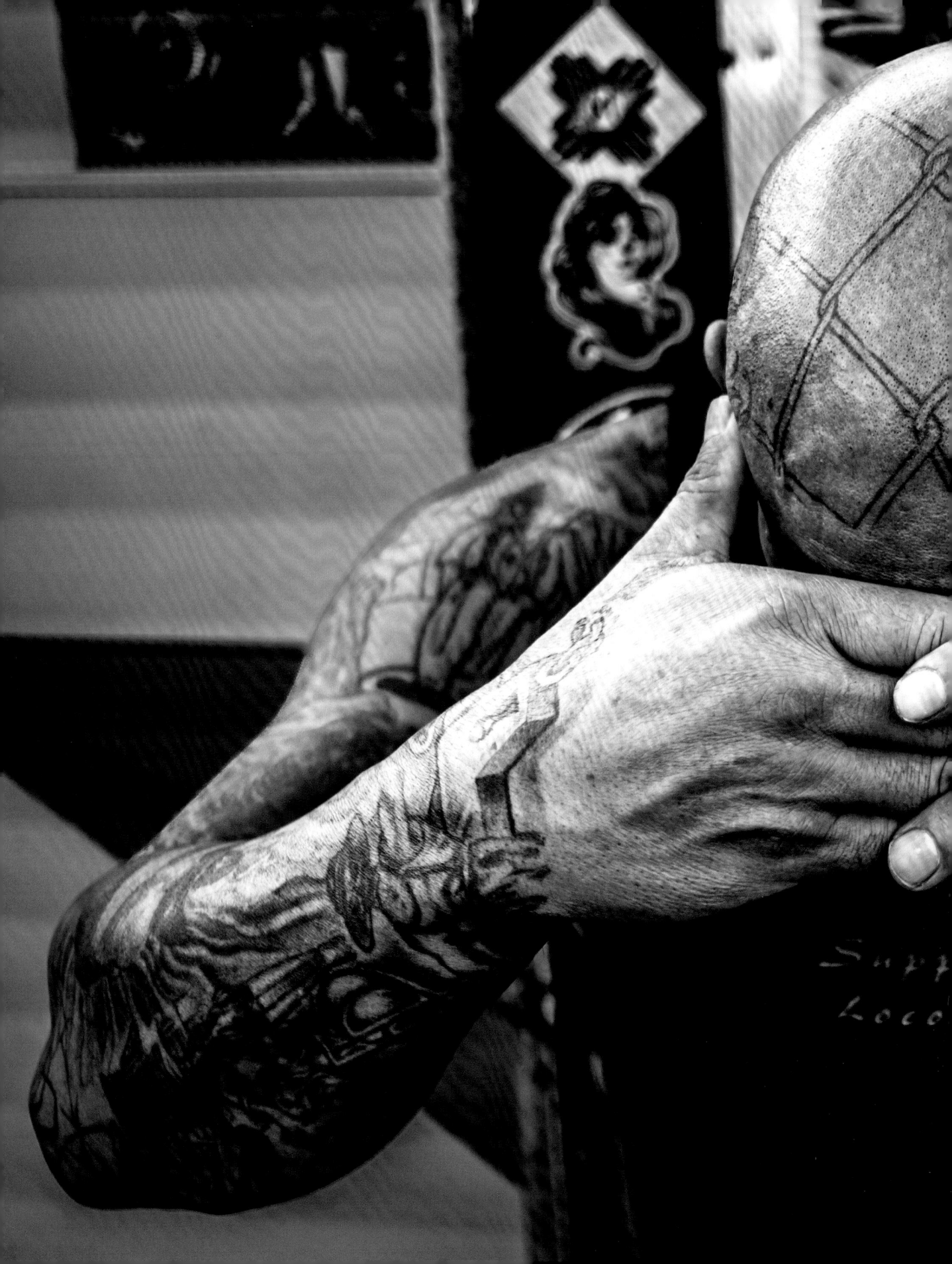

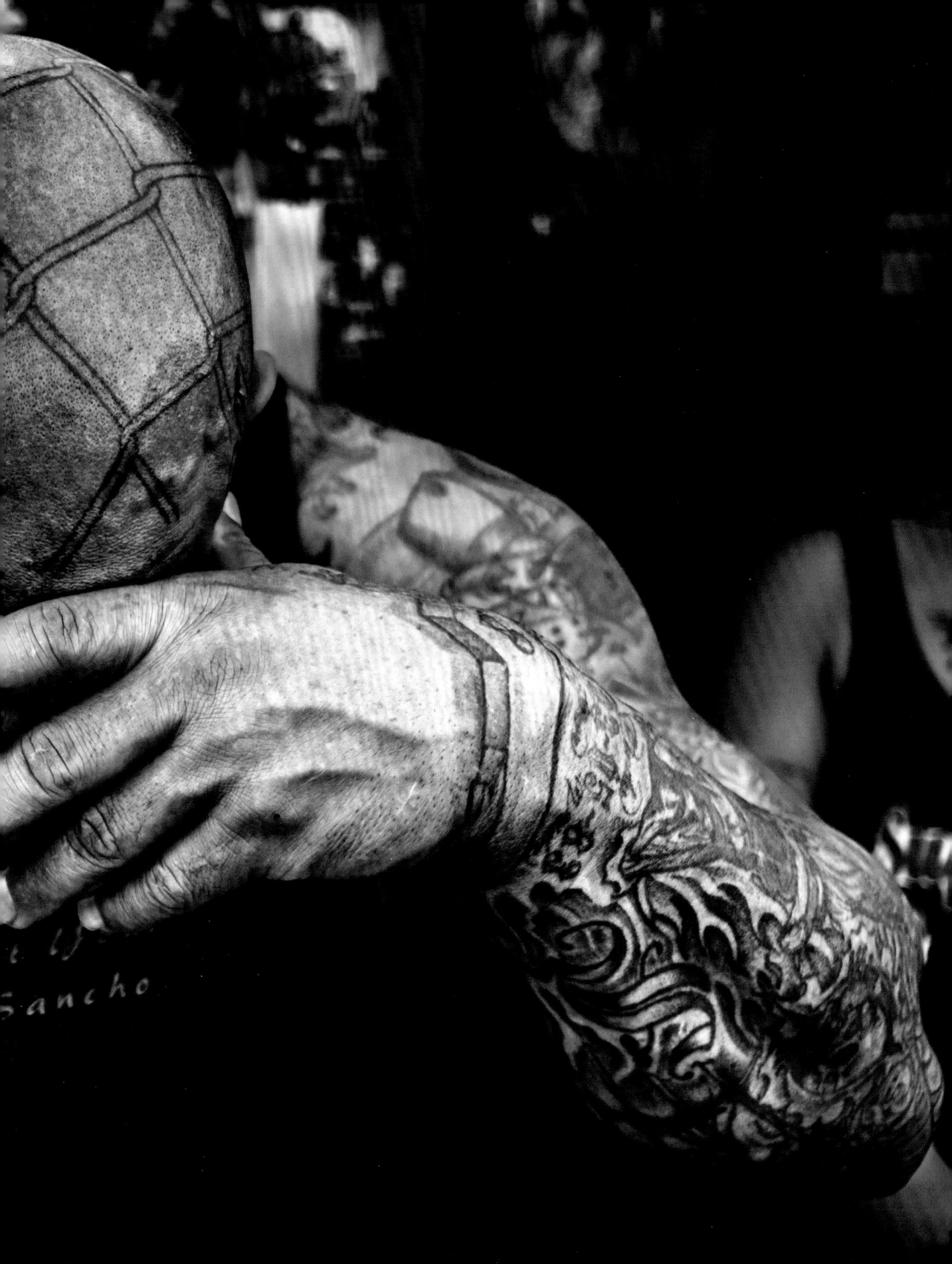

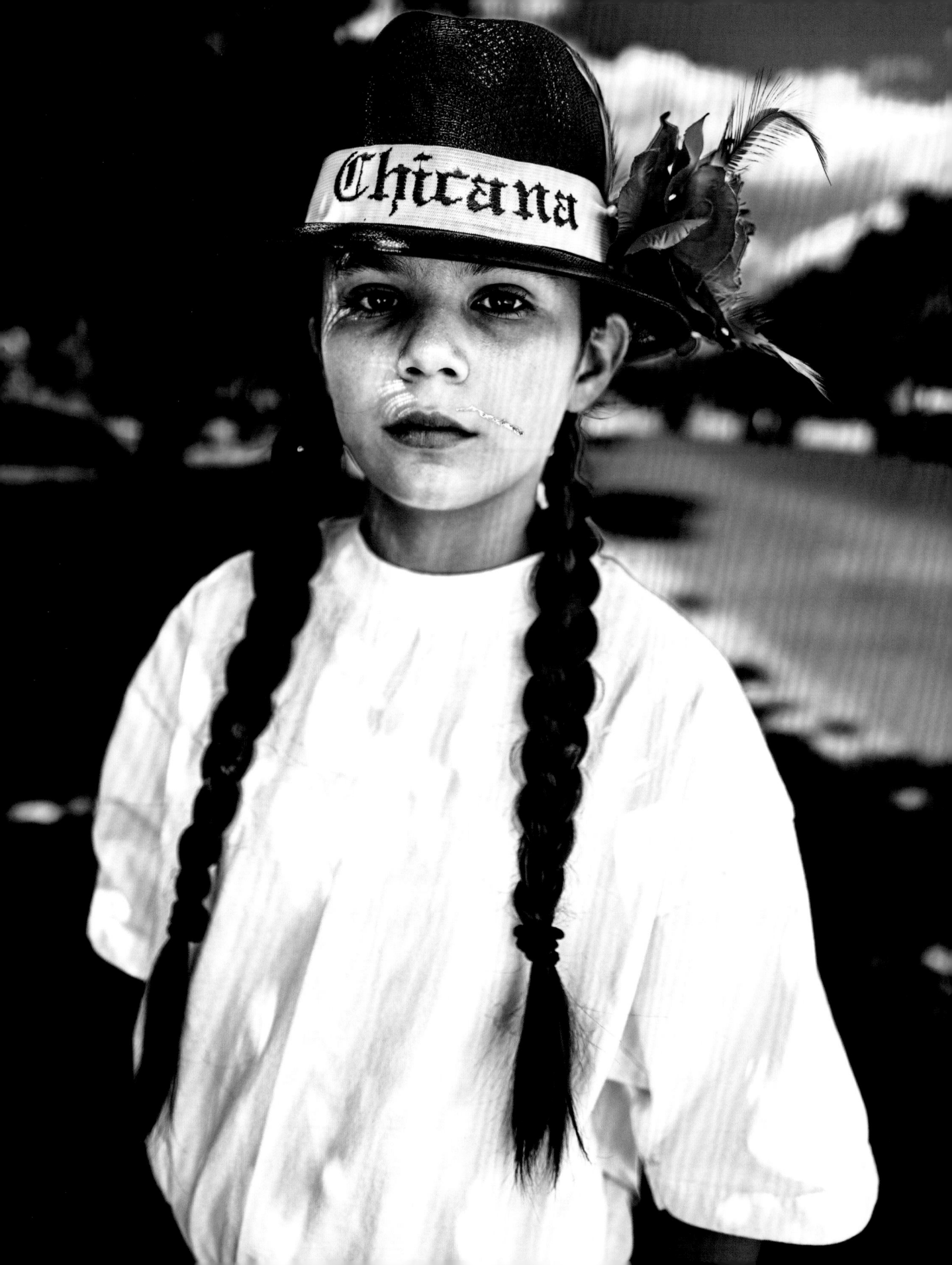

Pride/Orgullo

Manuel González

On the corner of 7th and Central in the heart of Alburquerque BURQUE!
Pride
Orgullo
Who we are
Where we're from
What we represent
Chicano
Nuevo Mexicano
Low and slow
Slammed to the ground
Down and brown
Close to the *tierra*
Cultura
Familia
Compadres and *comadres*
Sunday afternoon car shows
Where some of us found our indigenous roots
In an airbrushed Aztec princess
On the hood of an Impala
Lowriding
Cruising down Central
Burque
Gente
It's more than cars
More than a lifestyle
It's an attitude
How we flash our magic in the gold flake
Meant to
Catch your eye
Old school pachucos
Cholos creased and sharp
Chicanas who hold it down and carry
Our ancestors in her arms

In *Burque*
We know what it means to have

Style
We're brought up knowing how to show
Respect
Veteranos in *Bombas*
Cholas with their locs on
Chicas
Fine *mamacitas*
Chingonas
Fashionistas with *barrio* pride
Modern-day warriors
Carrying the weight of our history
In a tattoo teardrop
Or on gold spoke rims

The arte we sketch onto panos
Onto our skin
Onto our souls
For our grandchildren to
Discover and celebrate
Traditions con respeto
In the Duke City
Burque
Albuquerque
to those from somewhere else
Who don't know about
El corazón de nuevo méxico
Panzas full of *pozole*
Cruising central on the west side
Happy Homes
Bringing out the whole *familia*
Todos los mocosos!
Having good times
In the name of lowriding
We hop past *politicos* in Santa Fe
On our holy pilgrimage to pick up
Holy sand

From Chimayo

So we can have Guadalupe's blessings

On our cruise

Through the heart of

Aztlan

Looking for *Tonantzin*

In the eyes of a *morenita*

With her fist in the air

Or a spray-painted

Aztec eagle

That echoes with ancestral vibrations

Striking a chord

In our heartstrings

Sounding like *rancheras*

Sung by a Hurricane

At a lowrider wedding

Or a funeral procession

Or the first time we took that trip to Taos

For no other reason

But the ride

Going through Jemez on the way back down

This is how we express who we are with

steel chrome and

carnales

When we're at our best

Clean and polished

Low and slow

Slammed to the ground

Making memories that define us

Remind us

When to give respect

And how to show pride

Orgullo

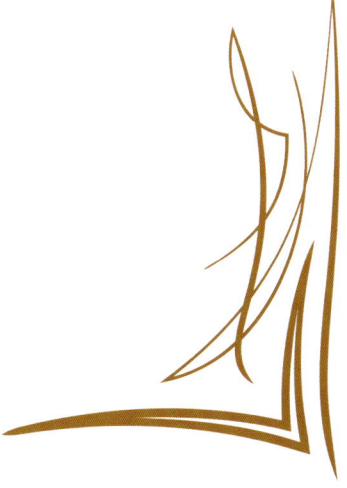

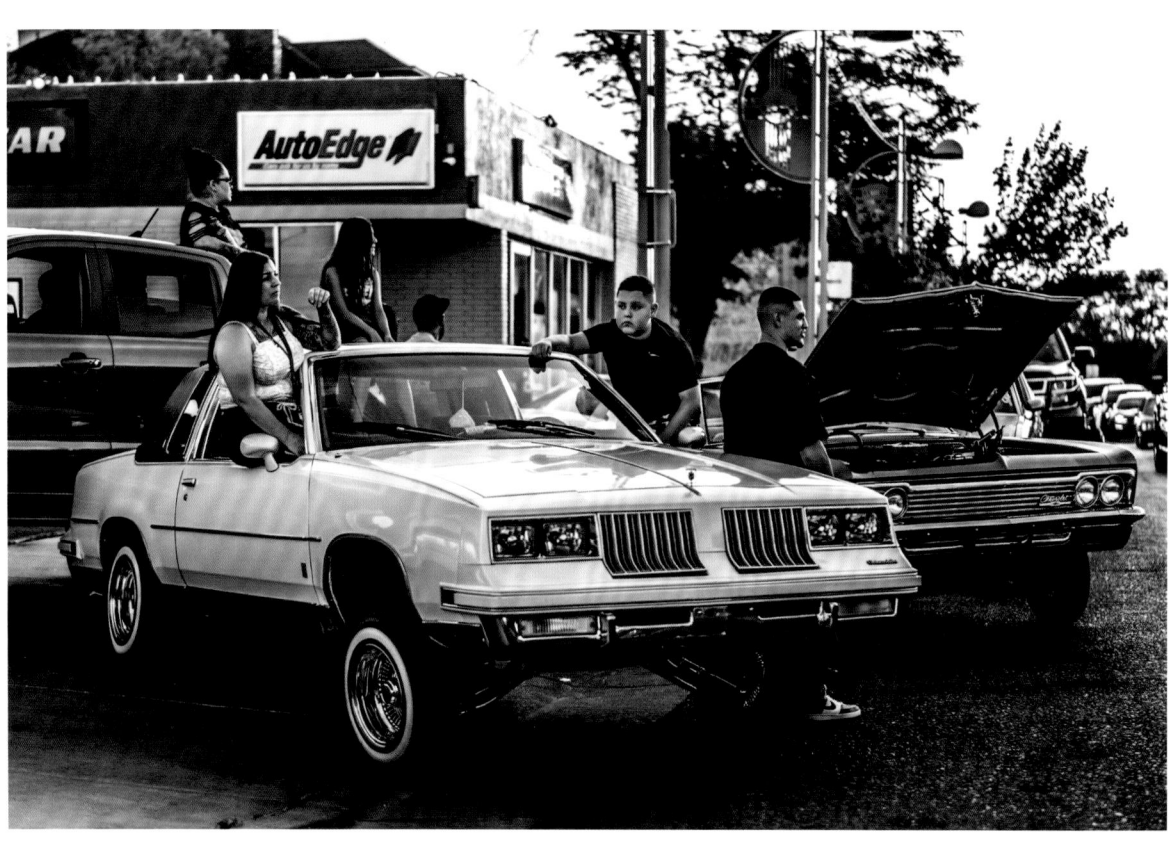

Tiana Martinez, her son Si, and Joel Leon, Seventh Street and Central Avenue, Downtown Albuquerque, 2022.

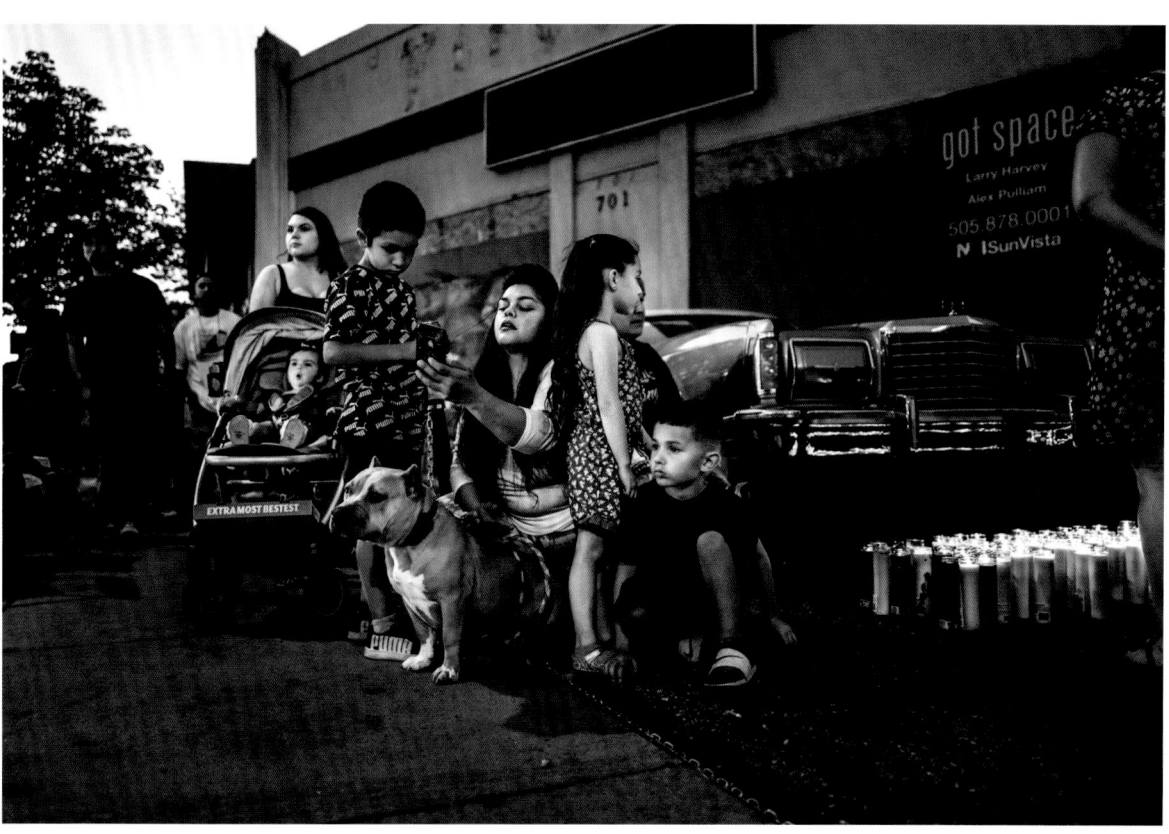

A family at a memorial for Stephen "Sparky" Gomez, Downtown Albuquerque, 2021.

(*following pages*) Fernando Ortega hops his lowrider, Downtown Albuquerque, 2024.

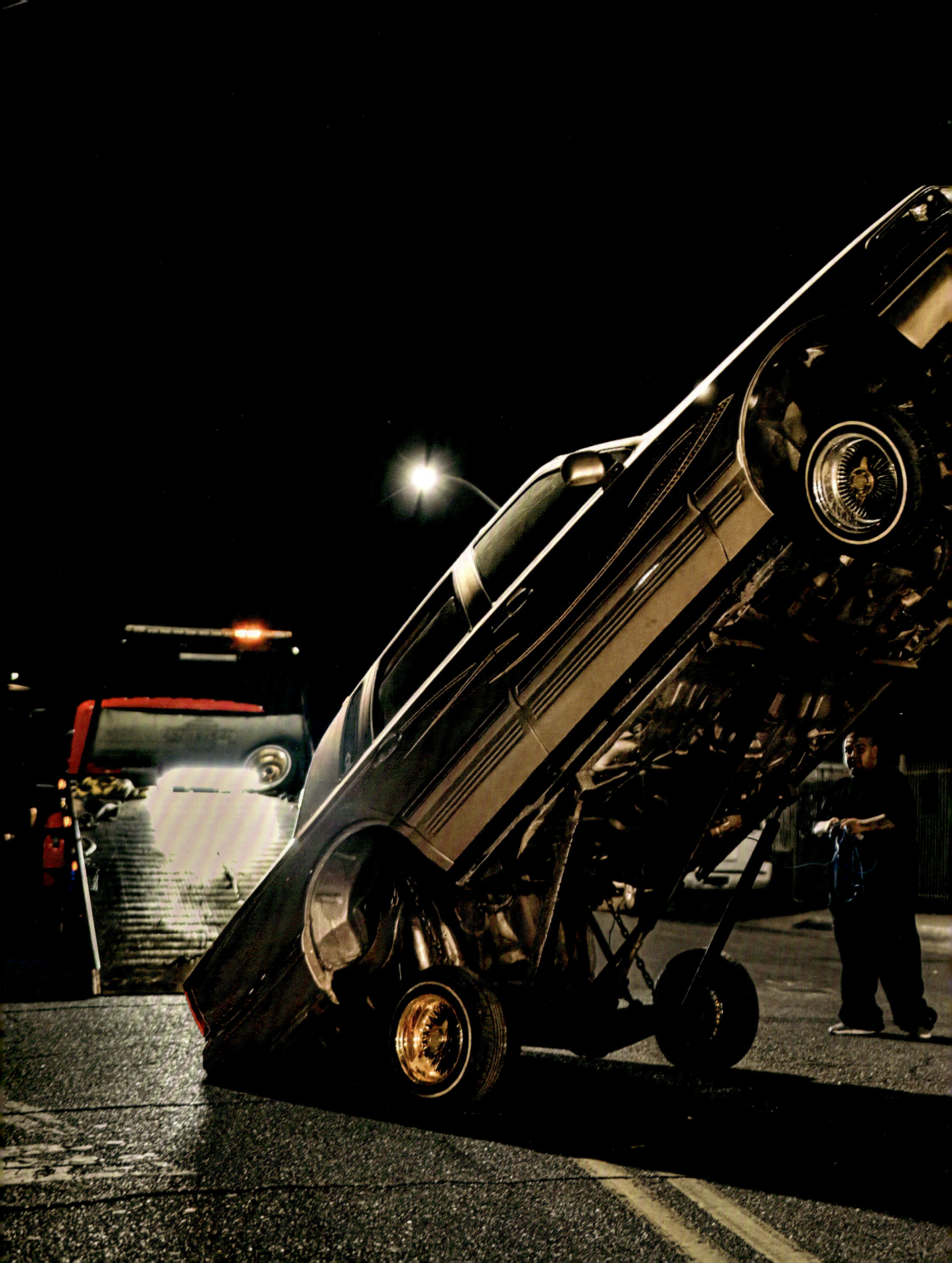

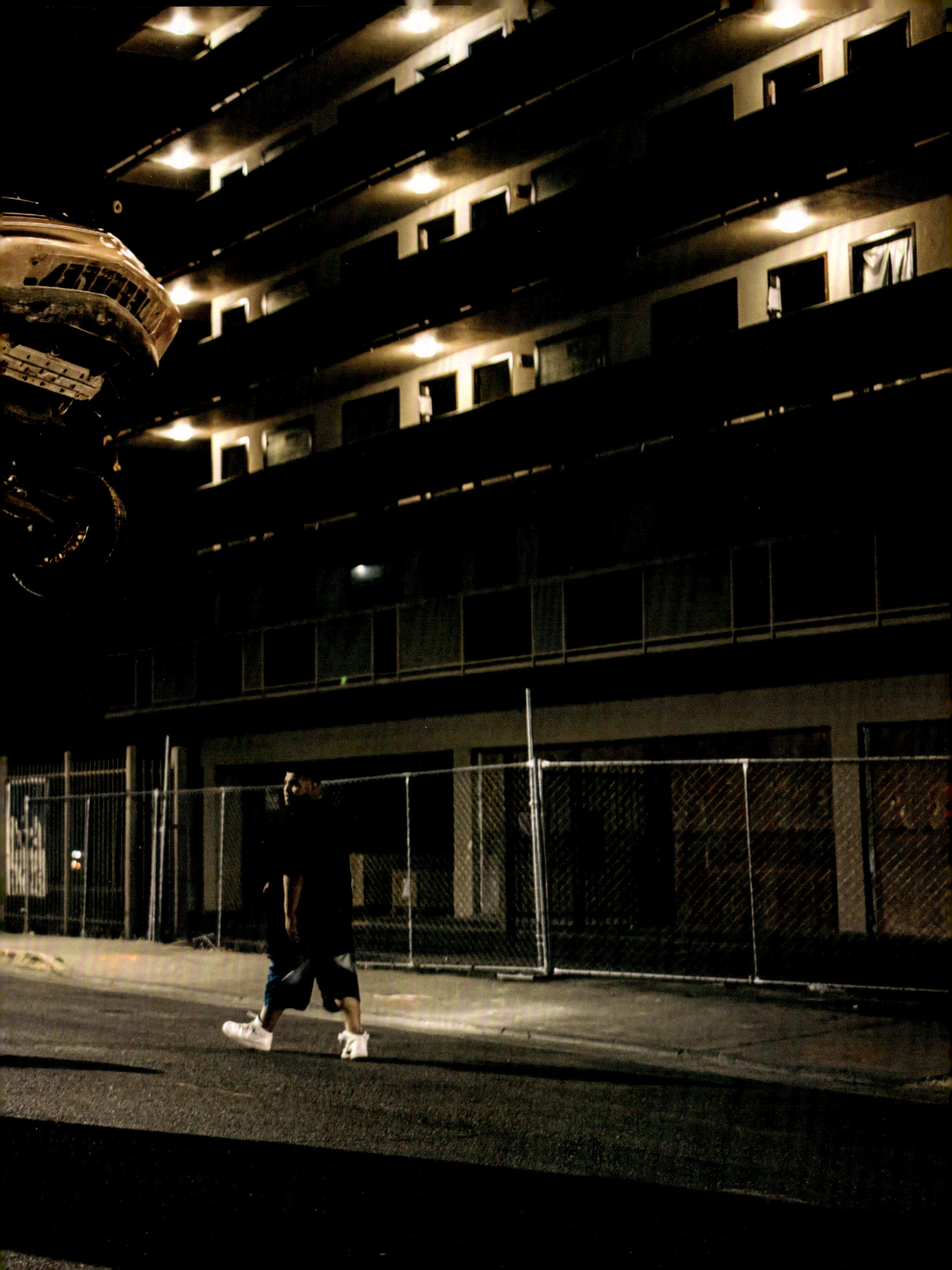

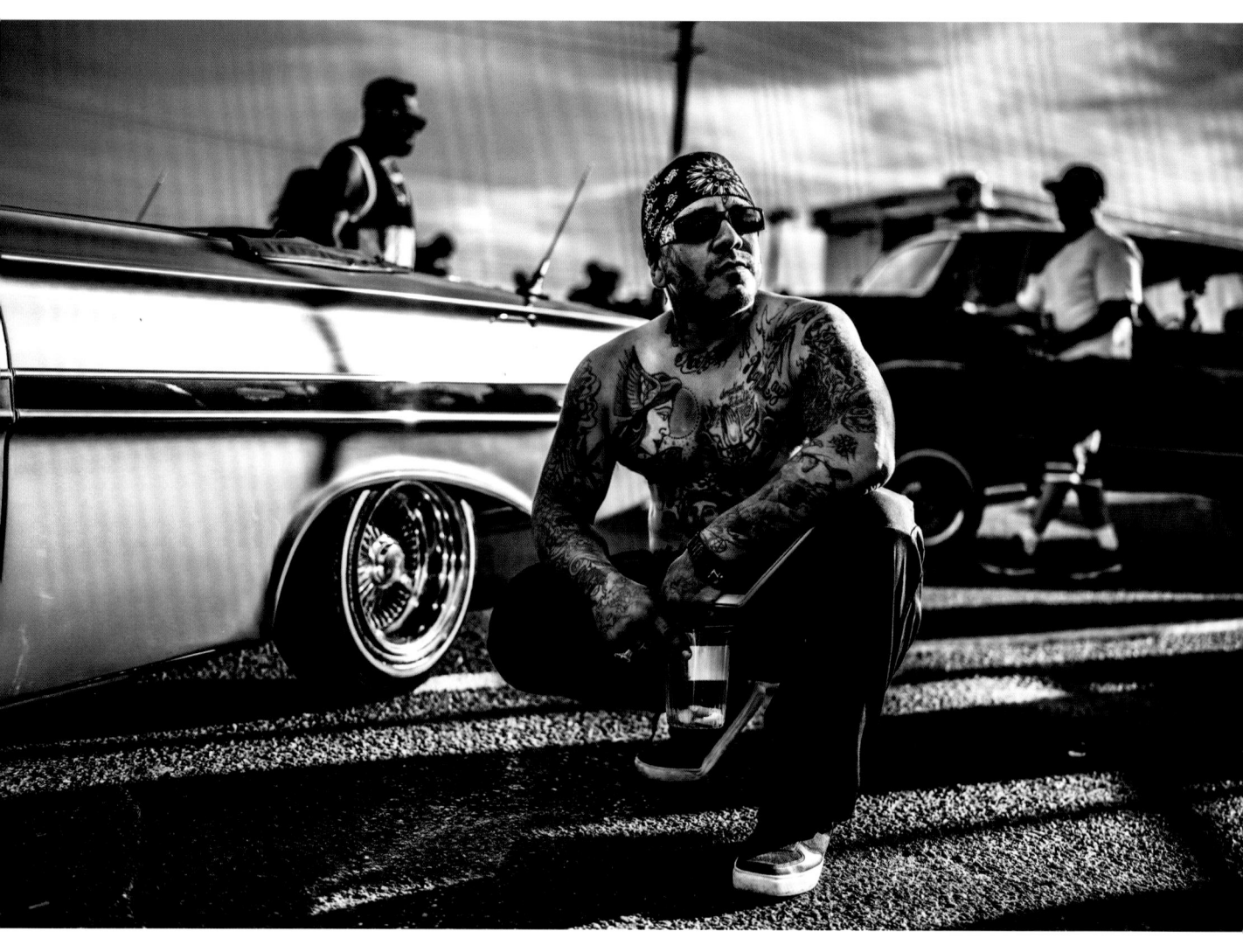

Second Annual Duke Day, Albuquerque, 2022.

(*opposite page*) Angelo, Barelas, Albuquerque, 2023.

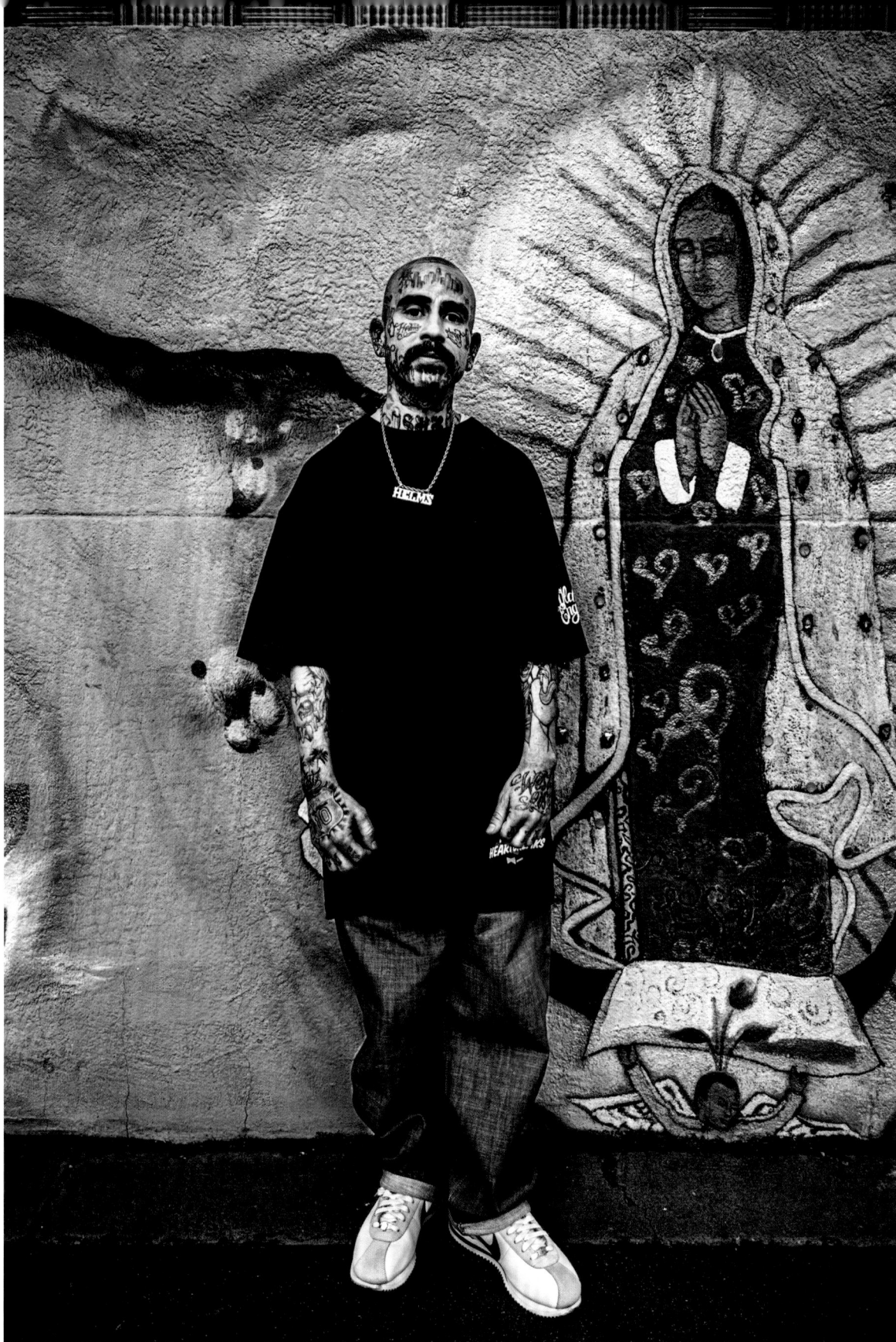

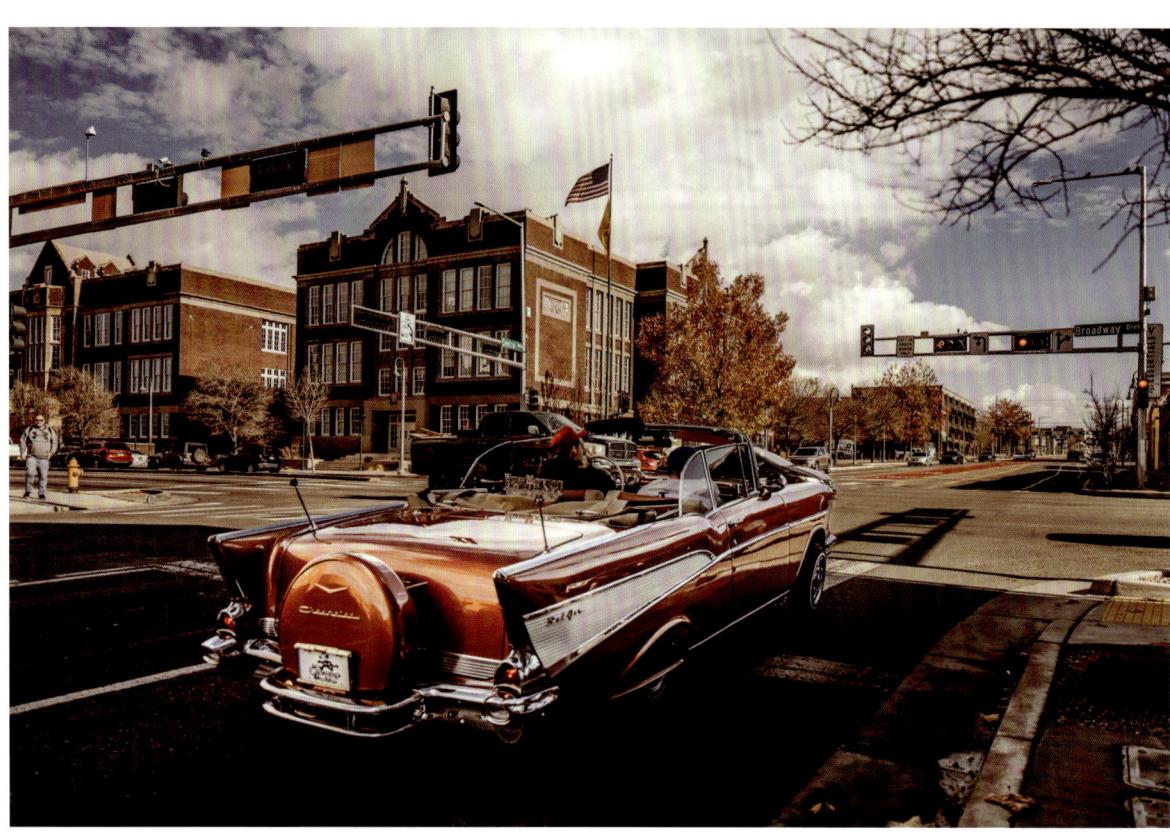

Marcos Jacquez with his Chevrolet Belair, Albuquerque, 2022.

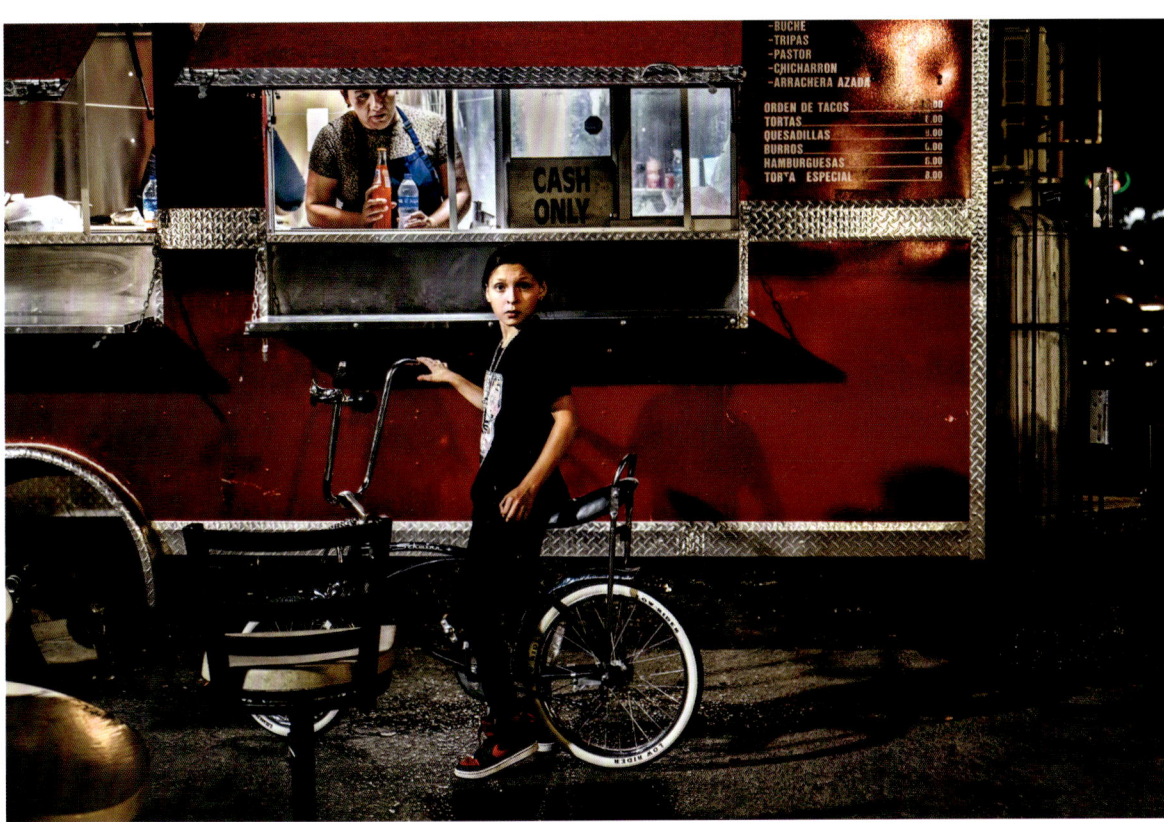

Waiting for tacos, Barelas, Albuquerque, 2023.

(*following pages*) Portrait of Matthew "Goof" Cordova with his six-day-old daughter, Ava, Albuquerque, July 10, 2022.

Portrait of Matthew "Goof" Cordova with his daughter, Ava, Albuquerque, June 4, 2023.

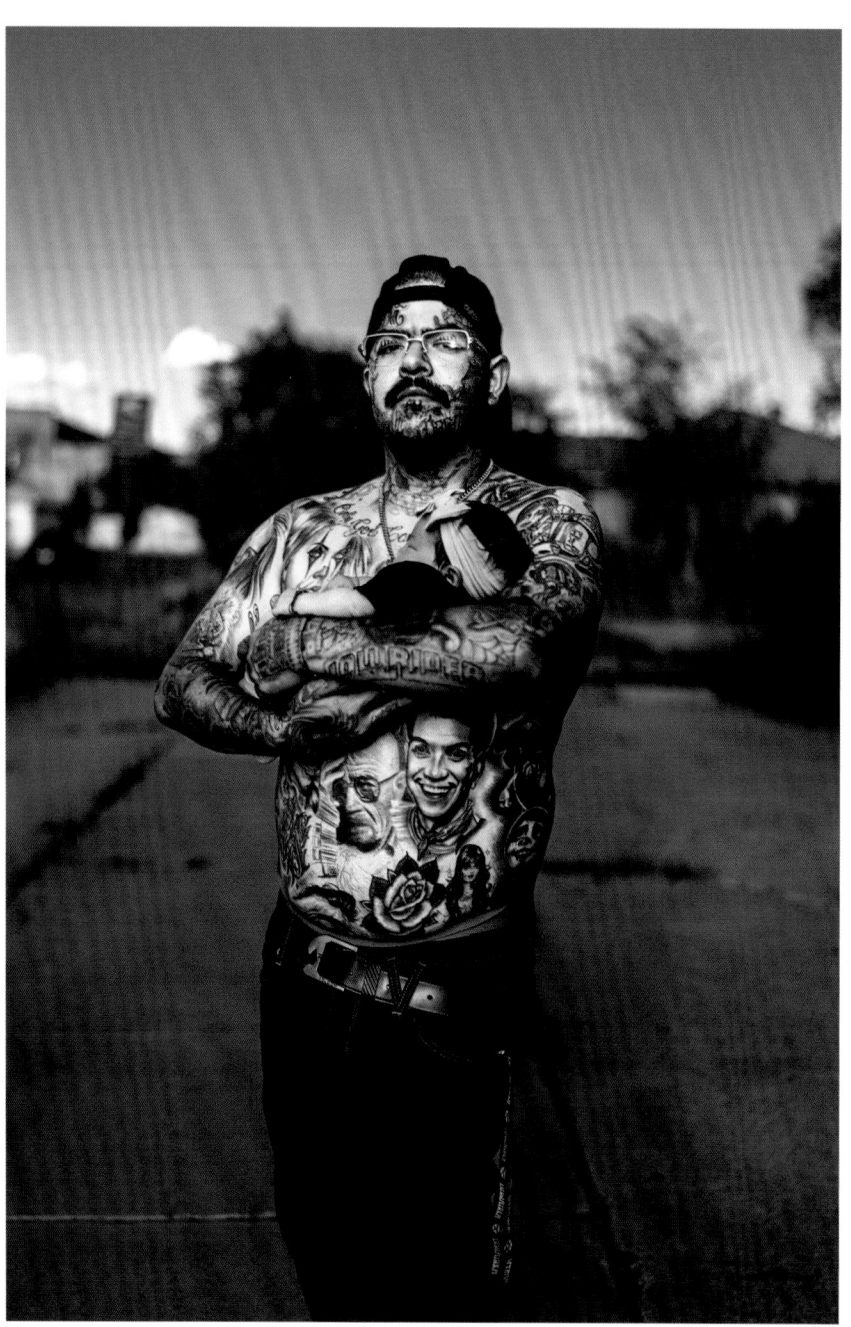

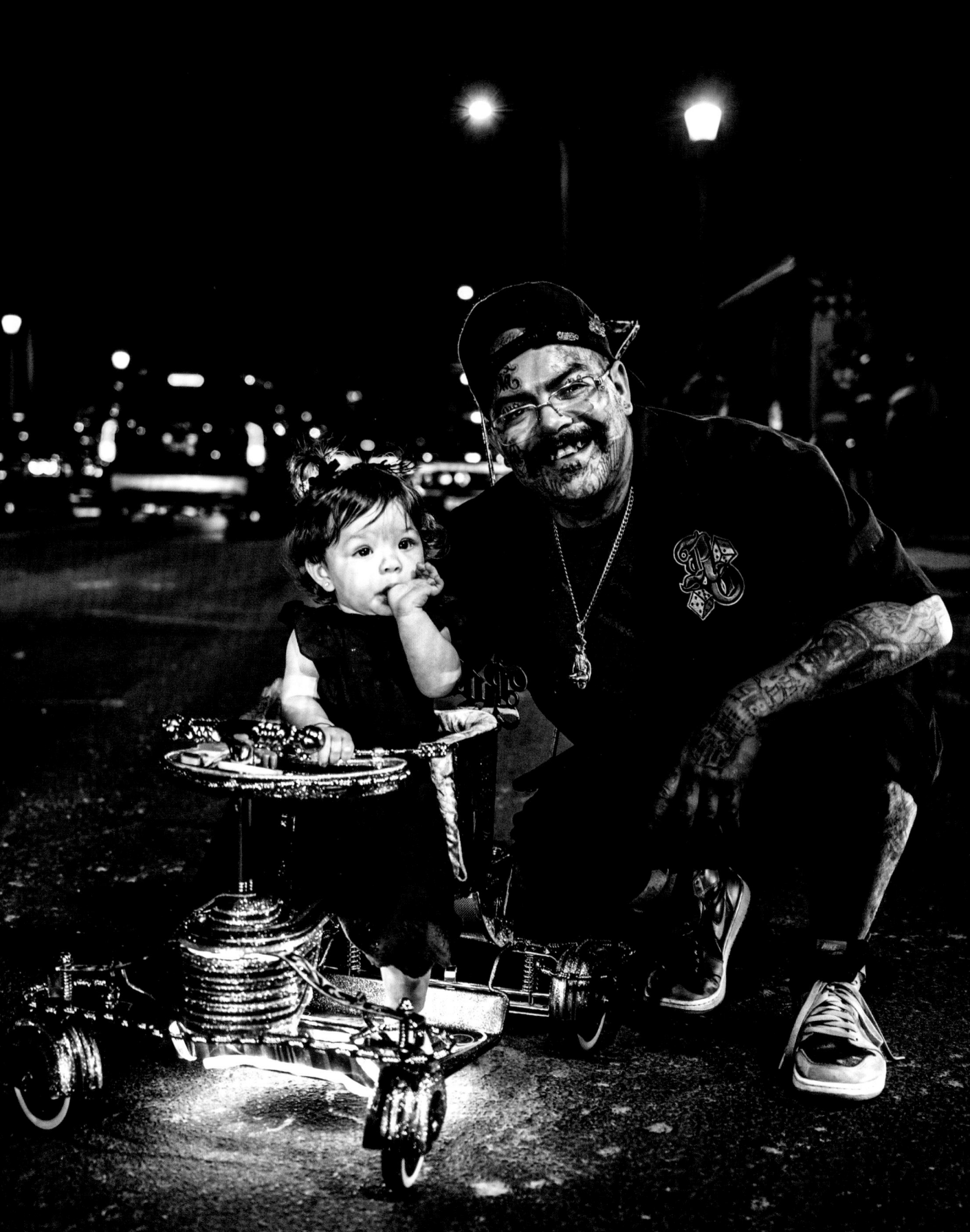

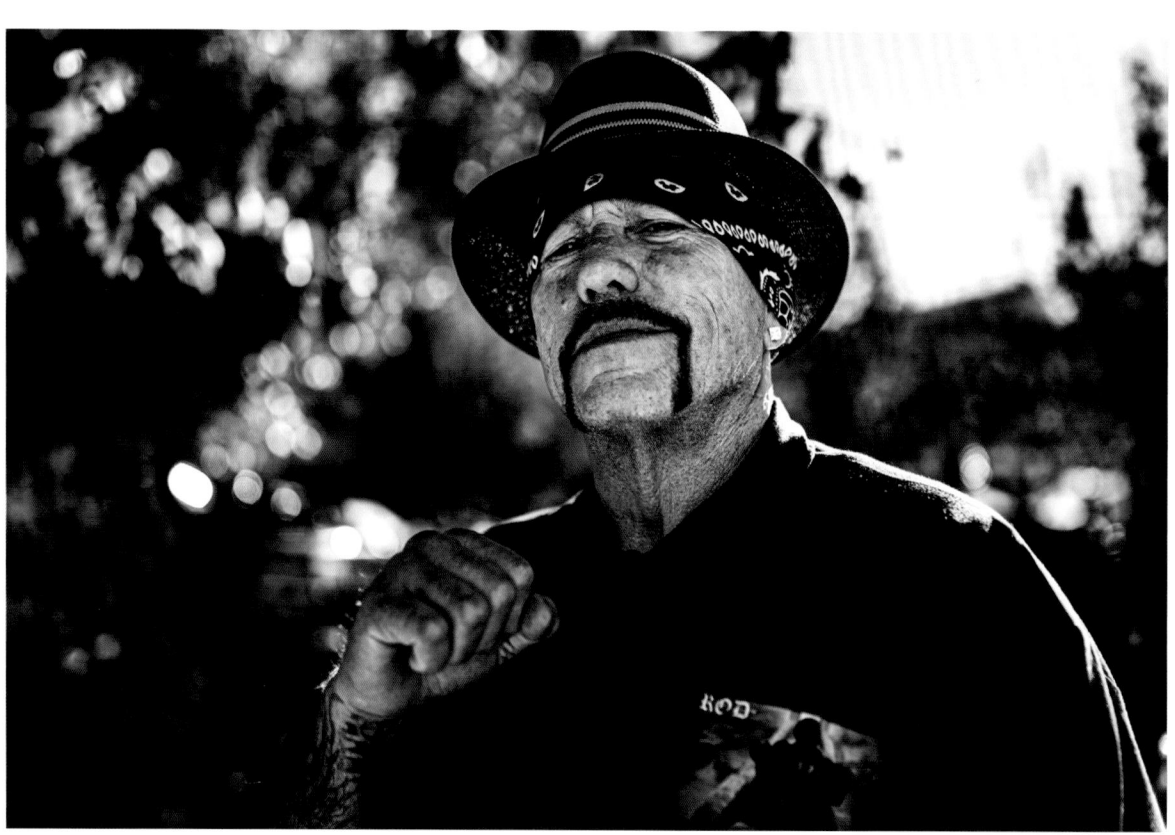

Downtown Albuquerque, 2023.

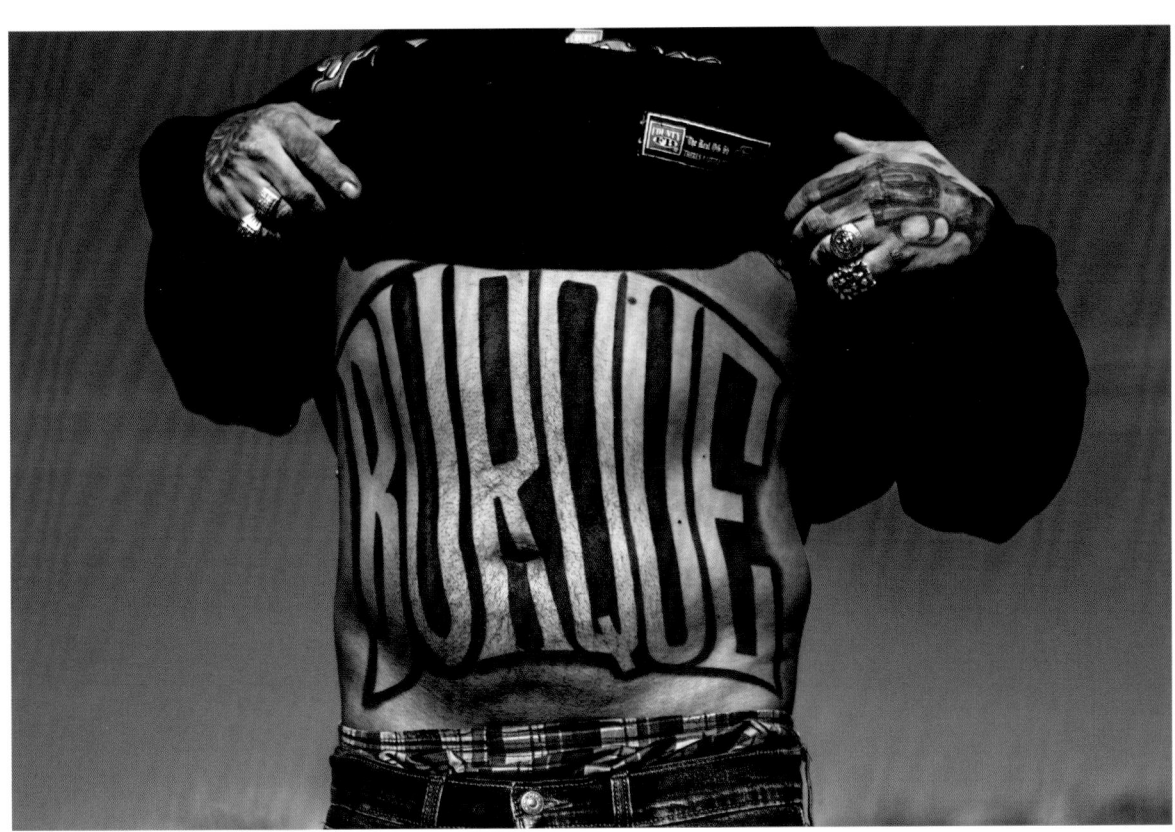

Burque tattoo, Albuquerque, 2024.

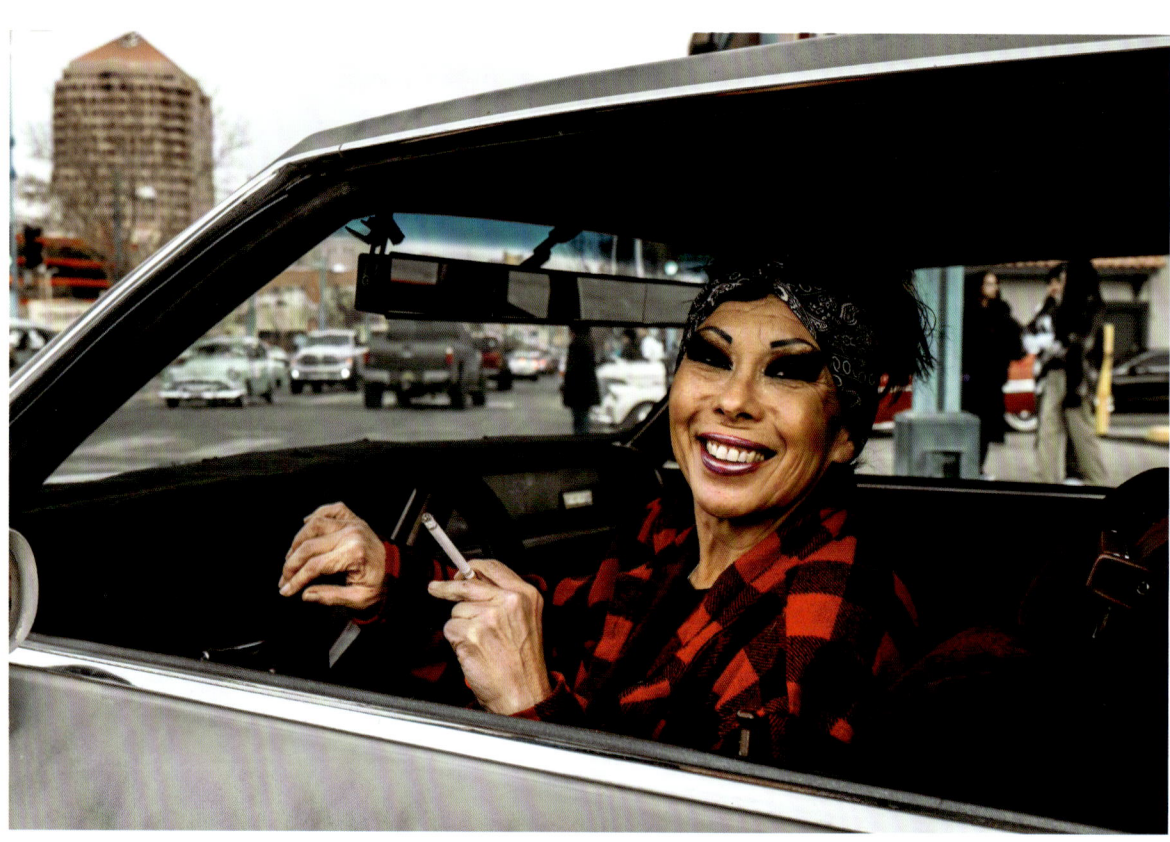

Cruising Central Avenue, Downtown Albuquerque, 2023.

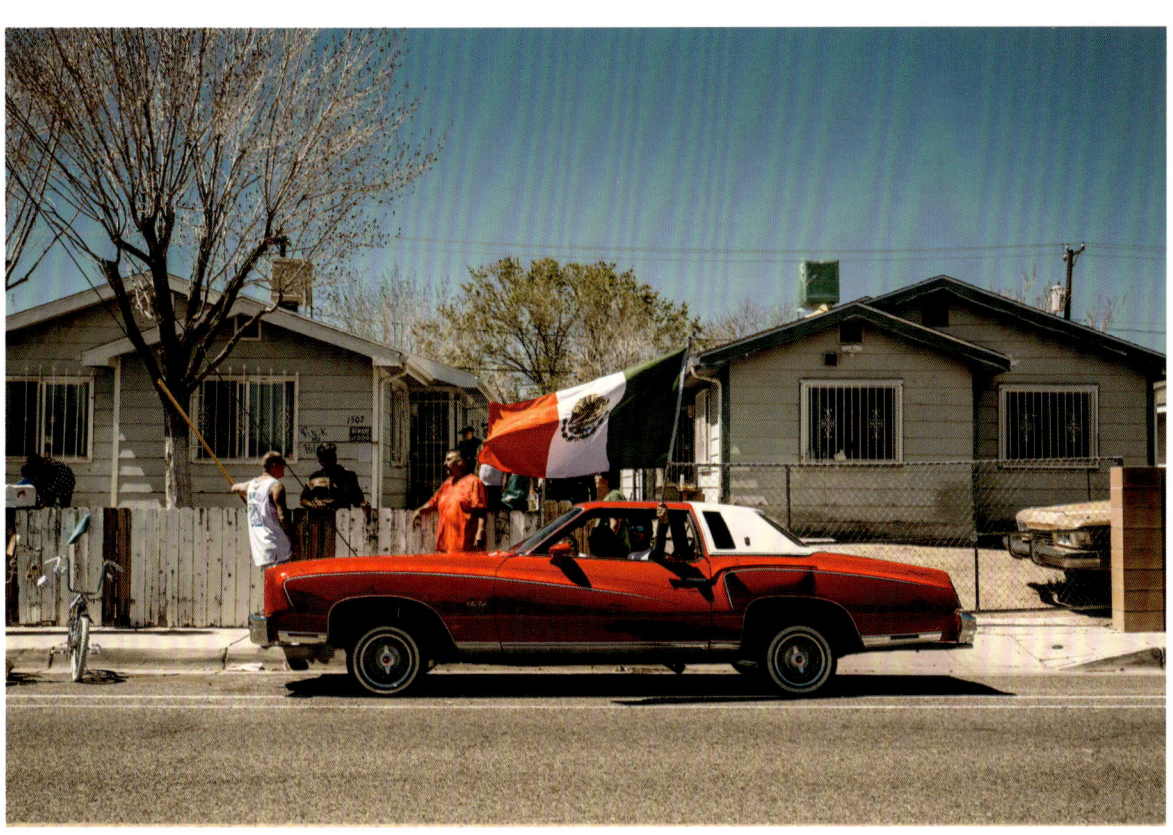

Uriel Vasquez and his Chevrolet Monte Carlo in front of Flaco's house, Barelas, Albuquerque, 2023.

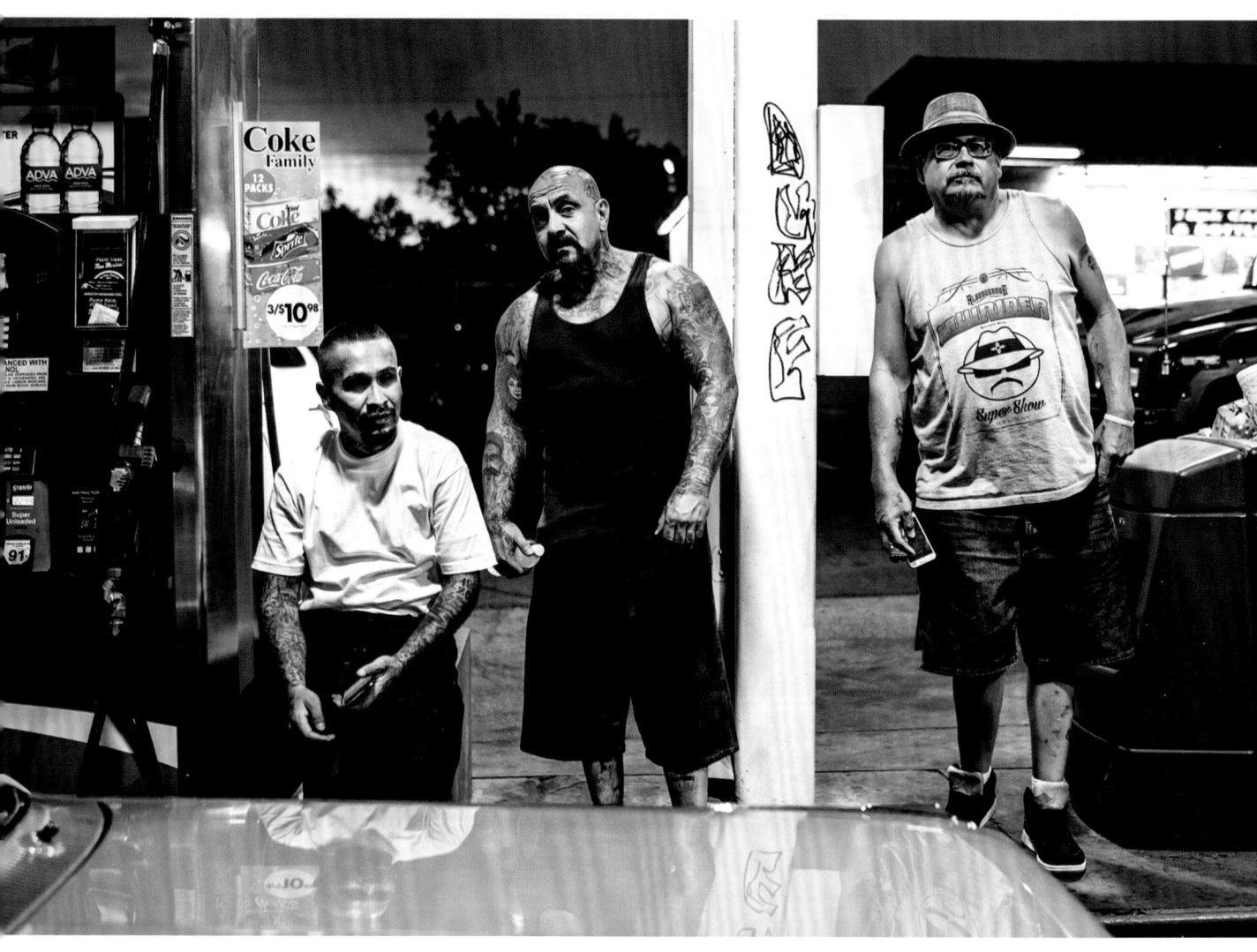

Sparky and friends at 7-Eleven, Albuquerque, 2016.

(*opposite page*) Pet snake, Downtown Albuquerque, 2023.

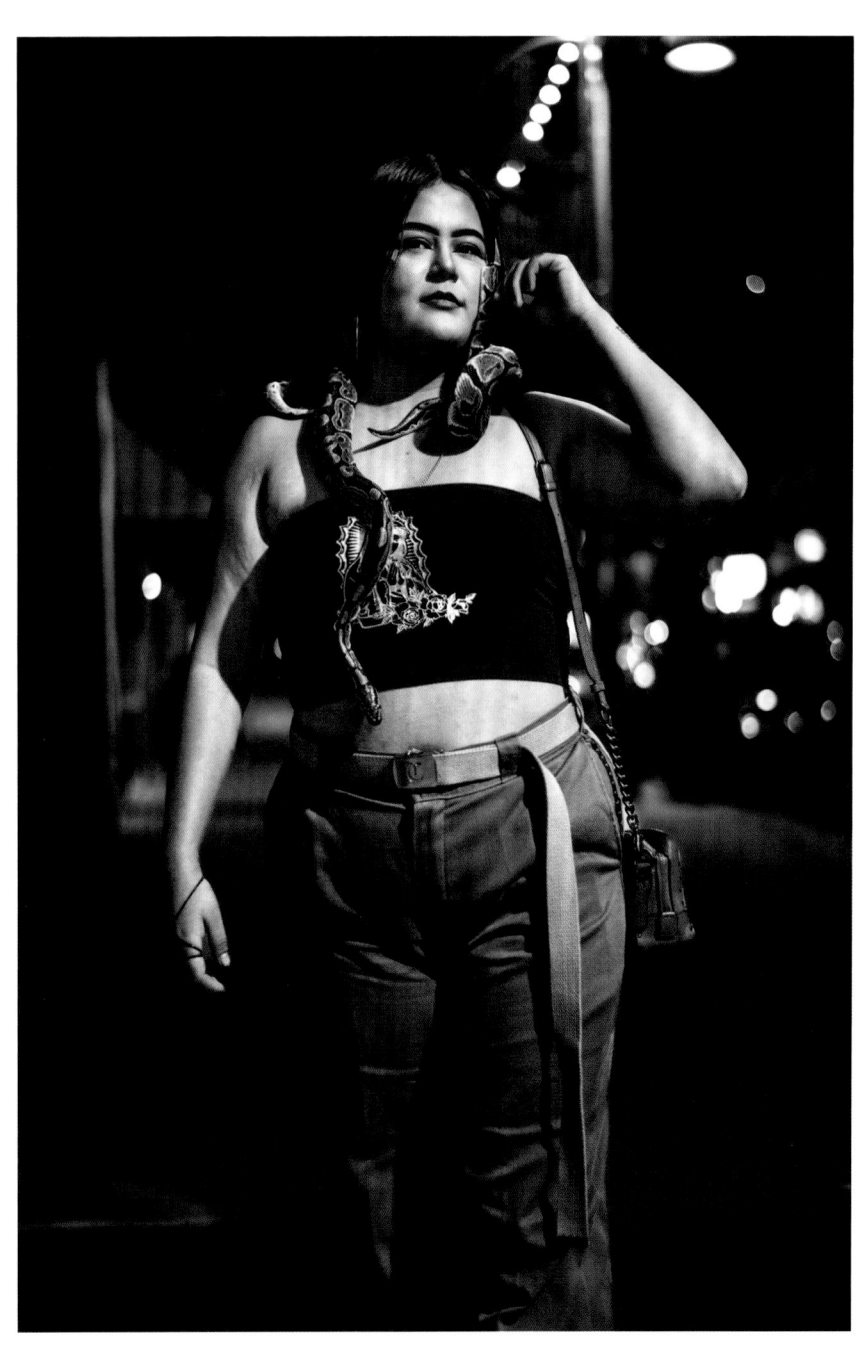

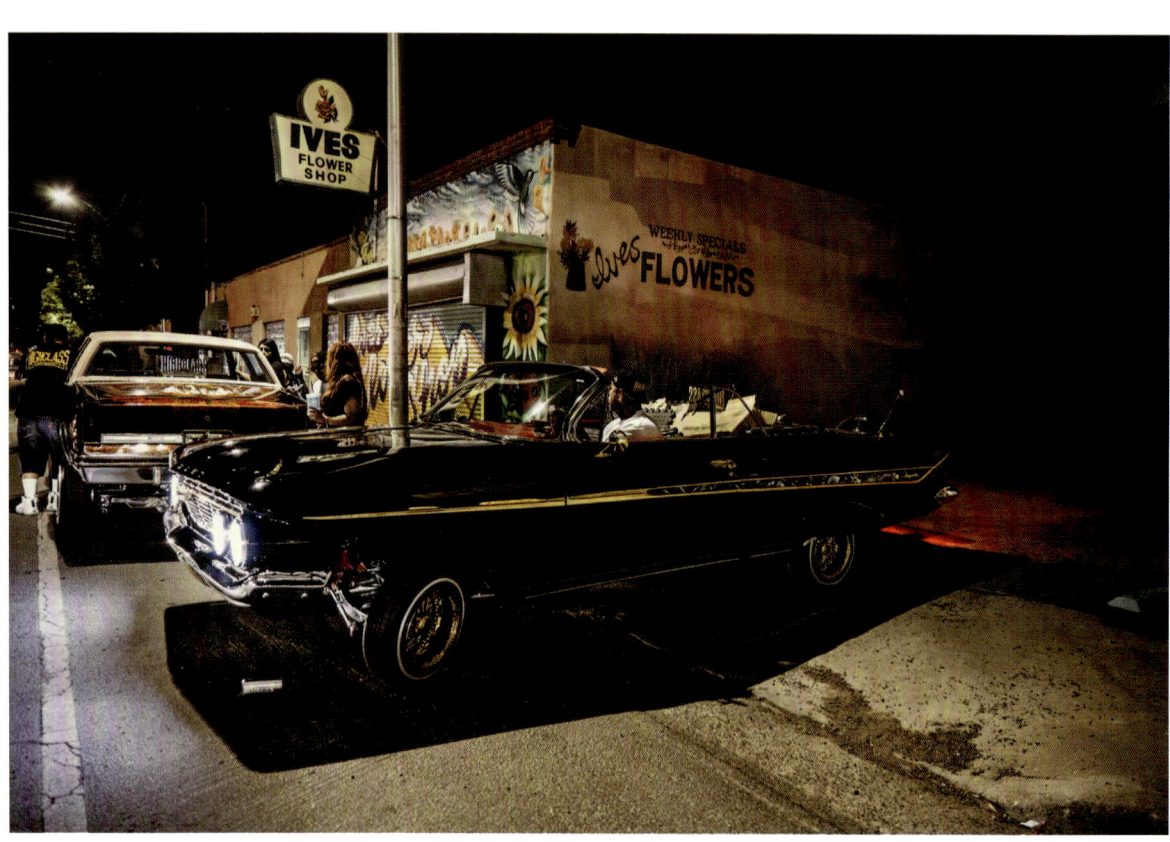

Ives Flower Shop, Barelas, Albuquerque, 2023.

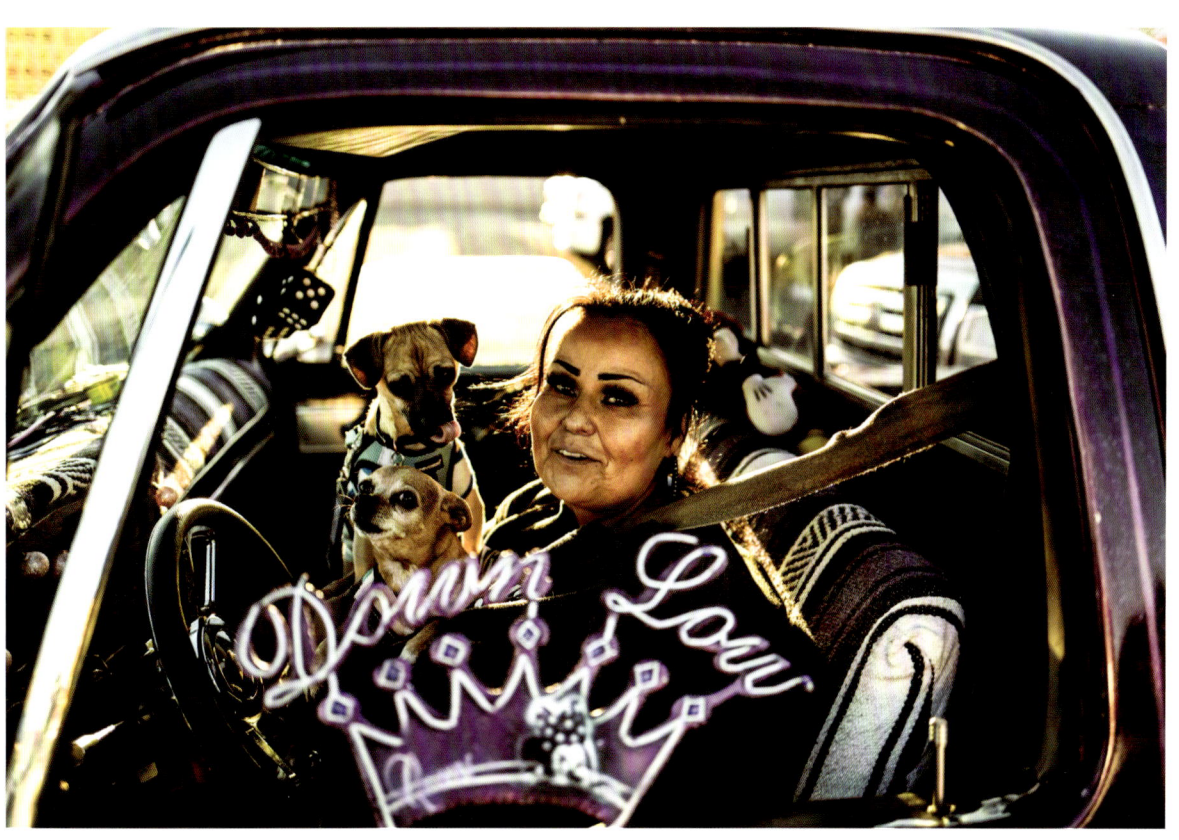

Downlow Queen and her dogs, Albuquerque, 2023.

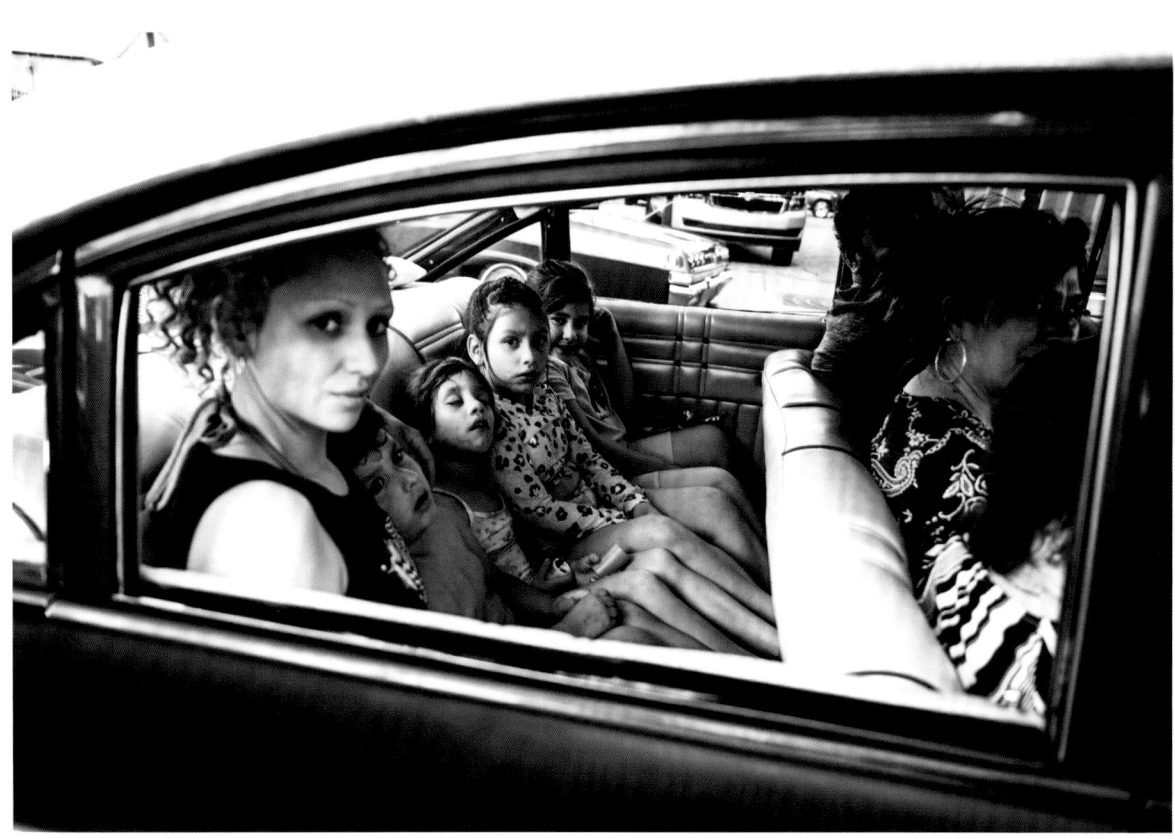

Many generations out for a cruise, Downtown Albuquerque, 2023.

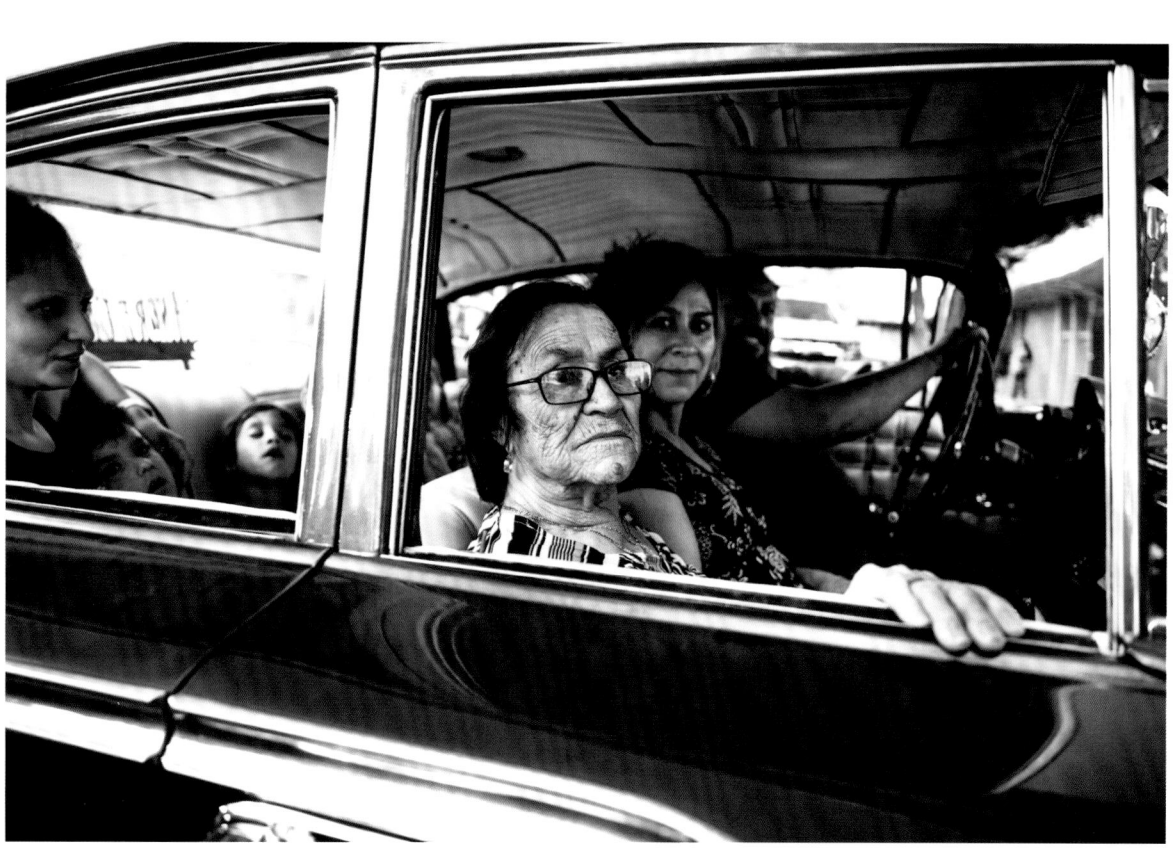

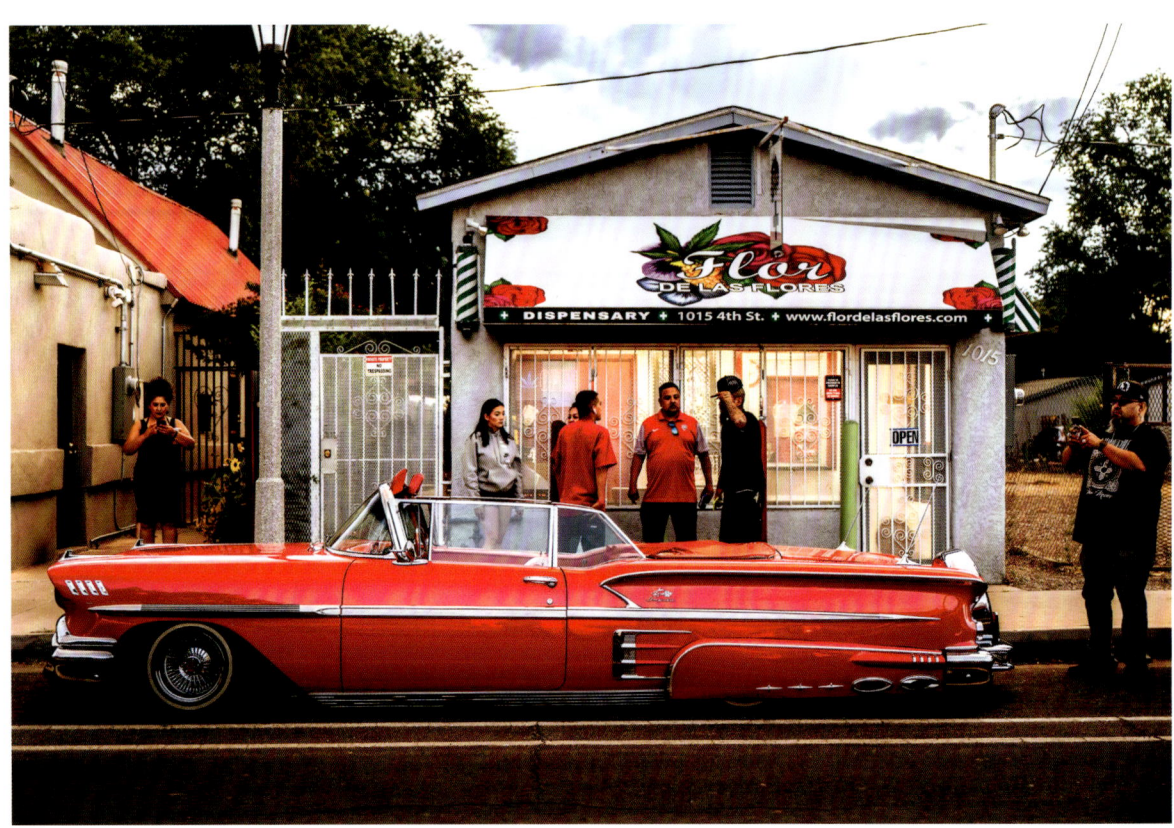

Friends hanging out, Barelas, Albuquerque, 2023.

(*opposite page*) Krystal Vigil and Dan Garcia, Barelas, Albuquerque, 2023.

(*following pages*) Juan Rey Sedillo shows his hand tattoos, Albuquerque, 2023.

Hand tattoos, Albuquerque, 2021–2024.

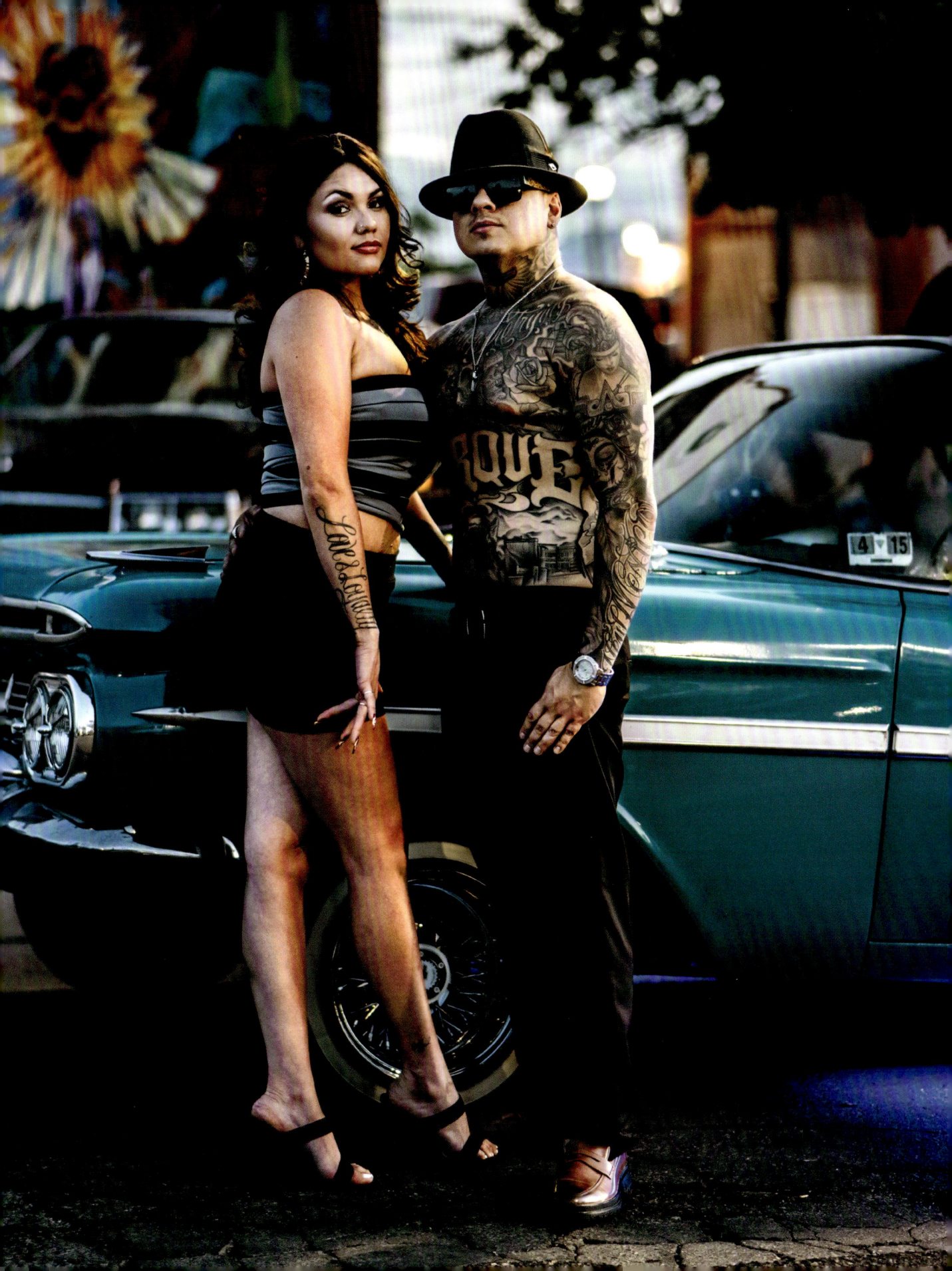

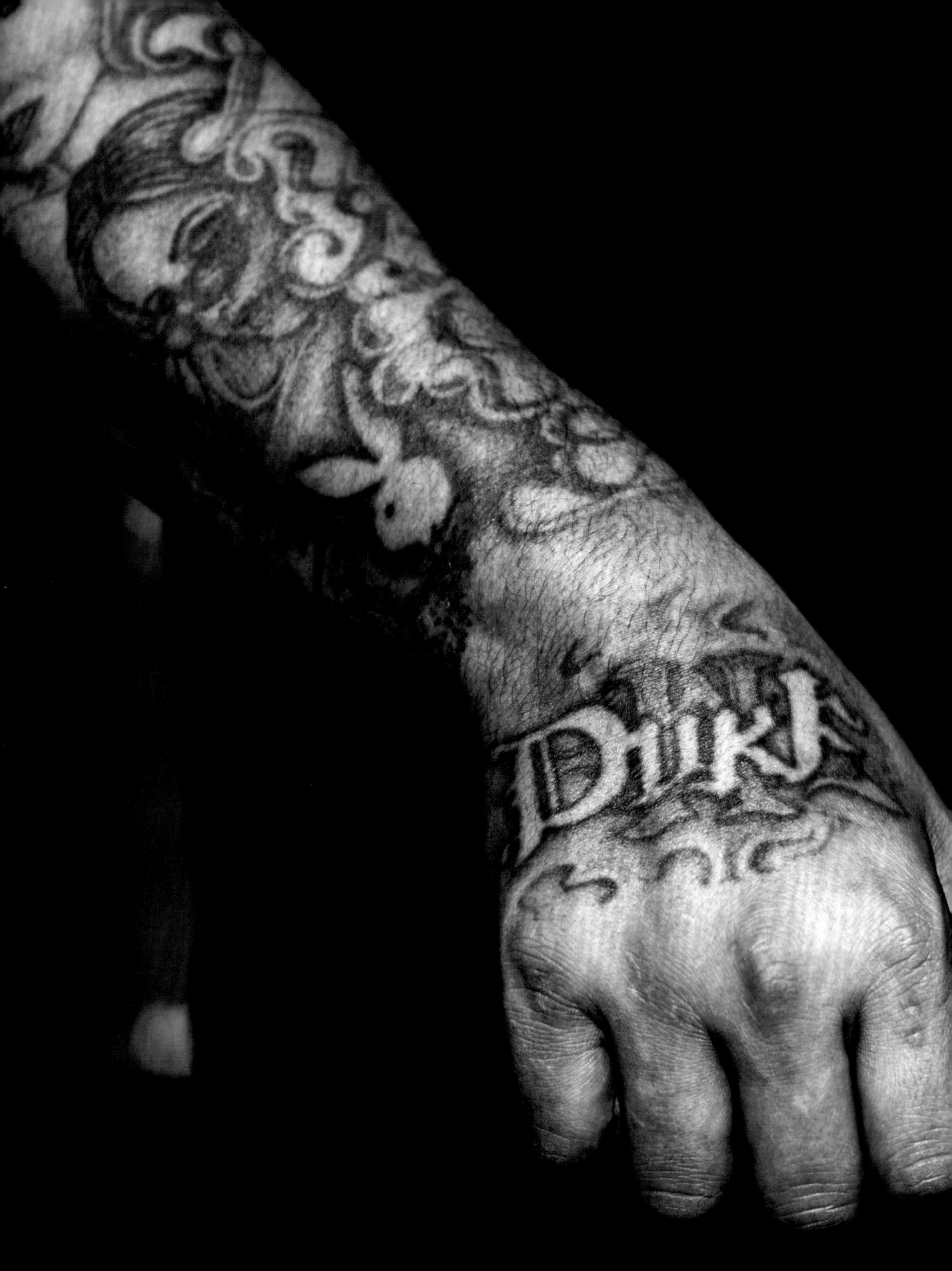

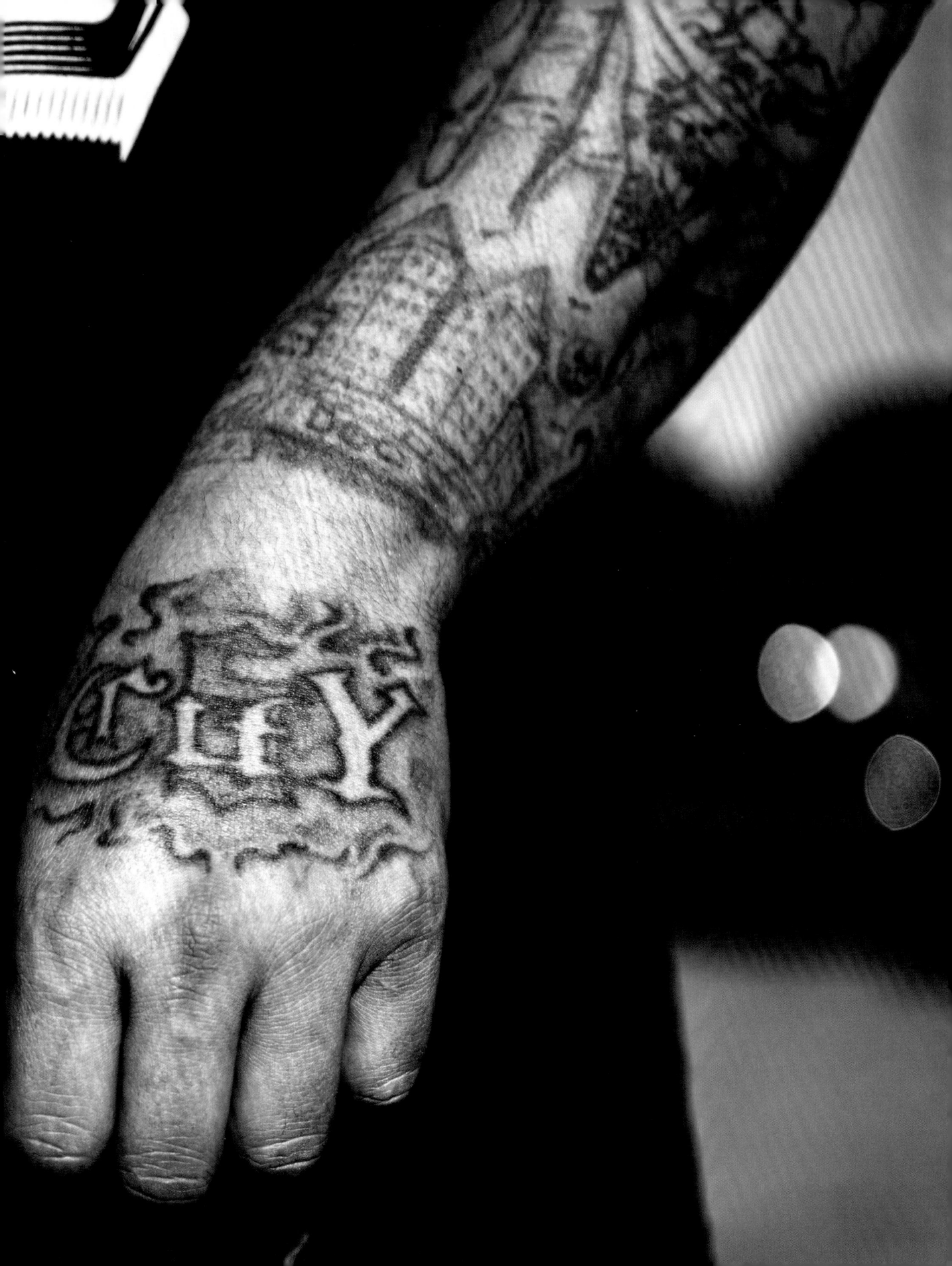

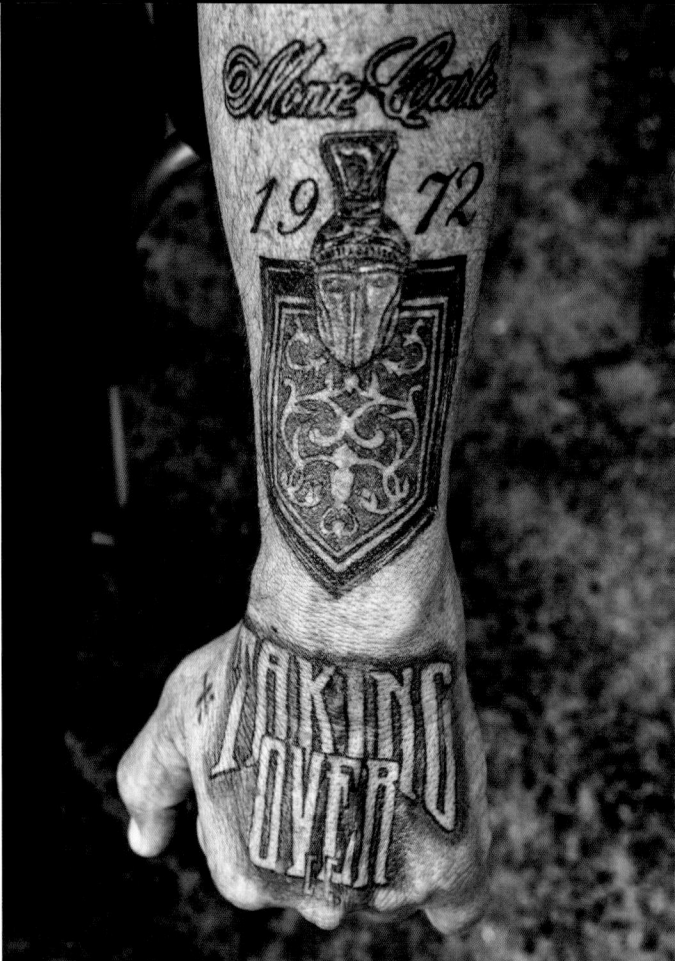

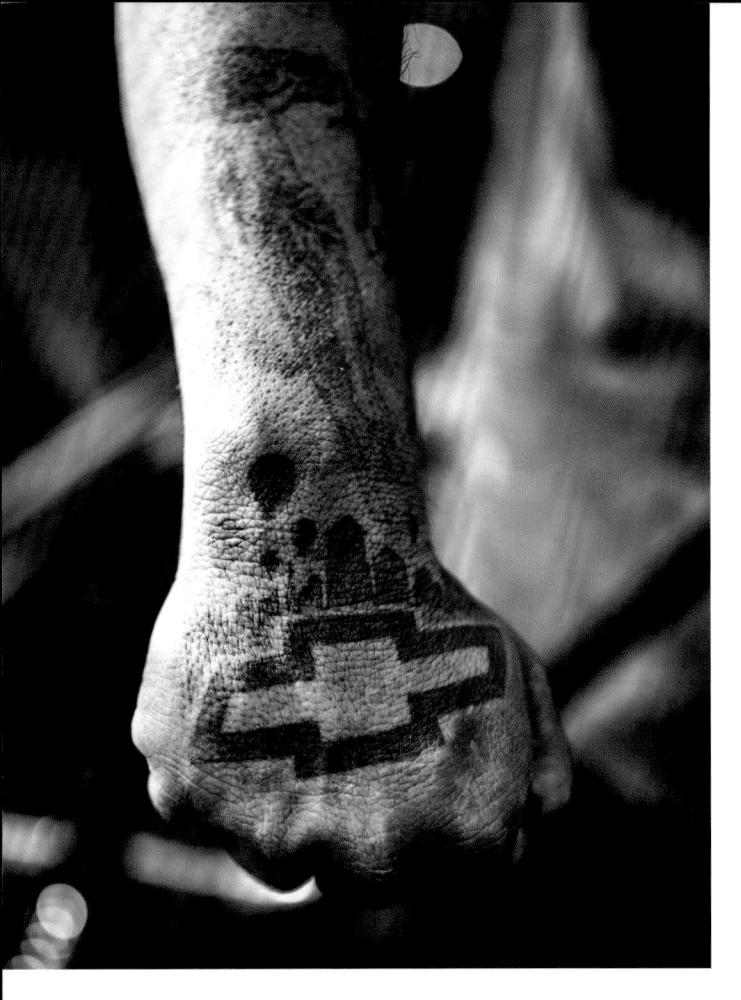

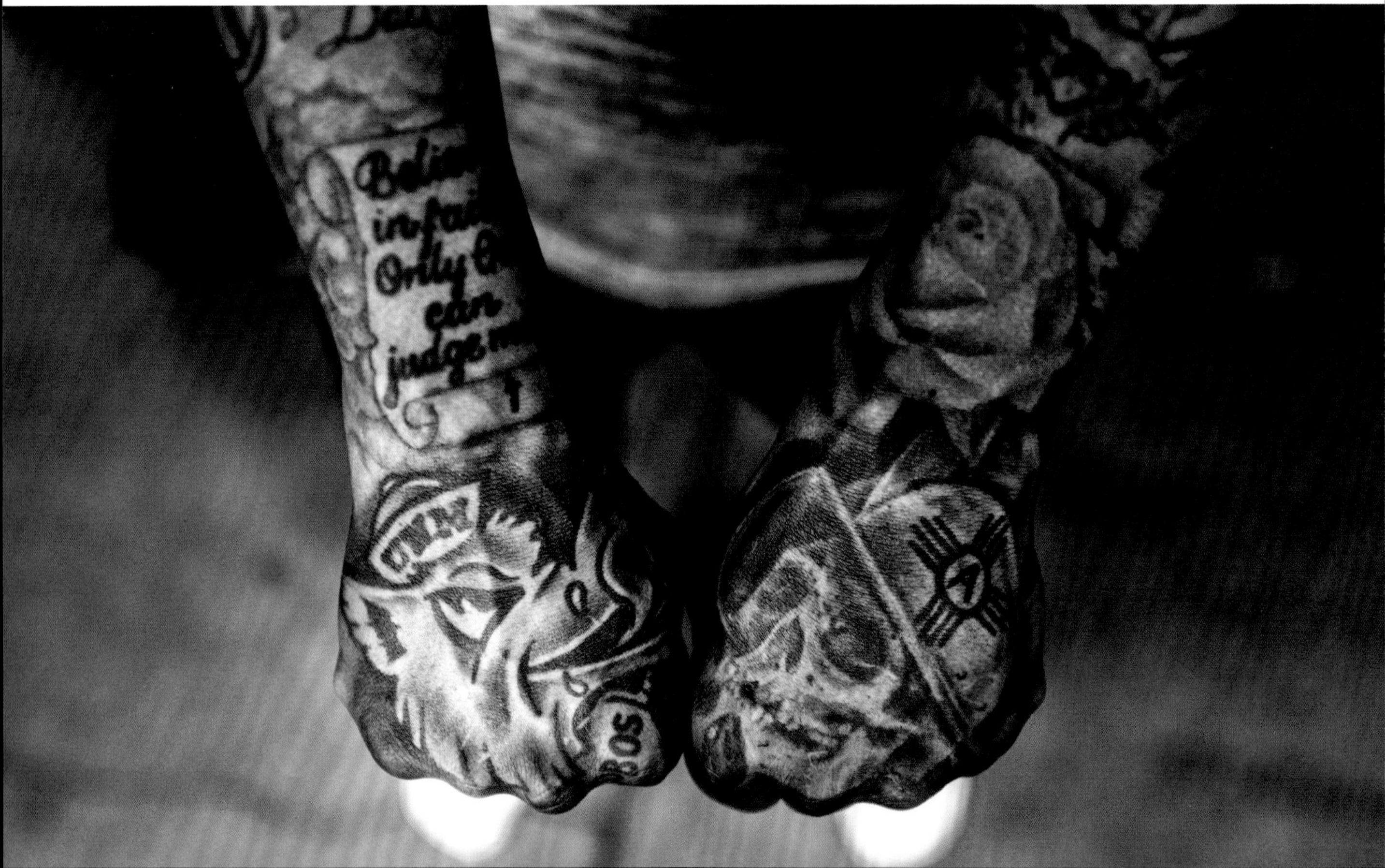

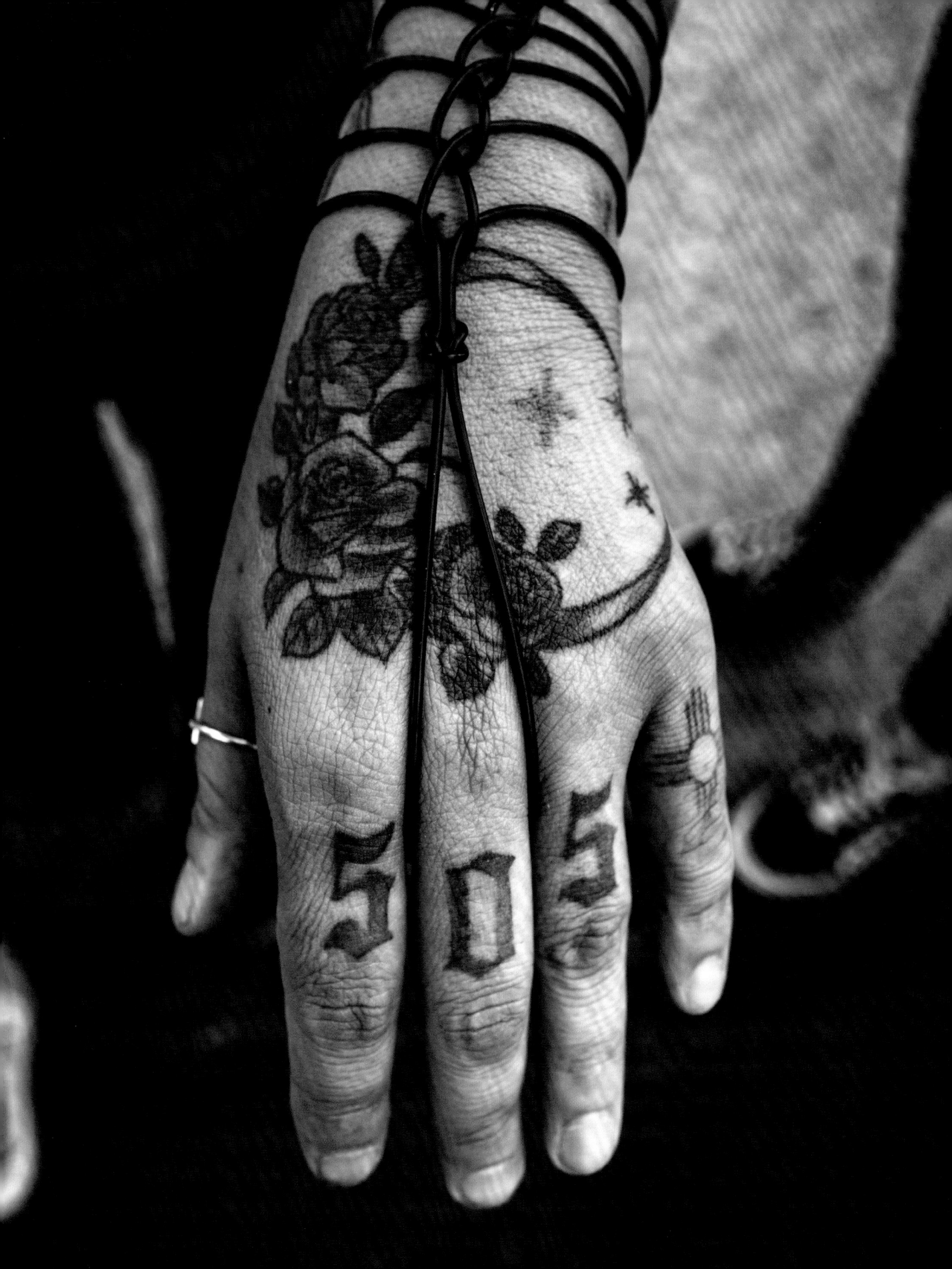

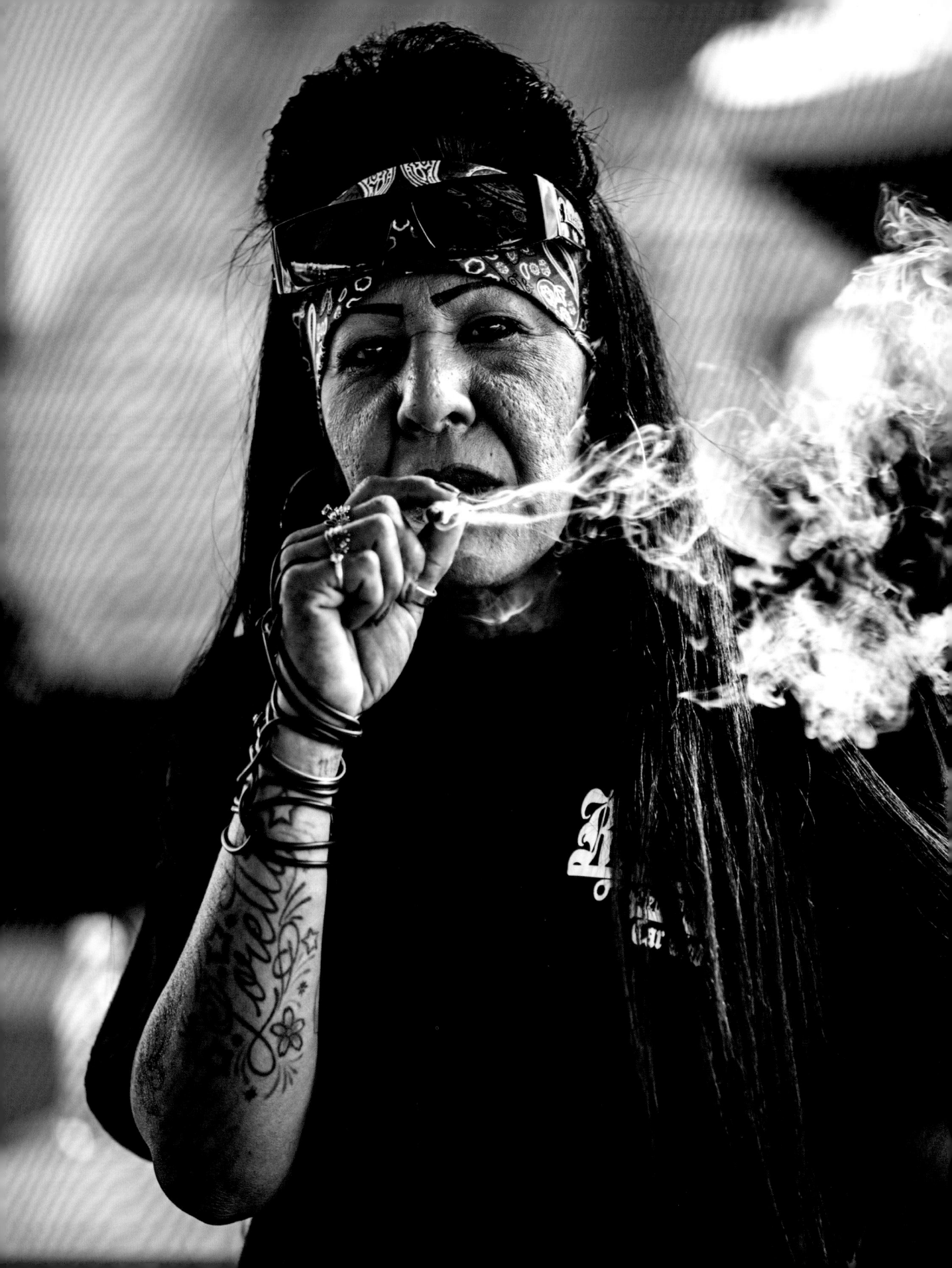

(*opposite page*) Rosa "La Chola" Lopez, Raza Unida Car Club, Albuquerque, 2023.

(*following pages*) Christopher with his RC lowrider, Albuquerque, 2024.

Pesa's 1964 Impala, San Francisco de Asis Catholic Church, Golden, New Mexico, 2024.

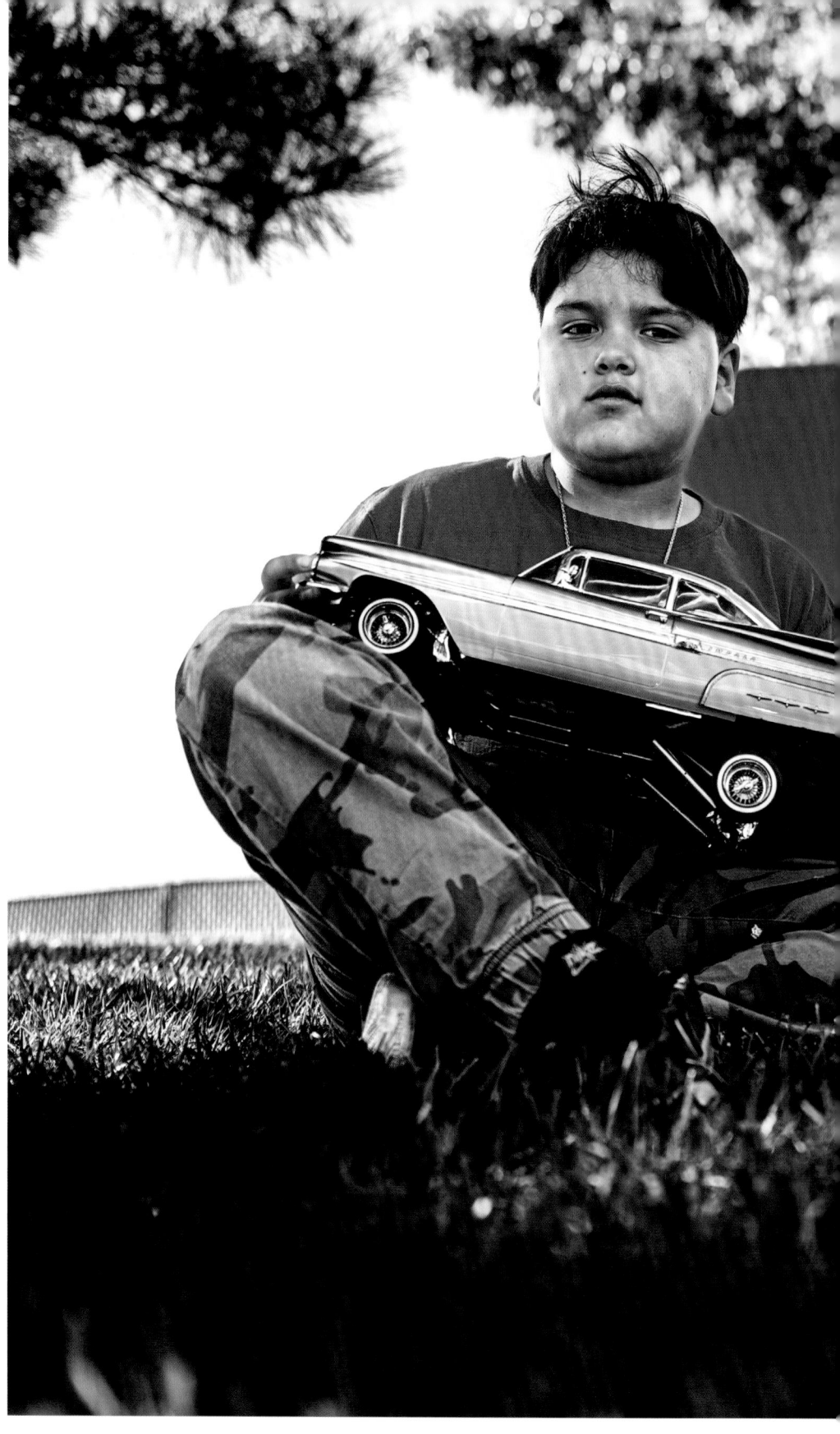

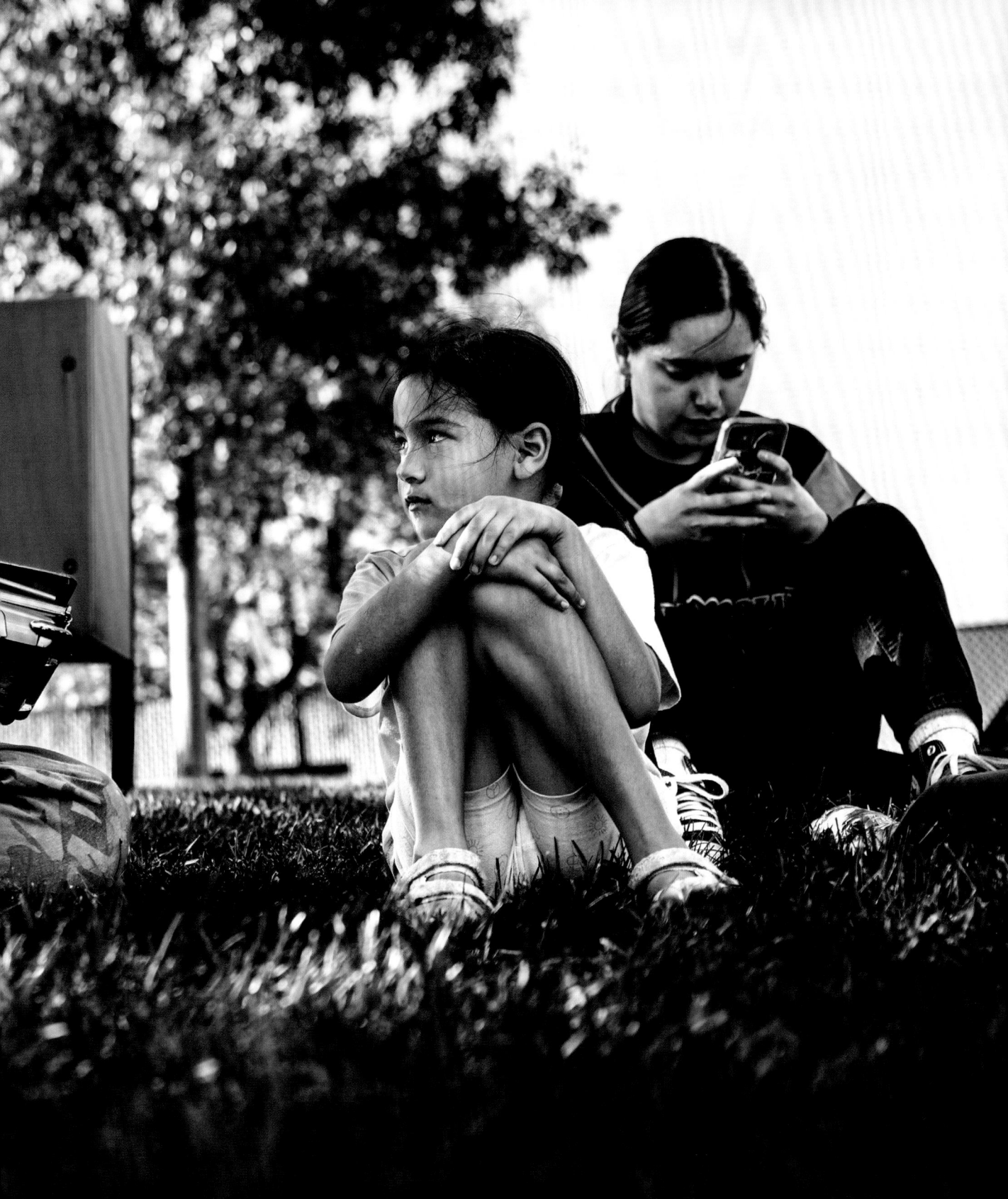

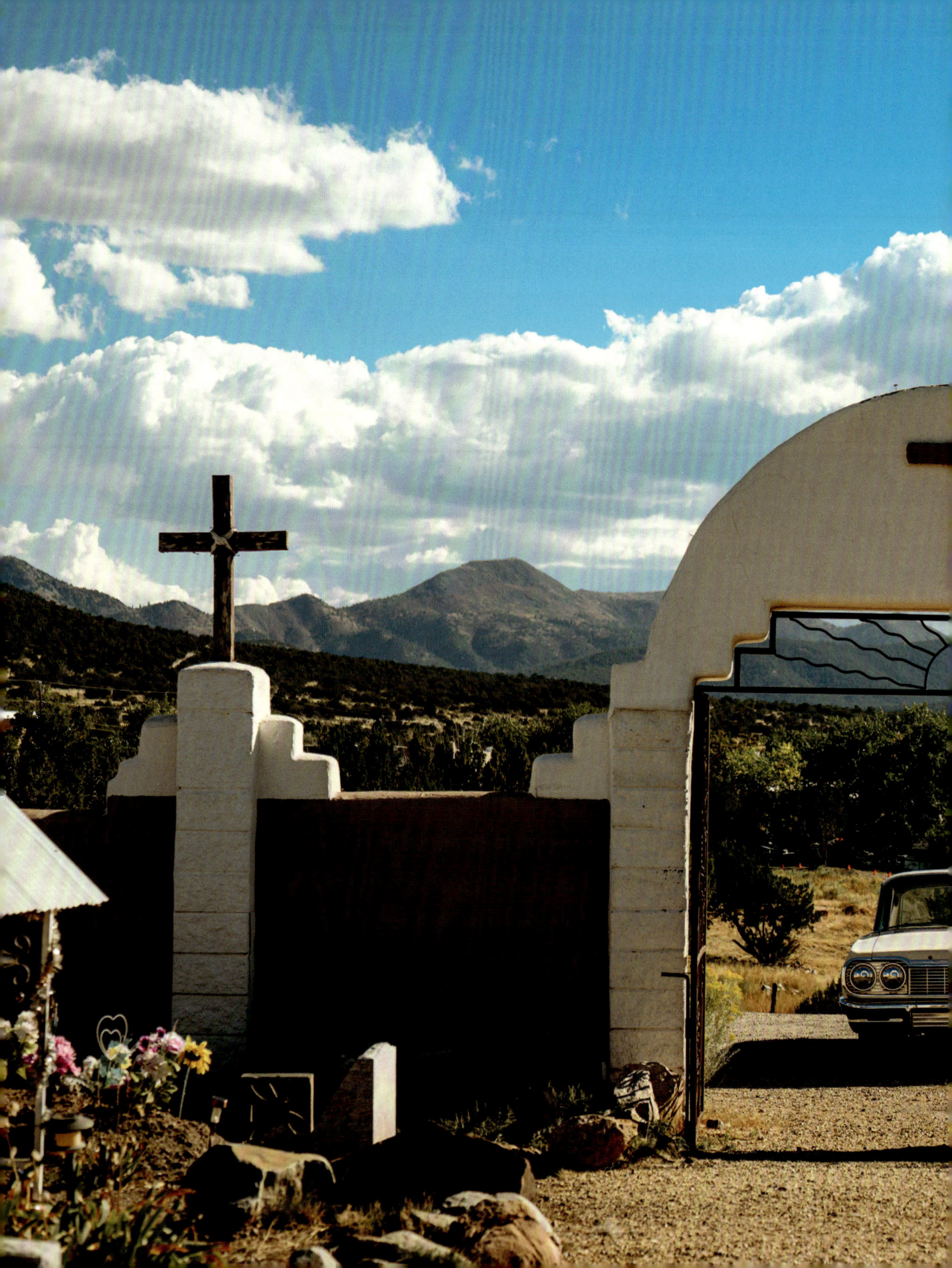

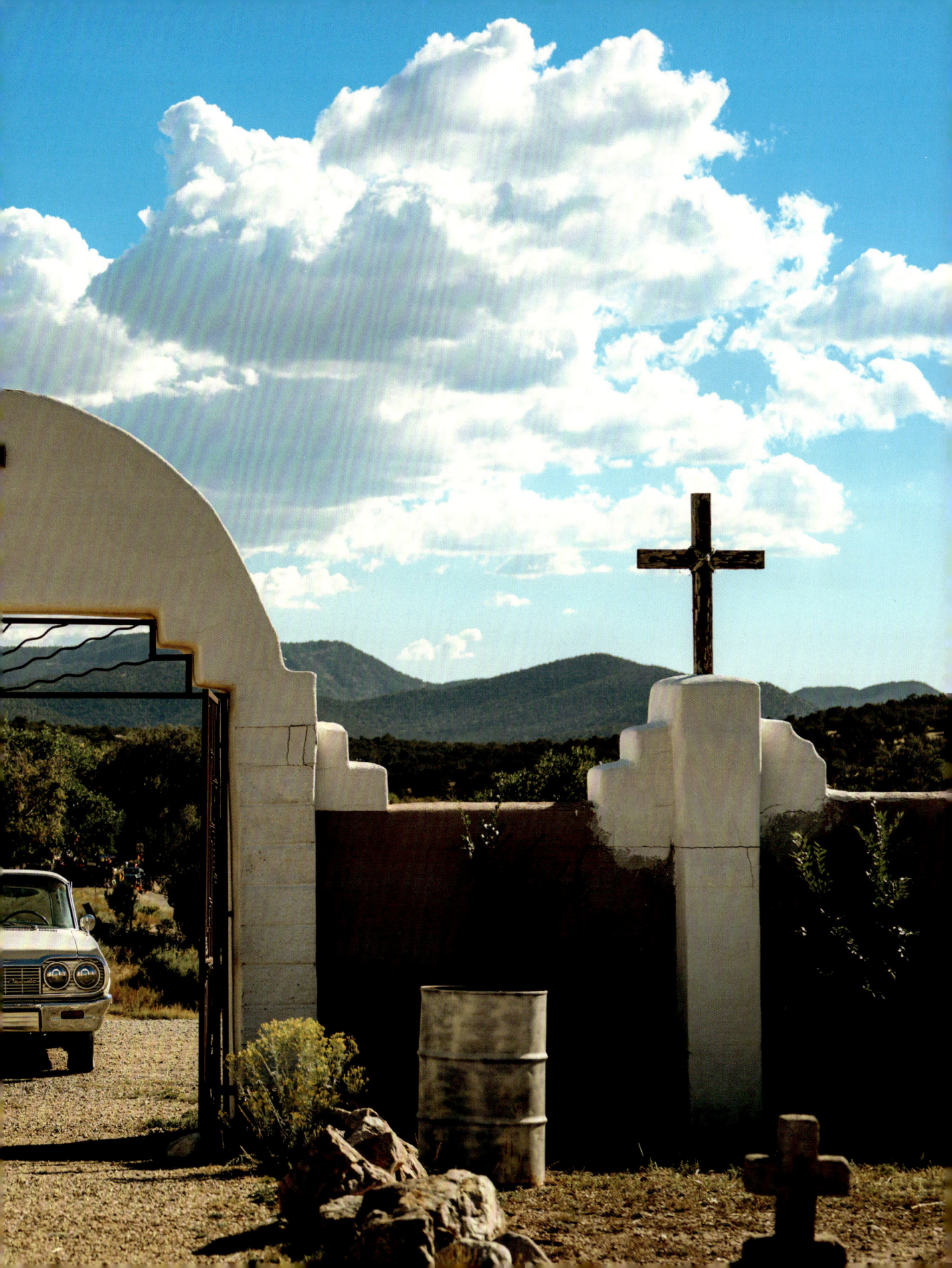

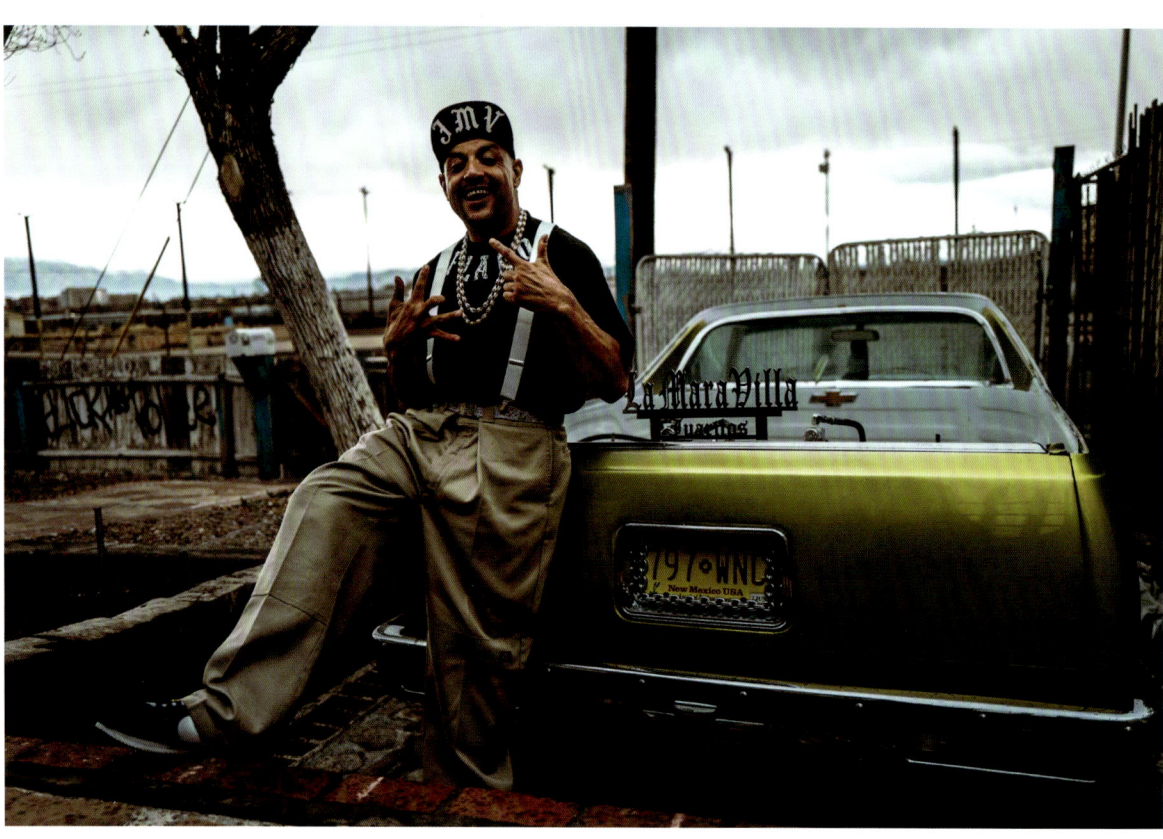

Flaco Garcia at home with his El Camino, Barelas, Albuquerque, 2024.

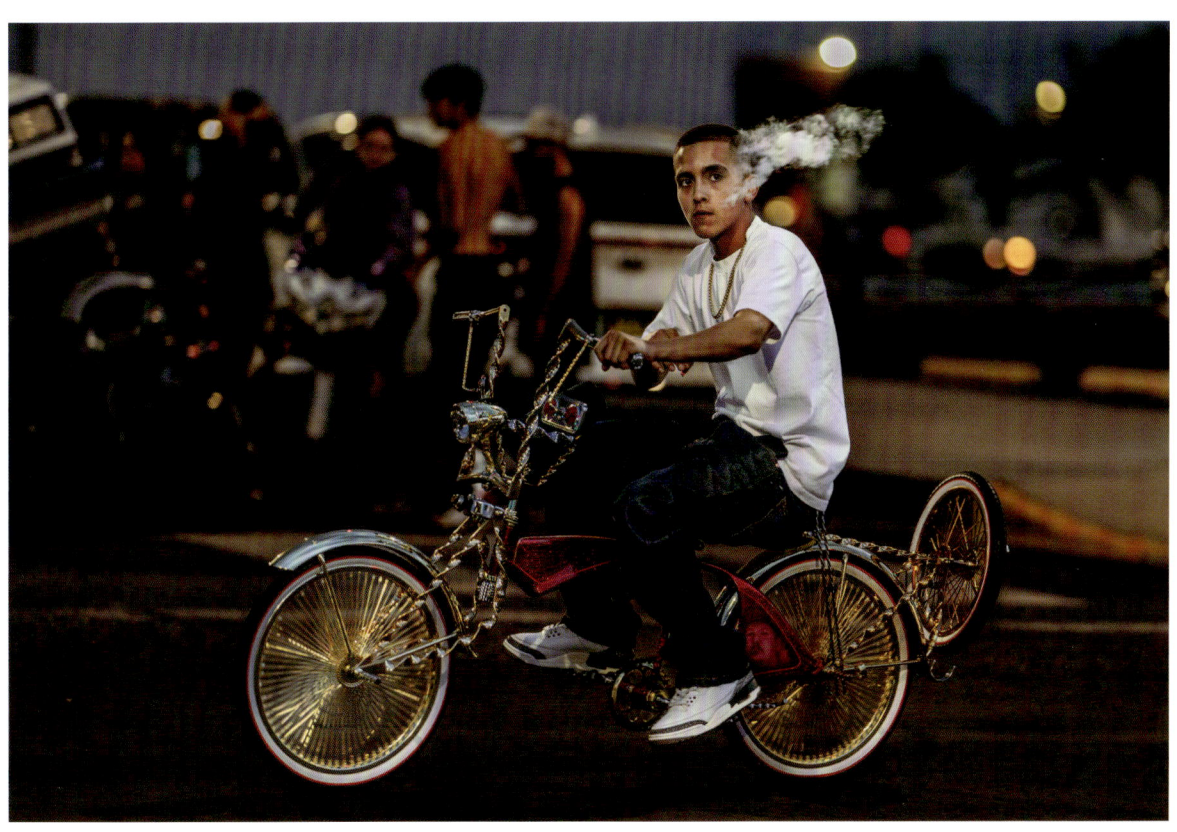

Candy Casares rolling through the intersection, Seventh Street and Central Avenue, Downtown Albuquerque, 2024.

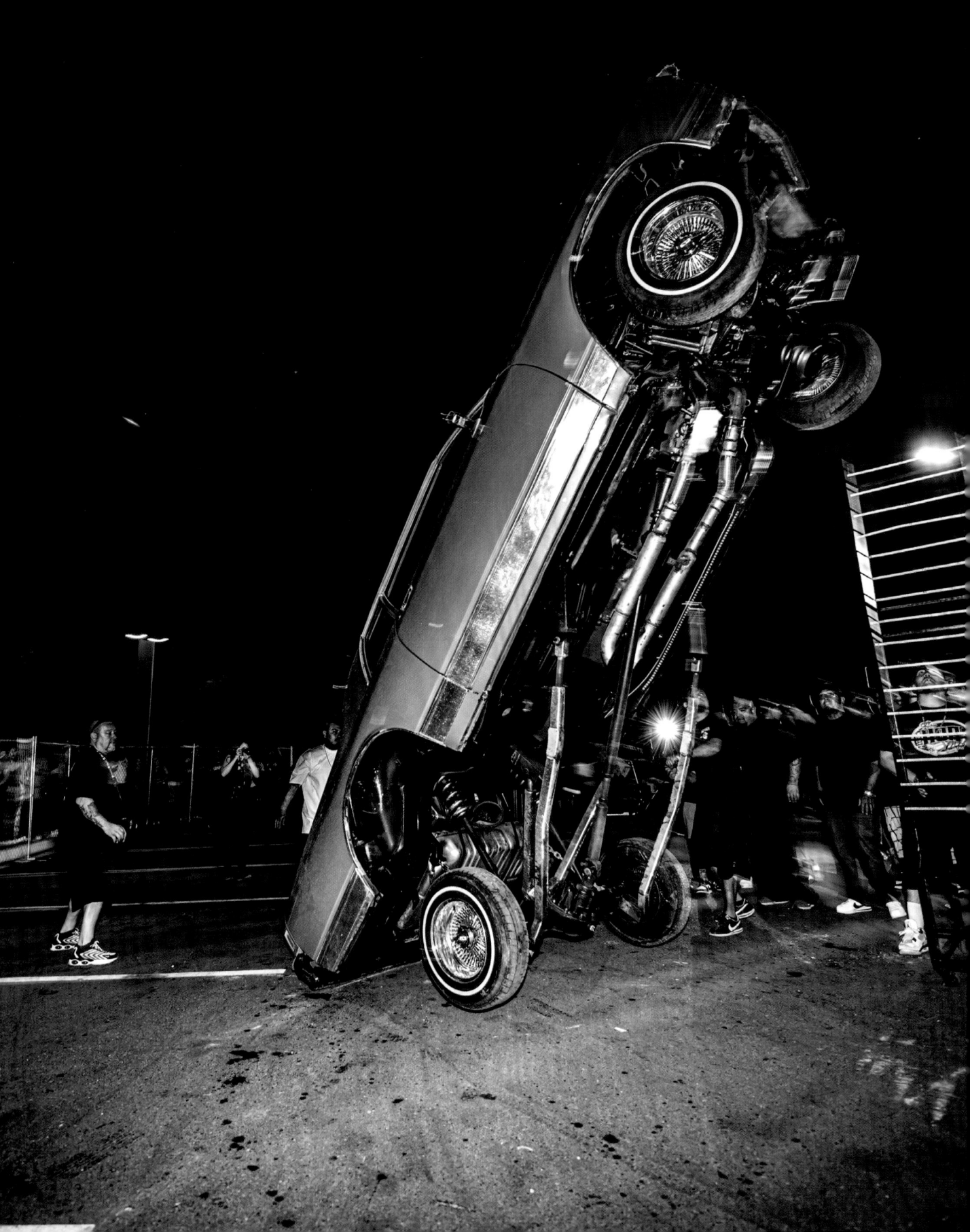

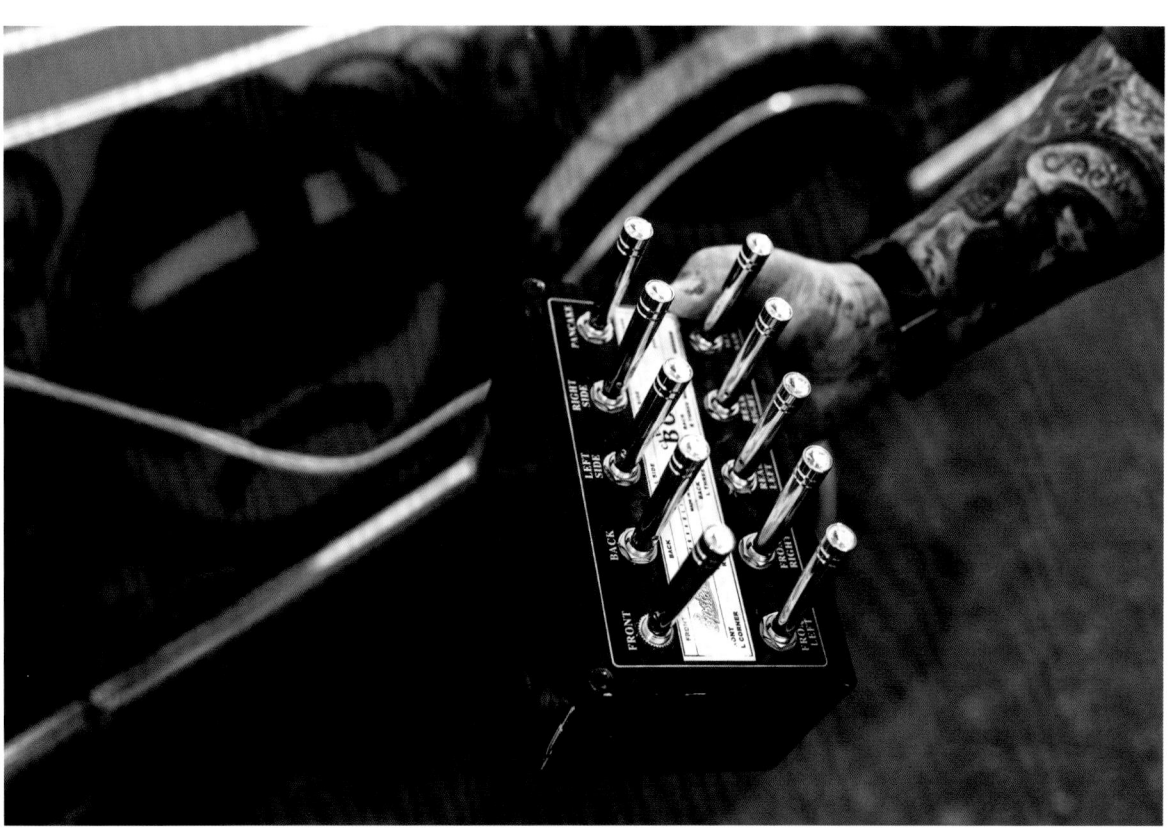

(*opposite page*) A car hops at a competition, Albuquerque, 2024.

Lowrider hydraulics controls, Albuquerque, 2022.

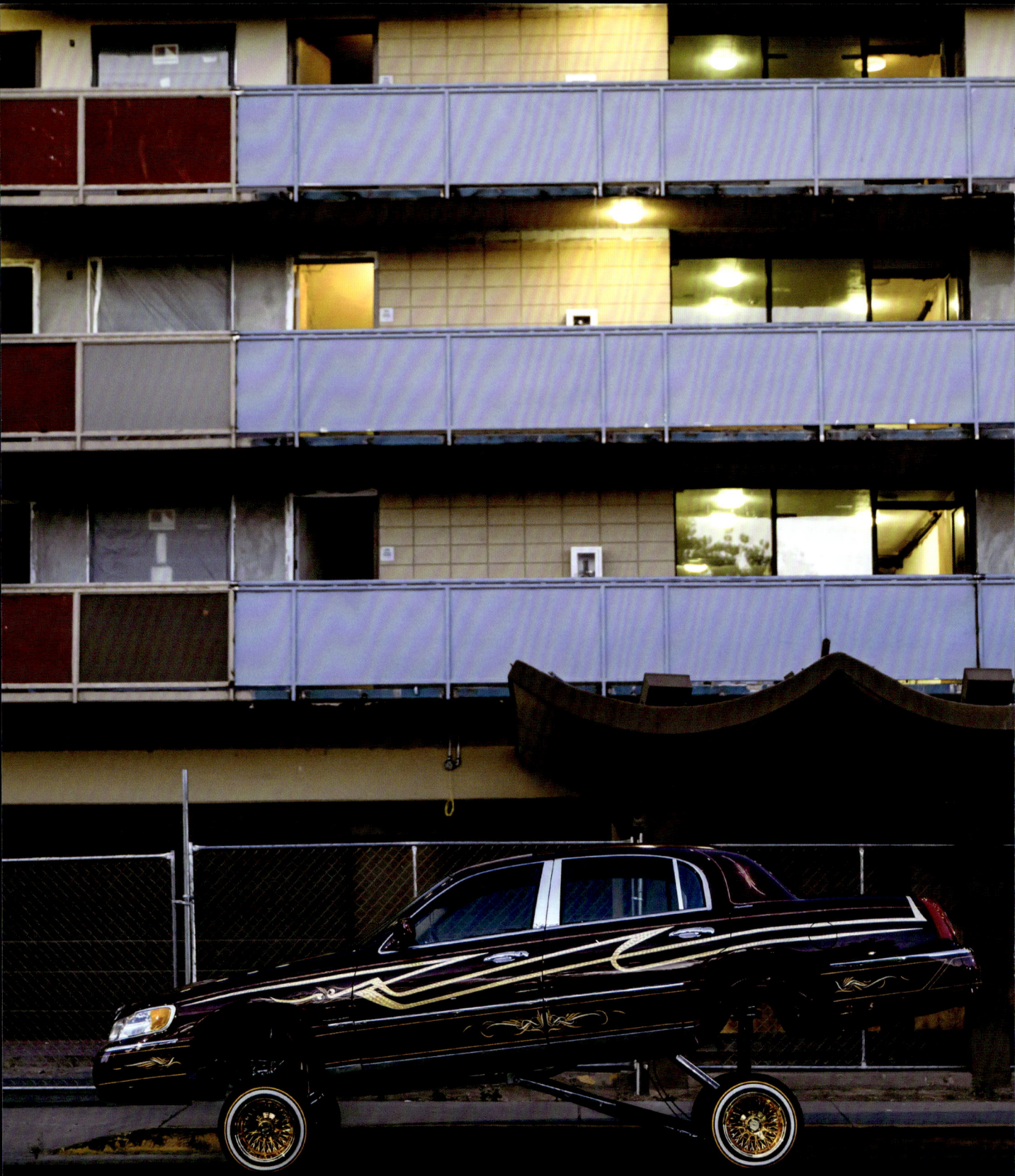

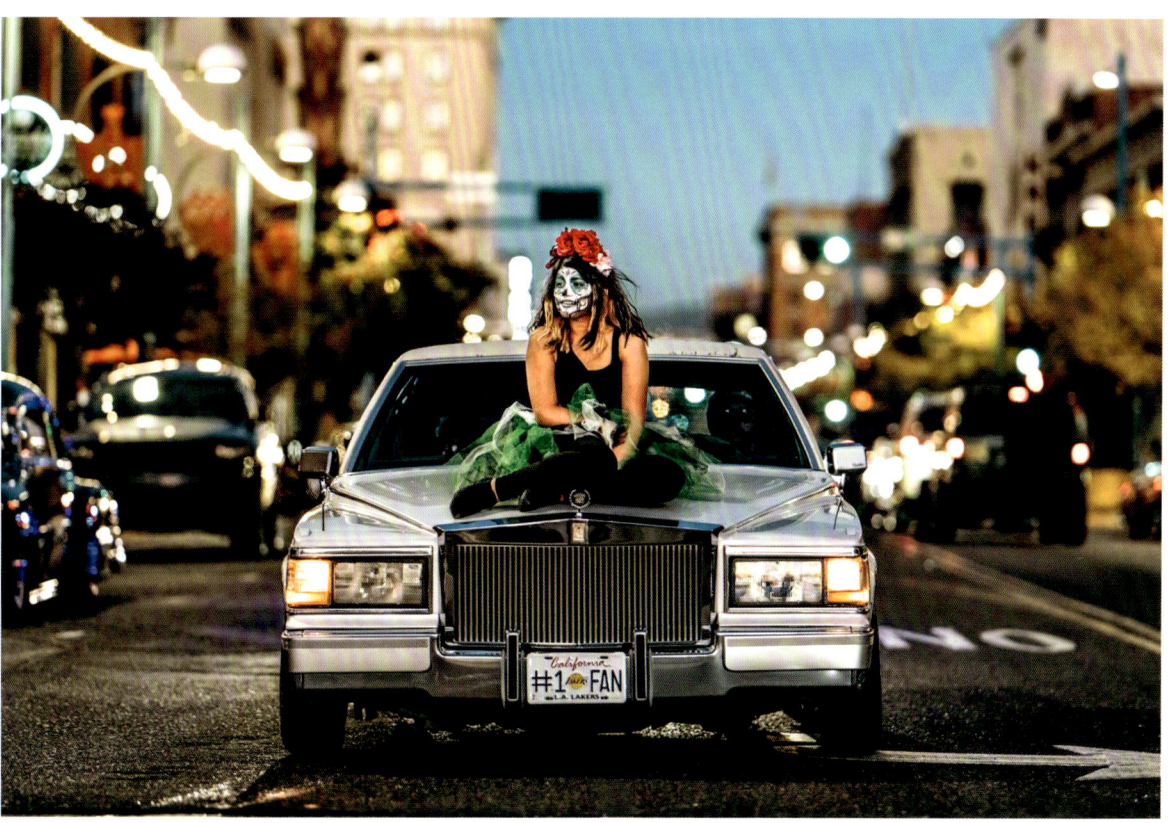

(*opposite page*) Larry Martinez's Lincoln Town Car, Eighth Street and Central Avenue, Downtown Albuquerque, 2024.

Riding on the hood of a car down Central Avenue, Día de los Muertos, Downtown Albuquerque, 2022.

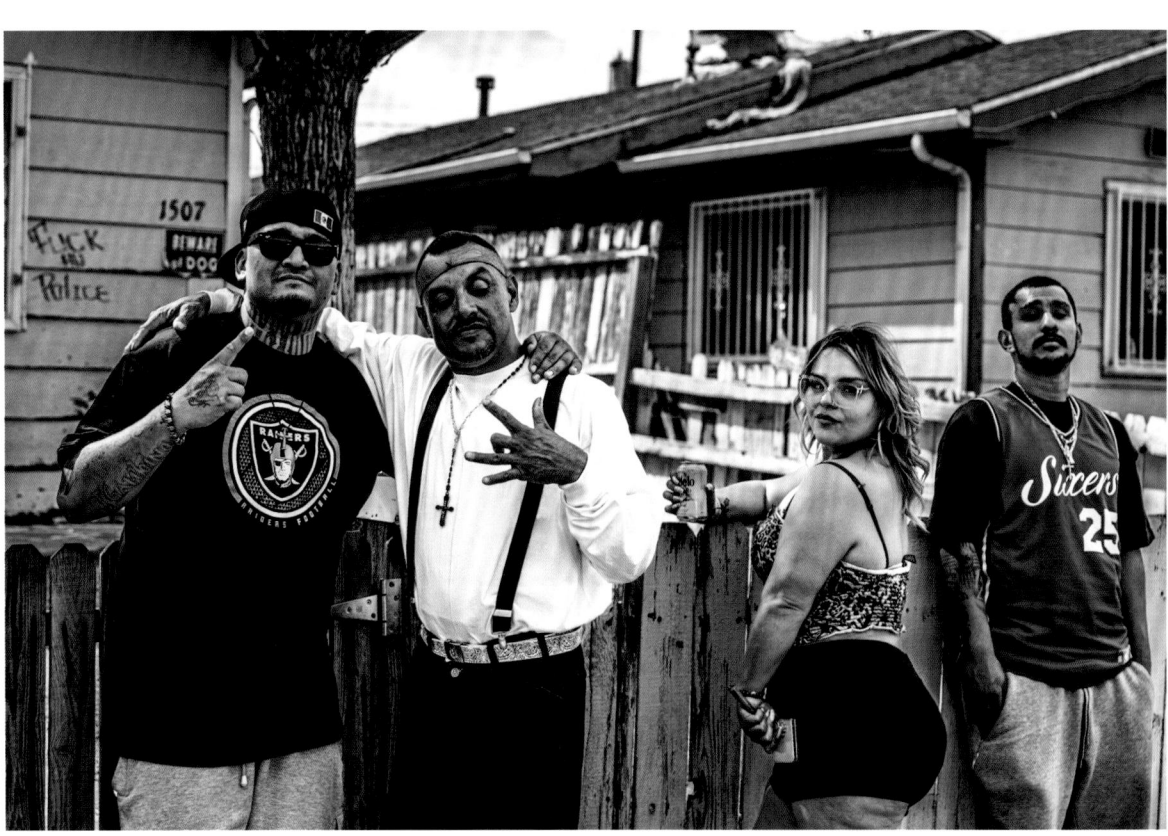

Juan and Flaco and their friends, Barelas, Albuquerque, 2023.

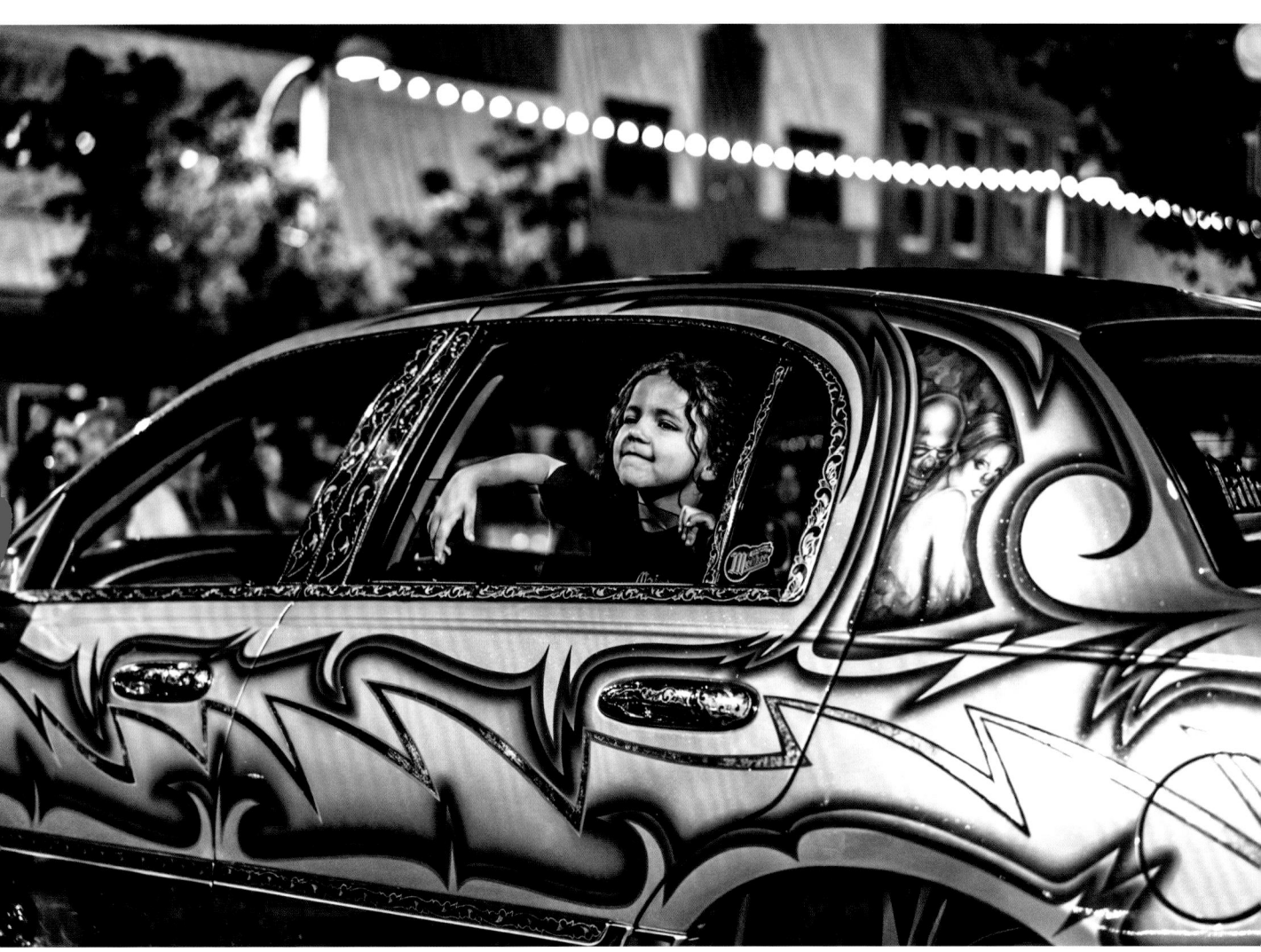

A girl looks out the window of her parents car, Downtown Albuquerque, 2022.

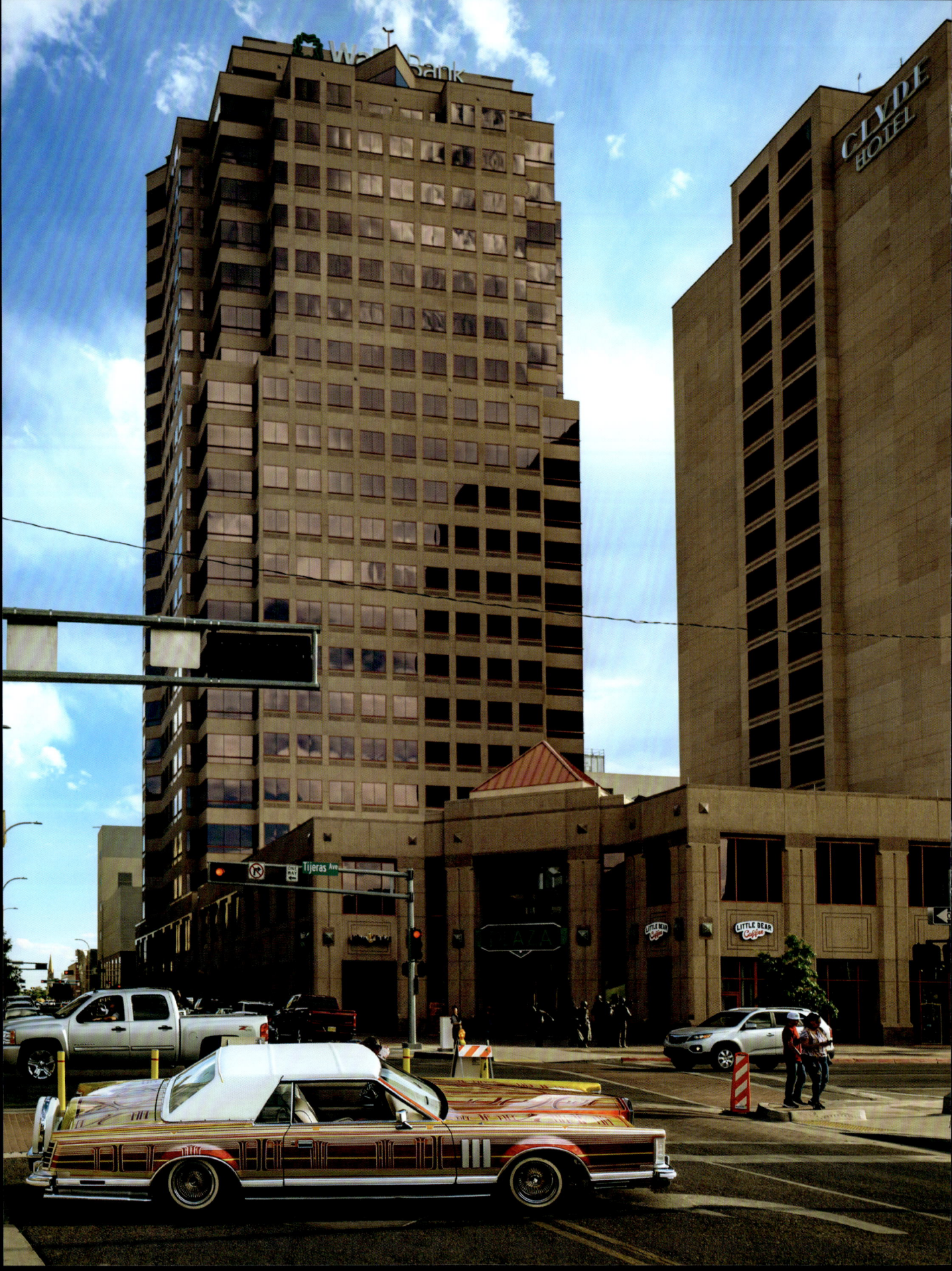

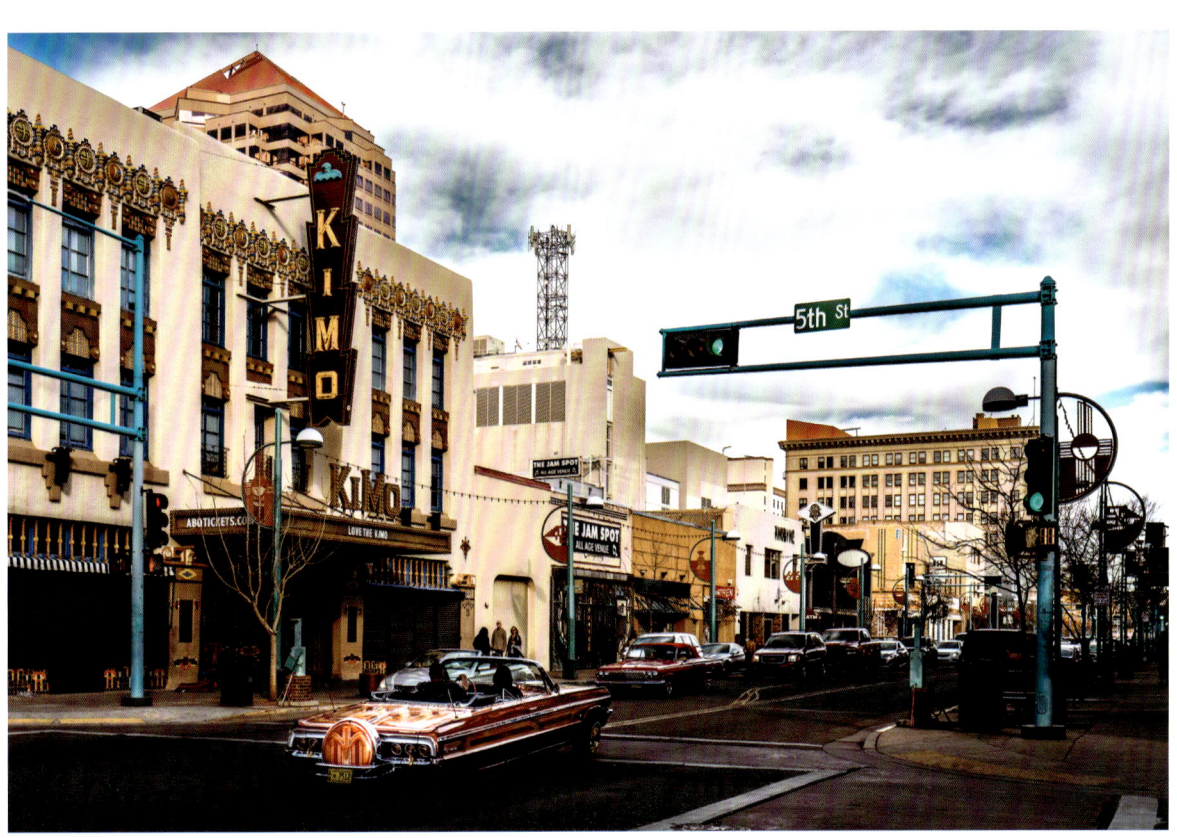

(*opposite page*) Lowrider, Downtown Albuquerque, 2024.

Fifth Street and Central Avenue, Downtown Albuquerque, 2022.

(*following pages*) Unique Lovato with her son King, Albuquerque, 2024.

Downtown Albuquerque, 2023.

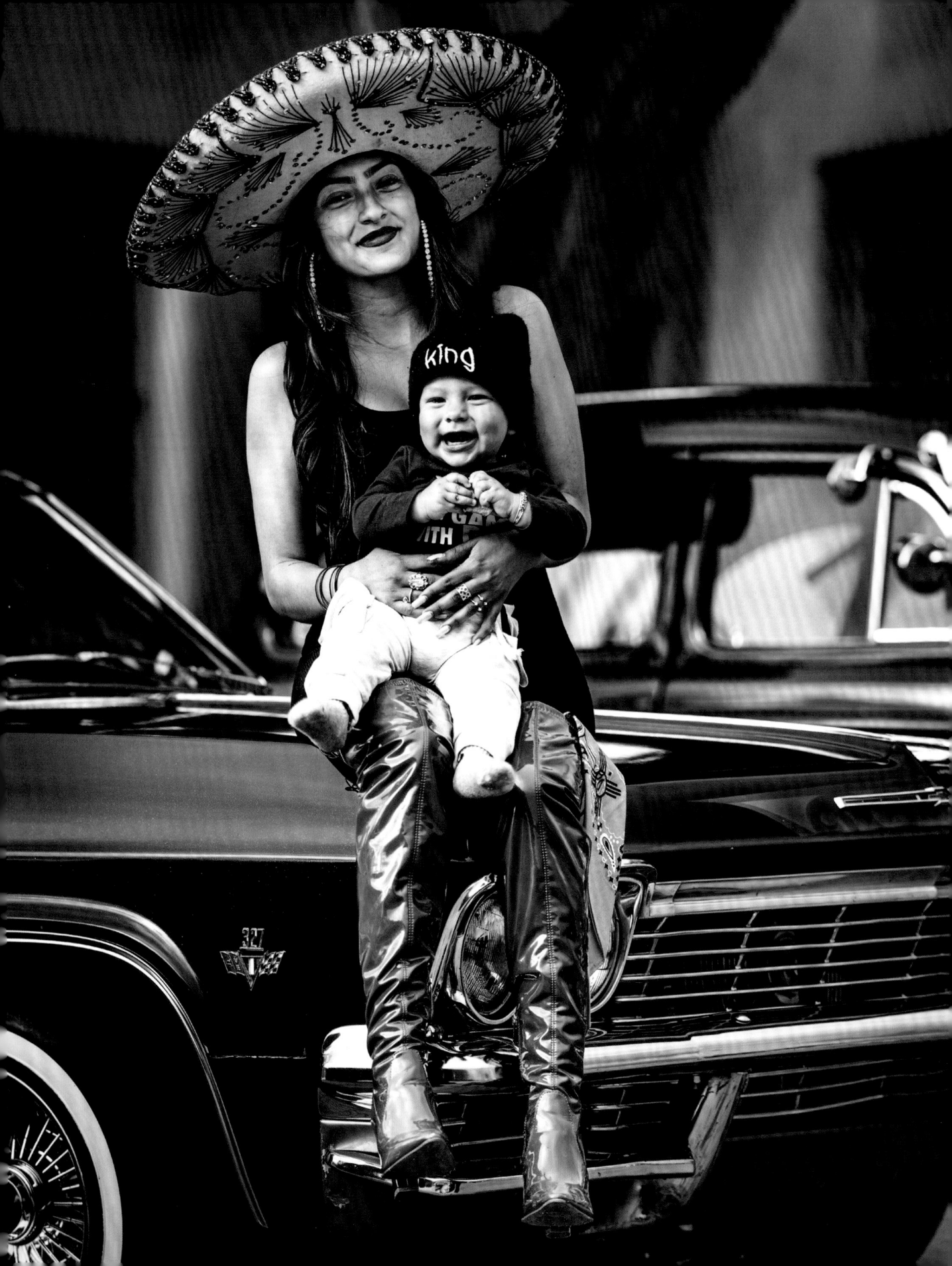

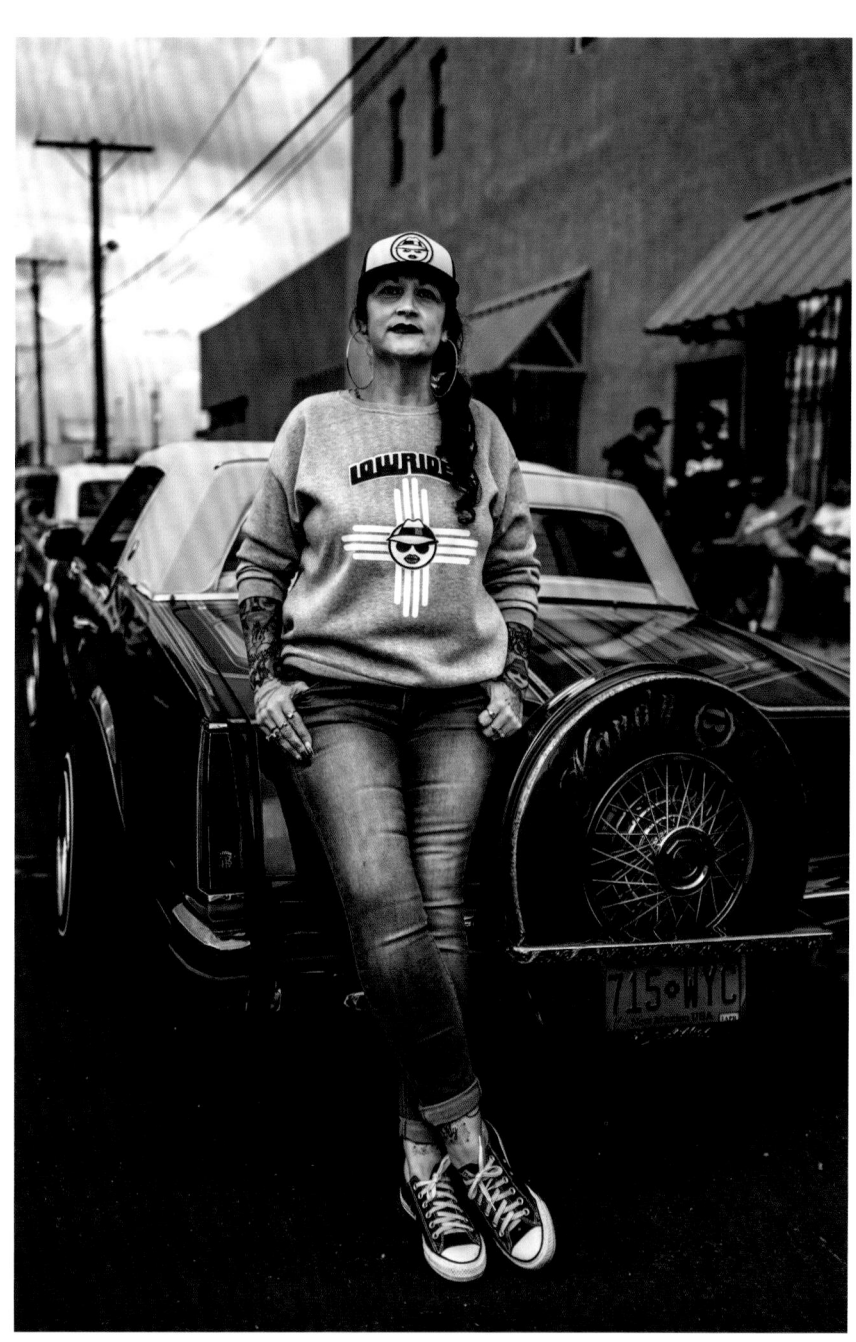

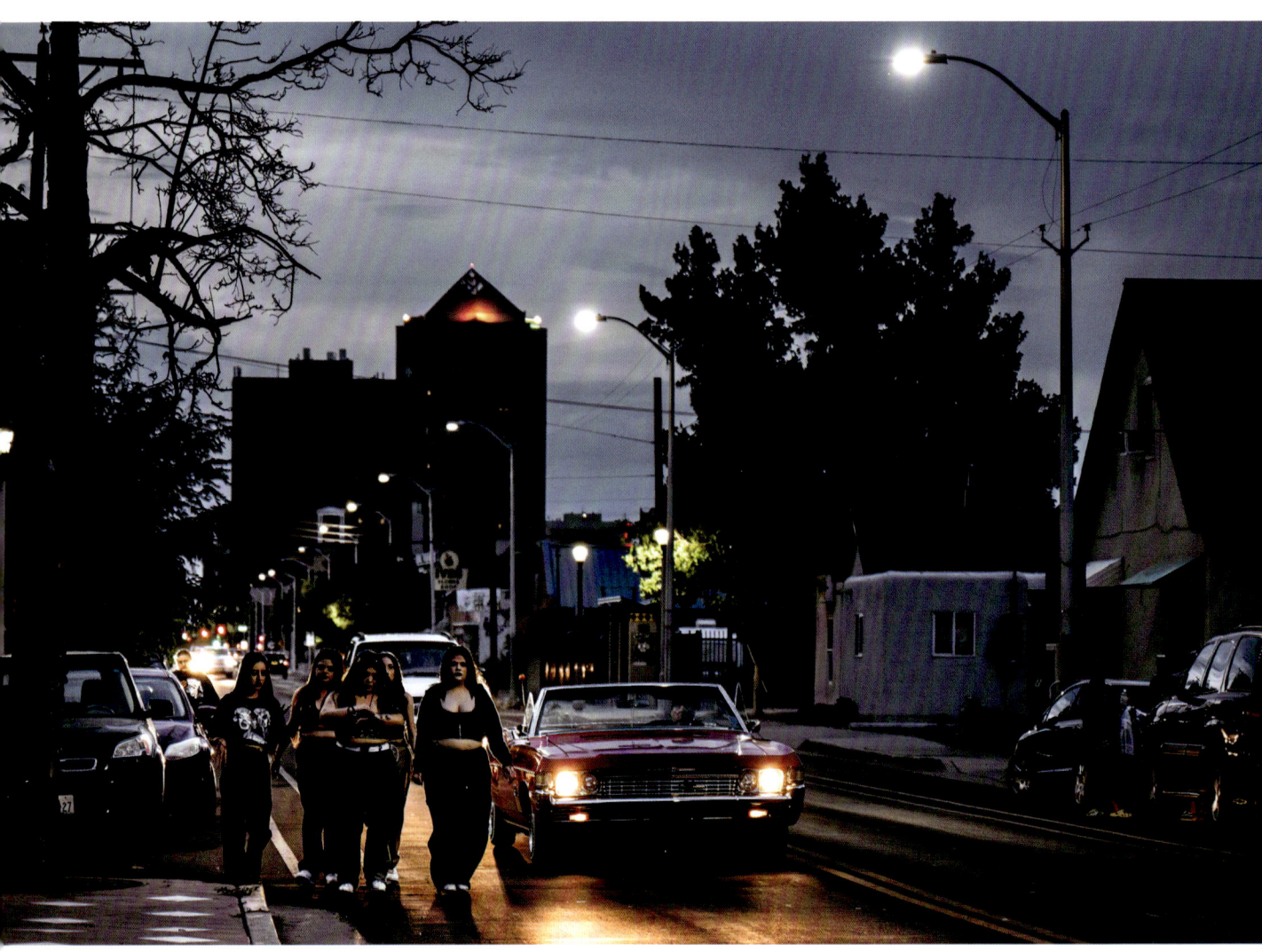

Sunday night on Fourth Street, Barelas, Albuquerque, 2023.

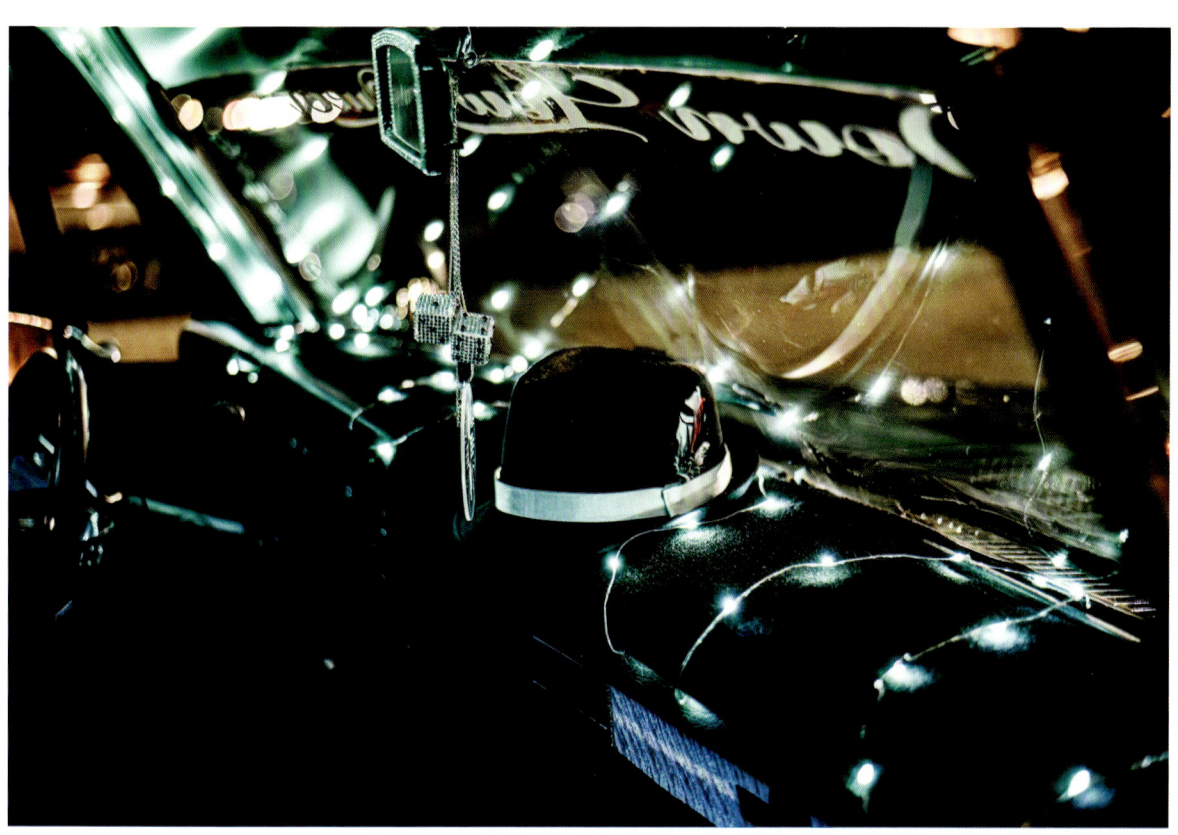

Interior of a lowrider, Downtown Albuquerque, 2023.

(*following pages*) Portrait of Angelo, Barelas, Albuquerque, 2023.

Portrait of Dan Garcia, Barelas, Albuquerque, 2023.

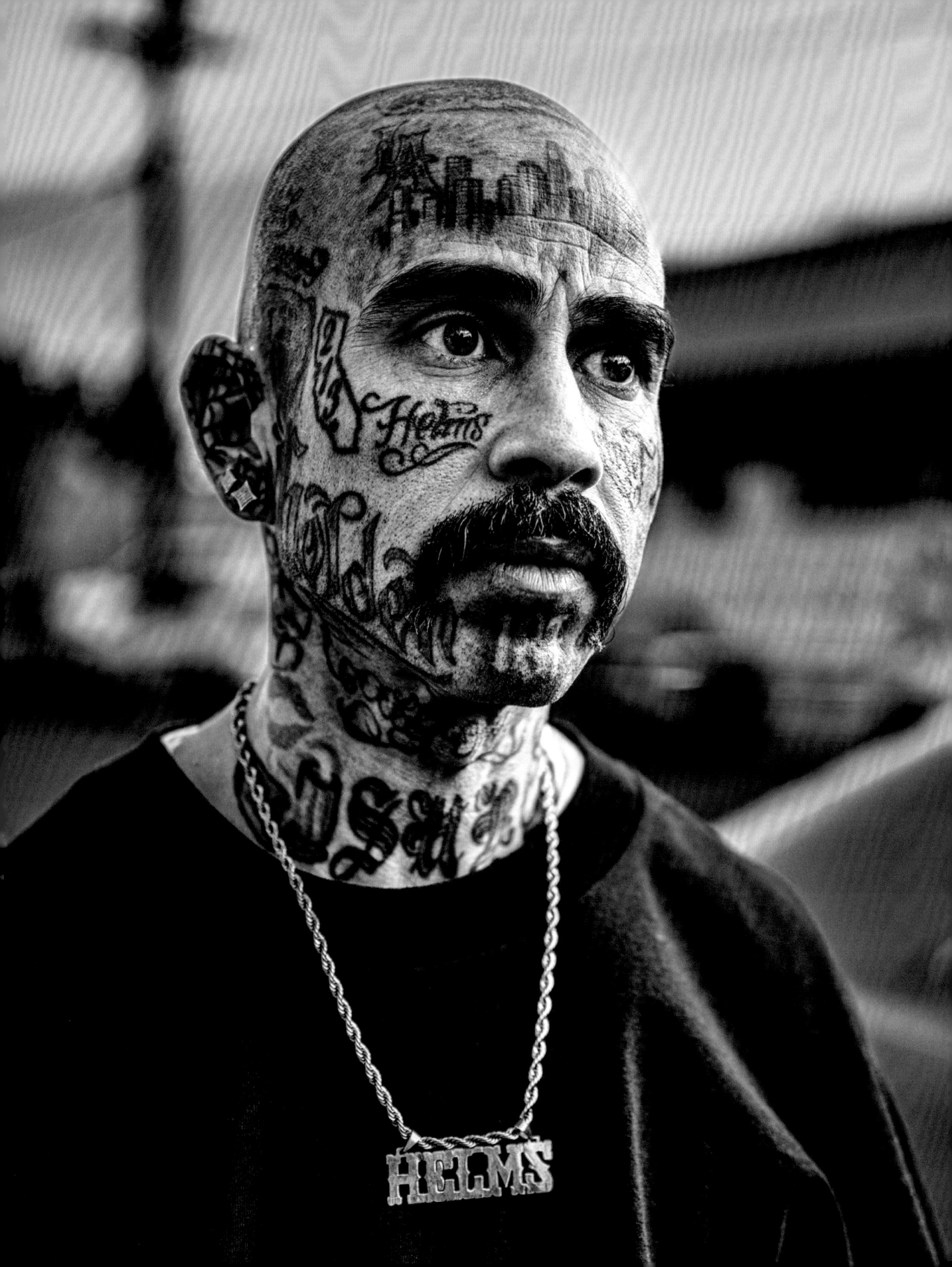

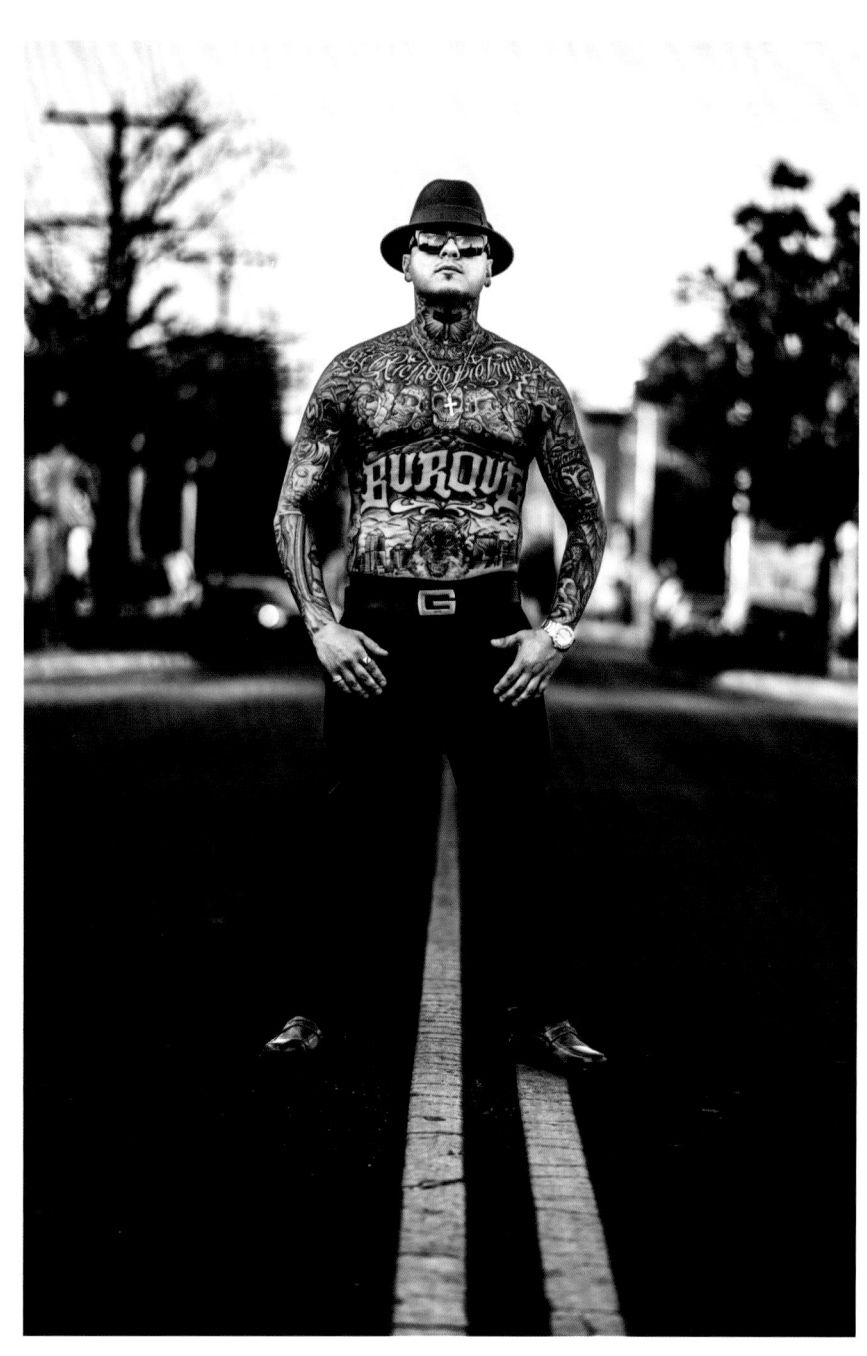

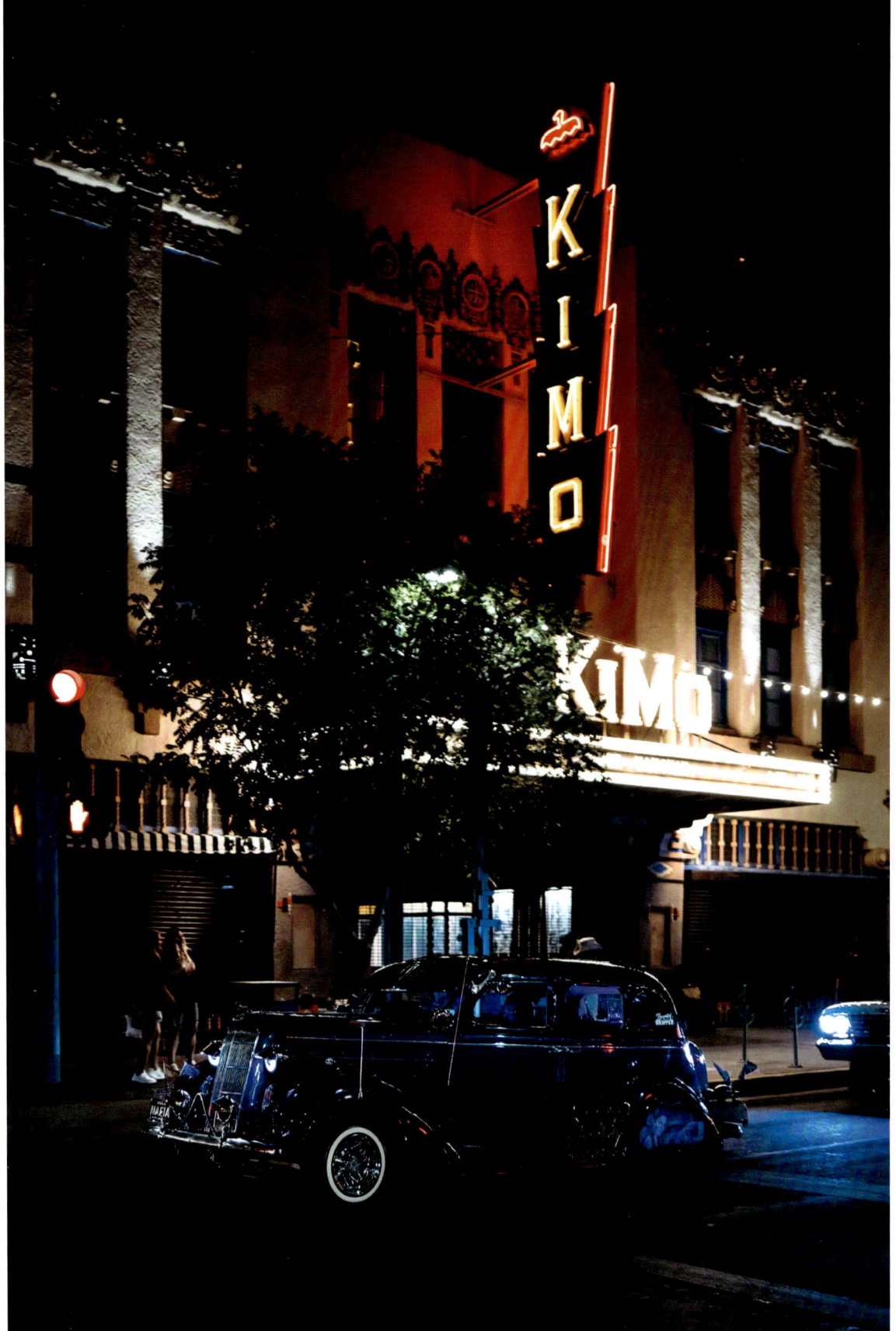

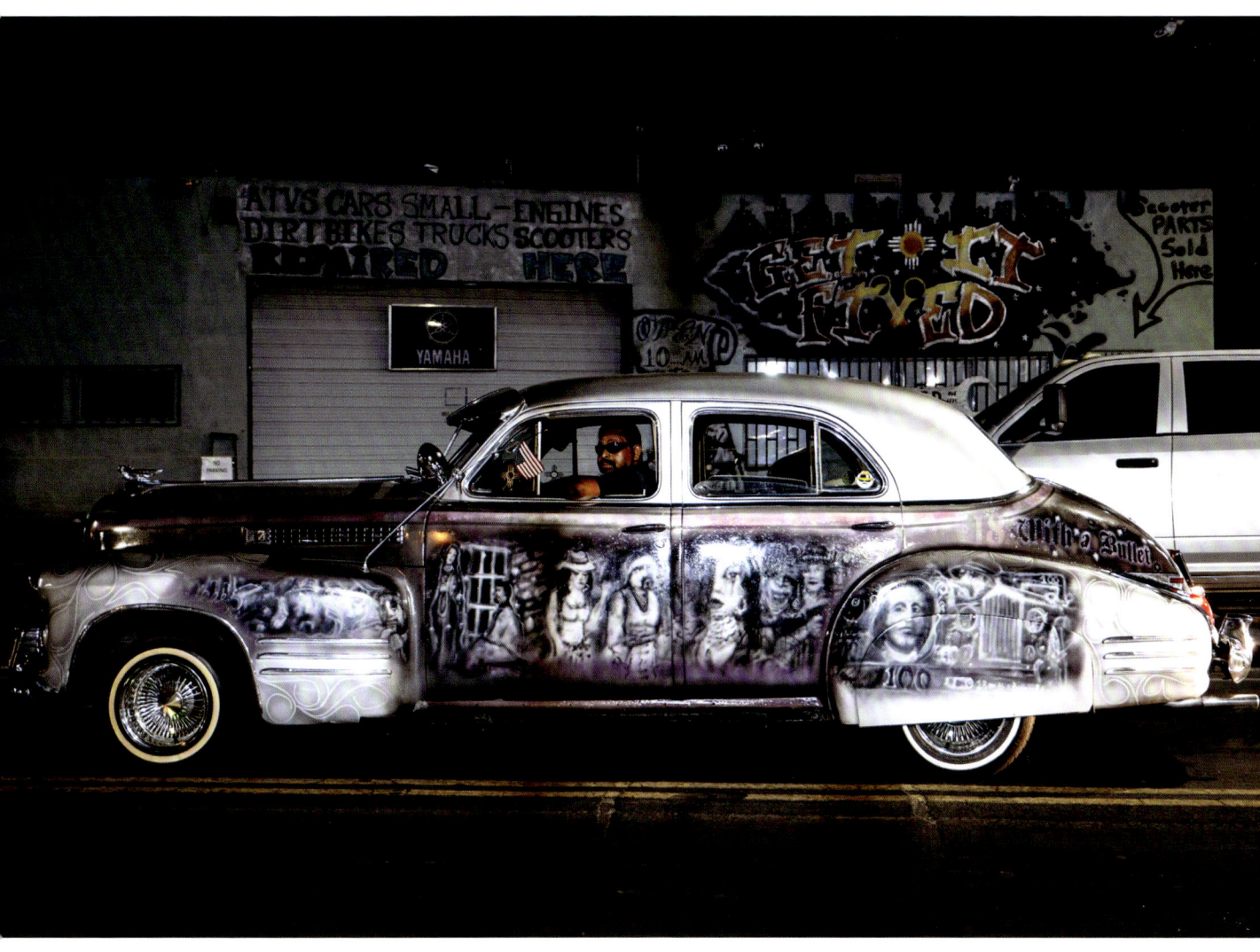

(*opposite page*) Kimo Theatre, Downtown Albuquerque, 2024.

Sunday night cruising, Barelas, 2023

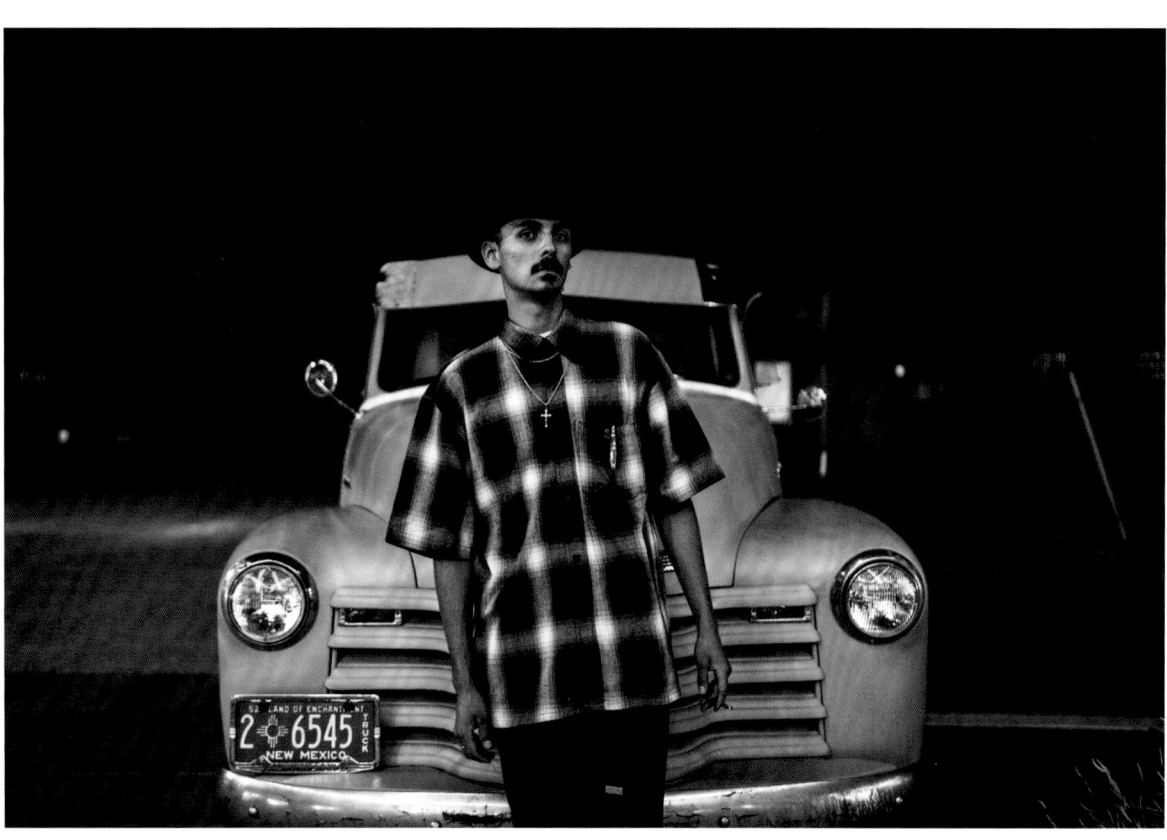

Michael Griego, Los Ranchos de Albuquerque, 2022.

(*opposite page*) Ariel Rodriguez, Barelas, Albuquerque, 2024.

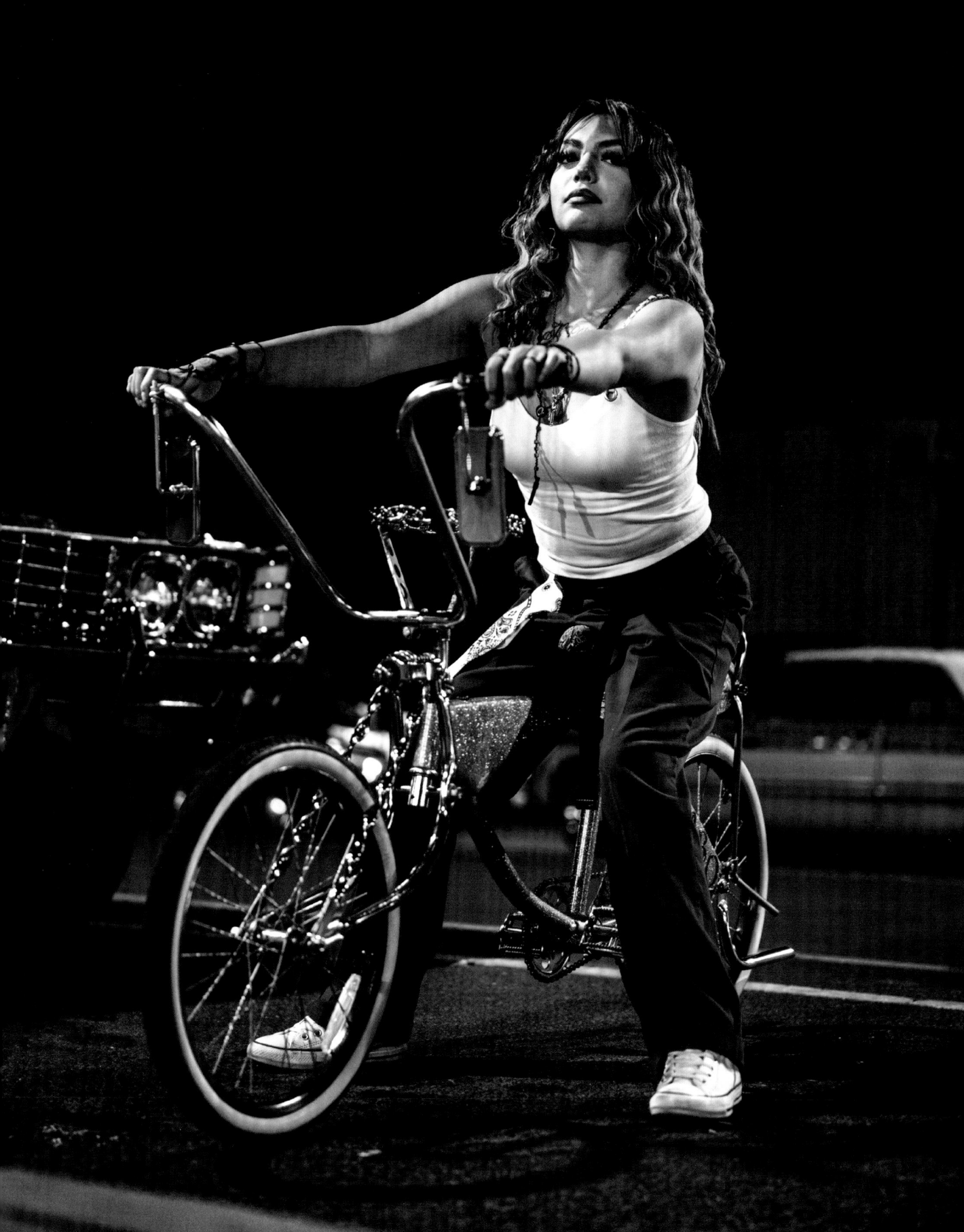

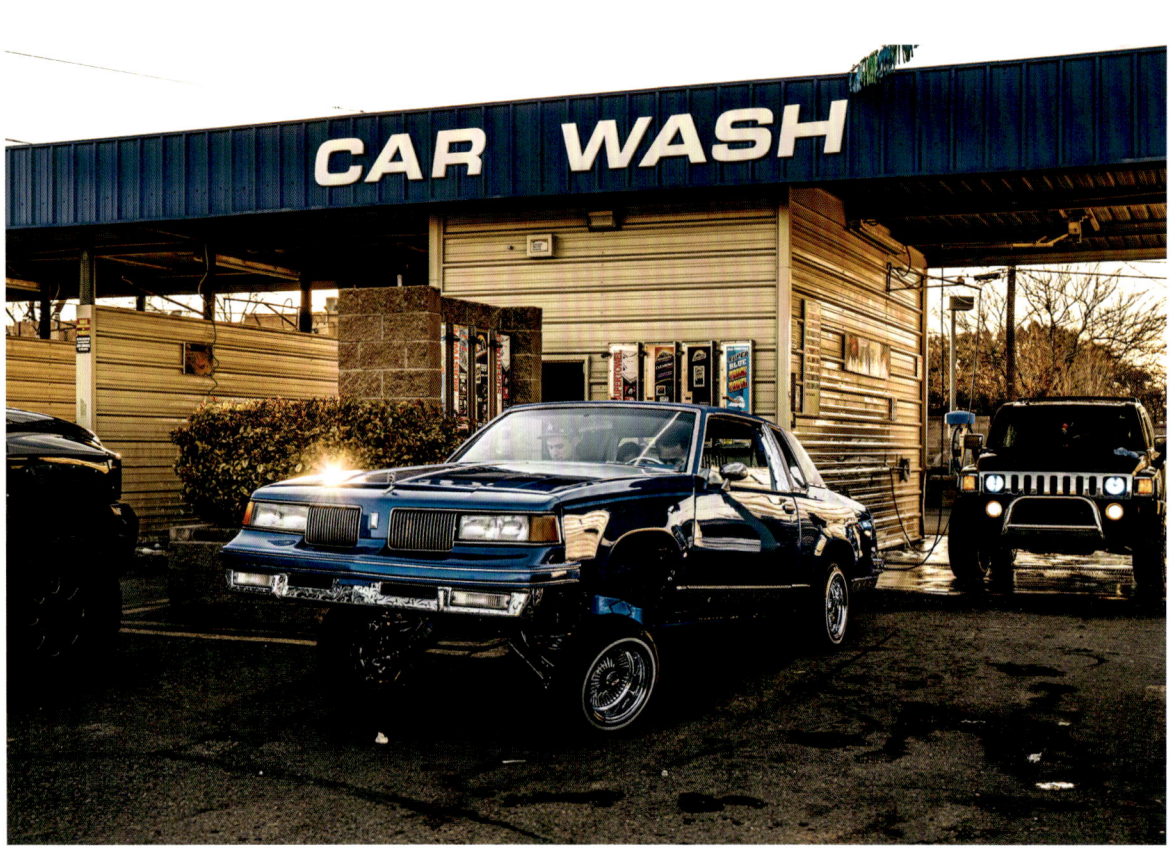

Carwash on San Mateo, Albuquerque, 2023.

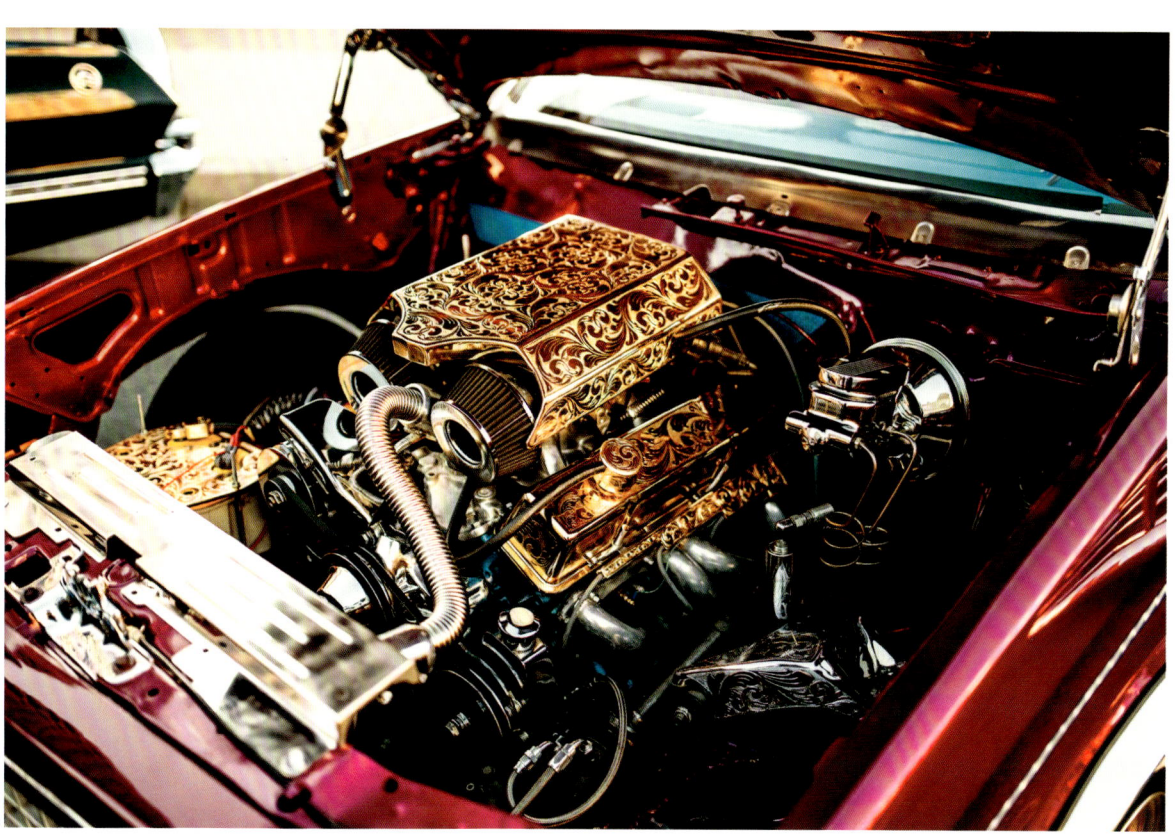

Lowrider engine, Downtown Albuquerque, 2023.

(*following pages*) Portrait of Mabel Chavez, Albuquerque, 2022.

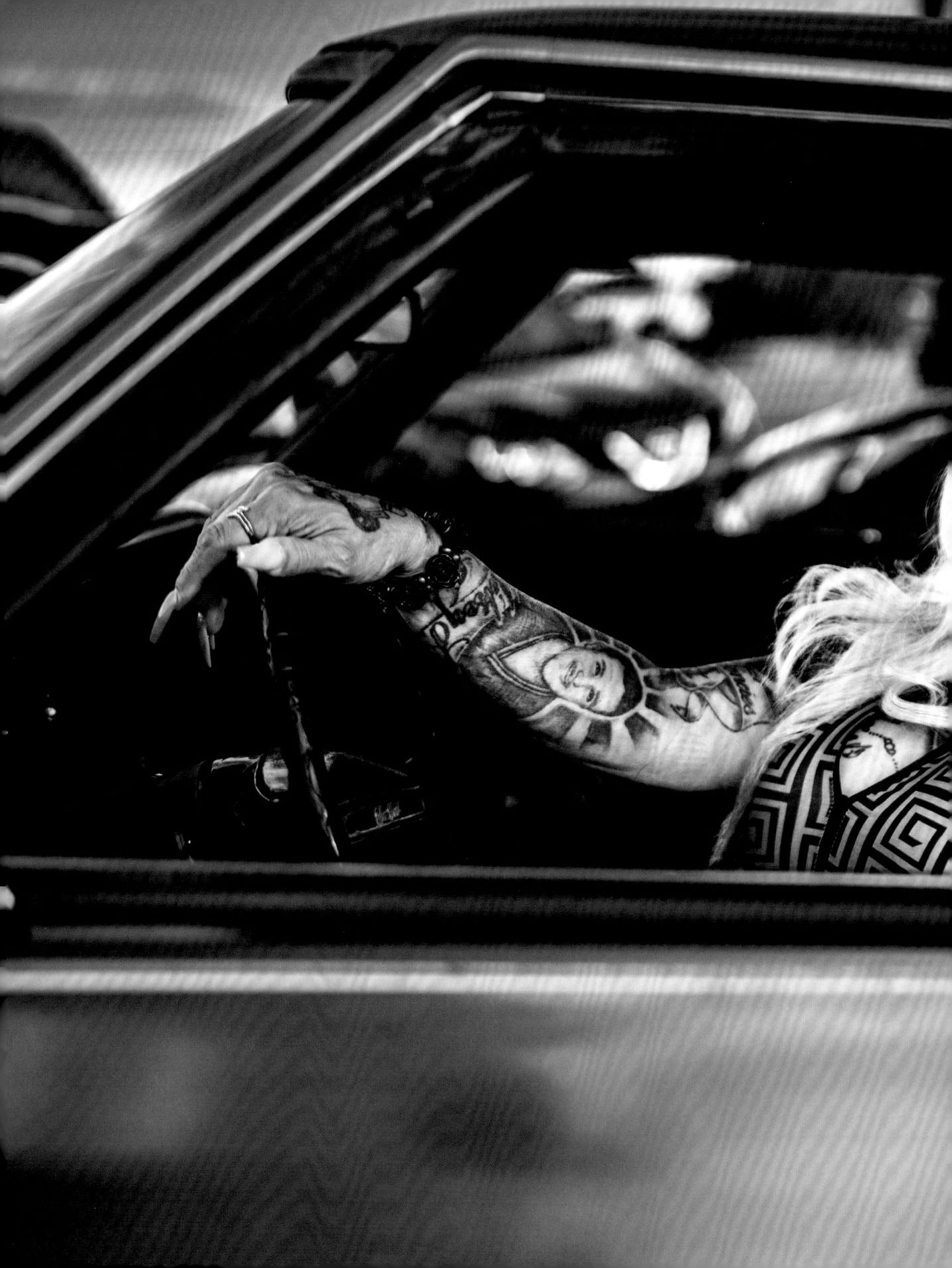

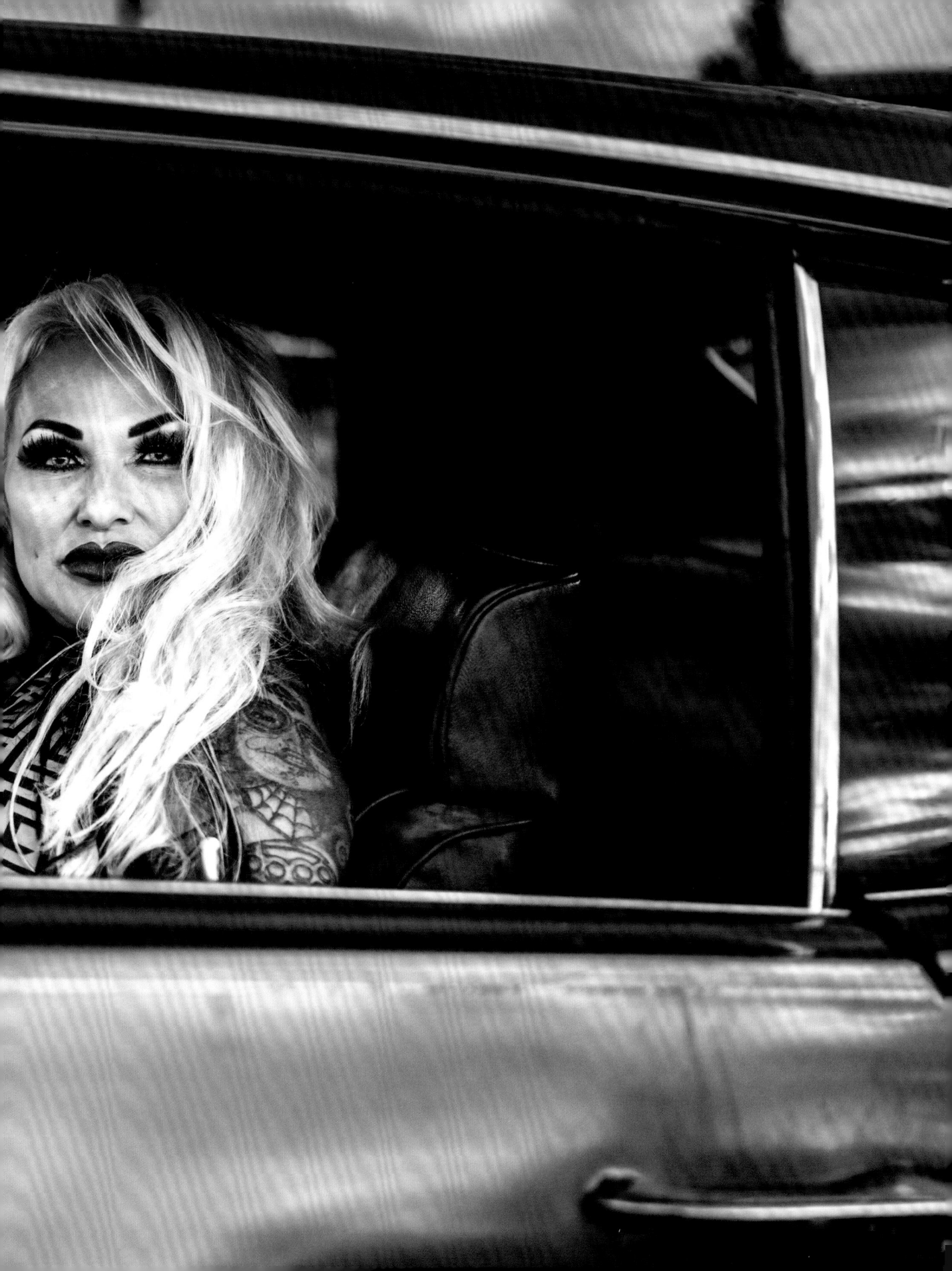

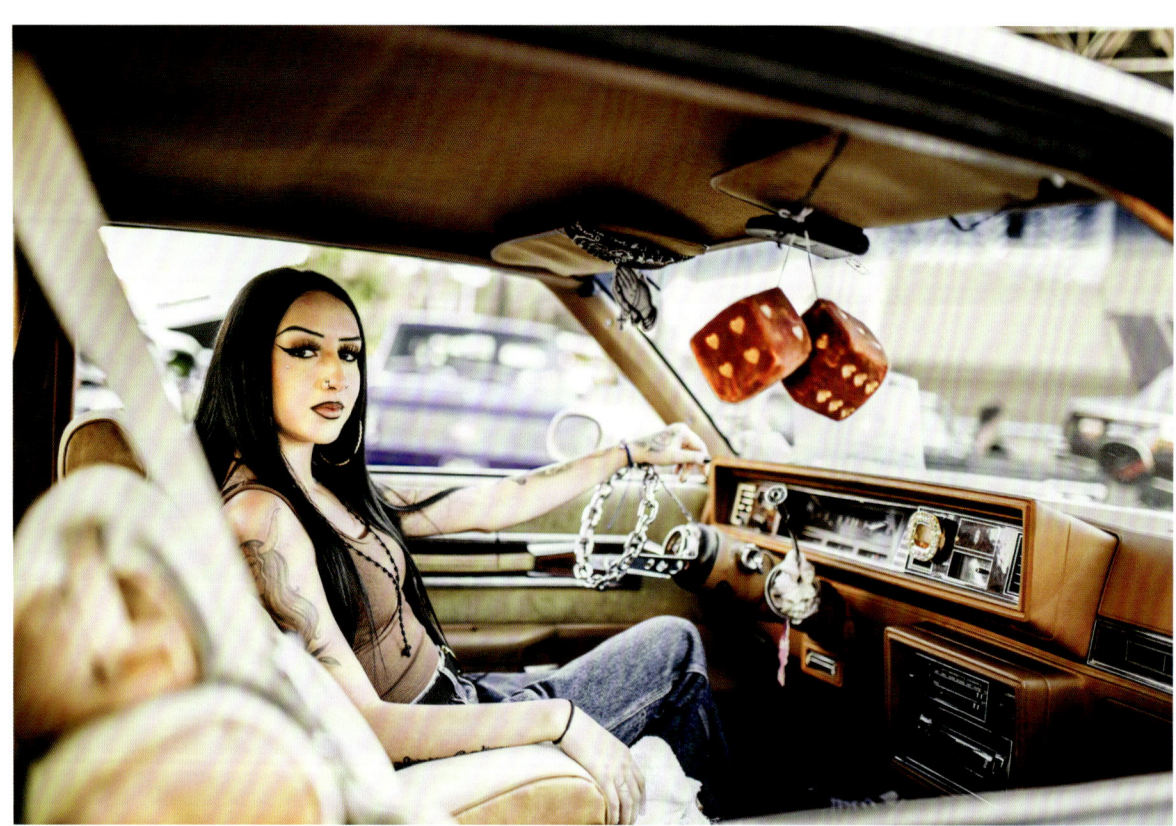

Amor Bustamante in her 1980 Oldsmobile Cutlass, Downtown Albuquerque, 2023.

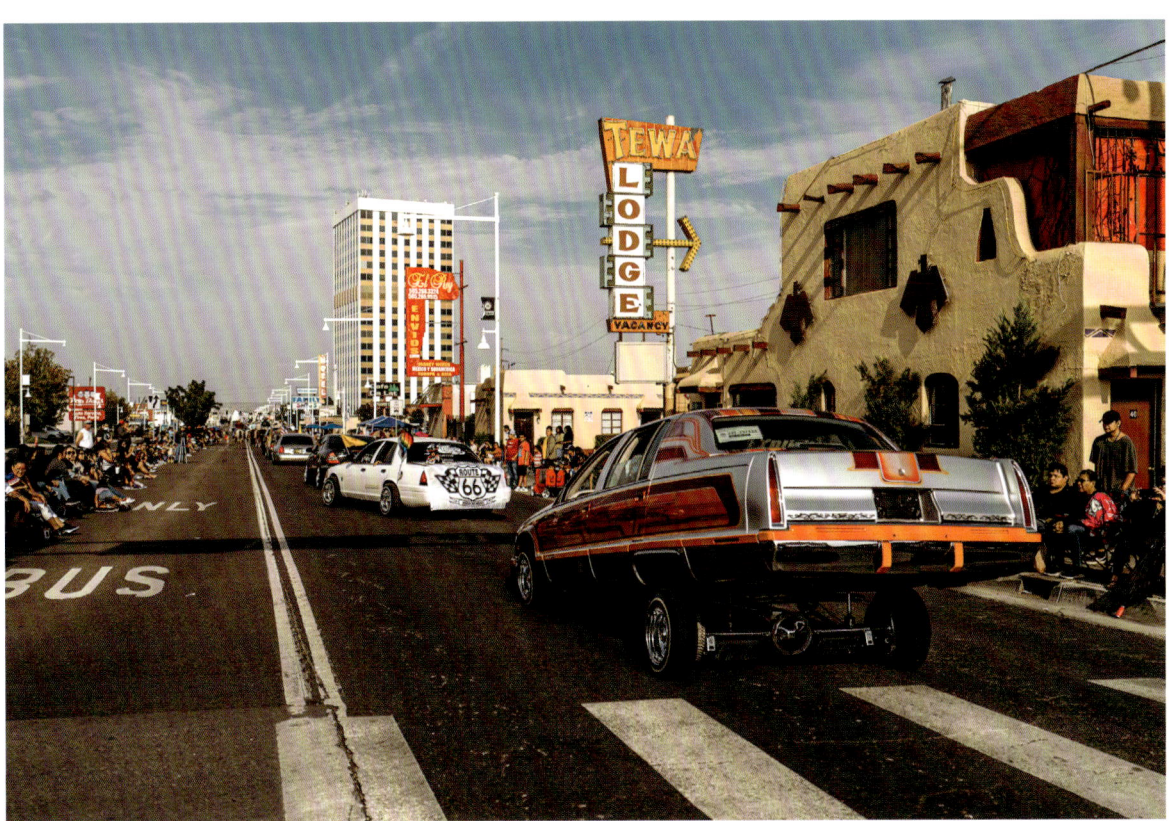

Lowriders cruise down Central Avenue in the State Fair Parade, Albuquerque, 2022.

(*following pages*) Portrait of a girl at the Lowrider Super Show, Albuquerque, 2024.

Portrait of Pedro, Albuquerque, 2021.

Jason Gomez in his garage, Albuquerque, 2024.

El Camino Motor Hotel, Los Ranchos de Albuquerque, 2023.

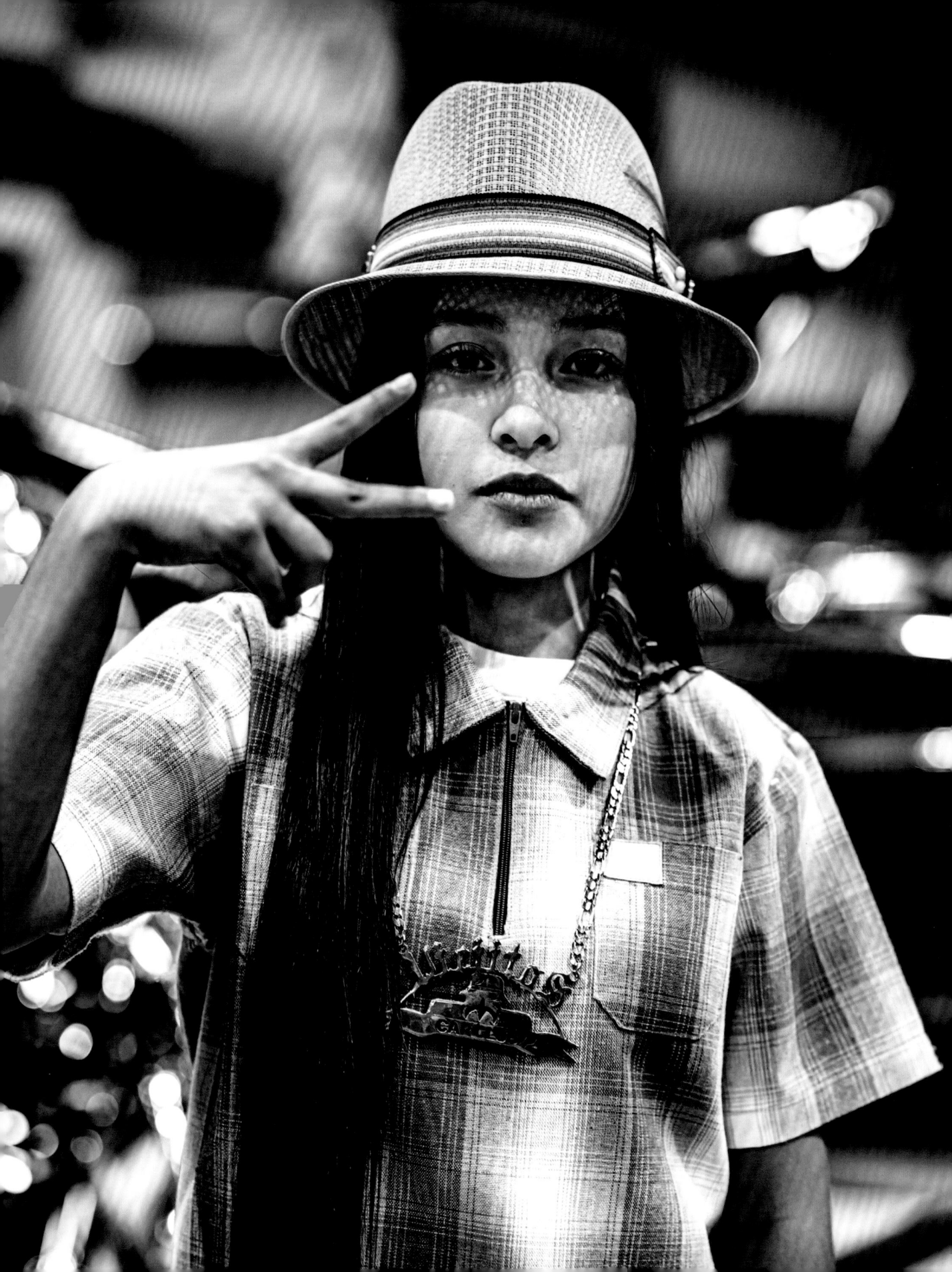

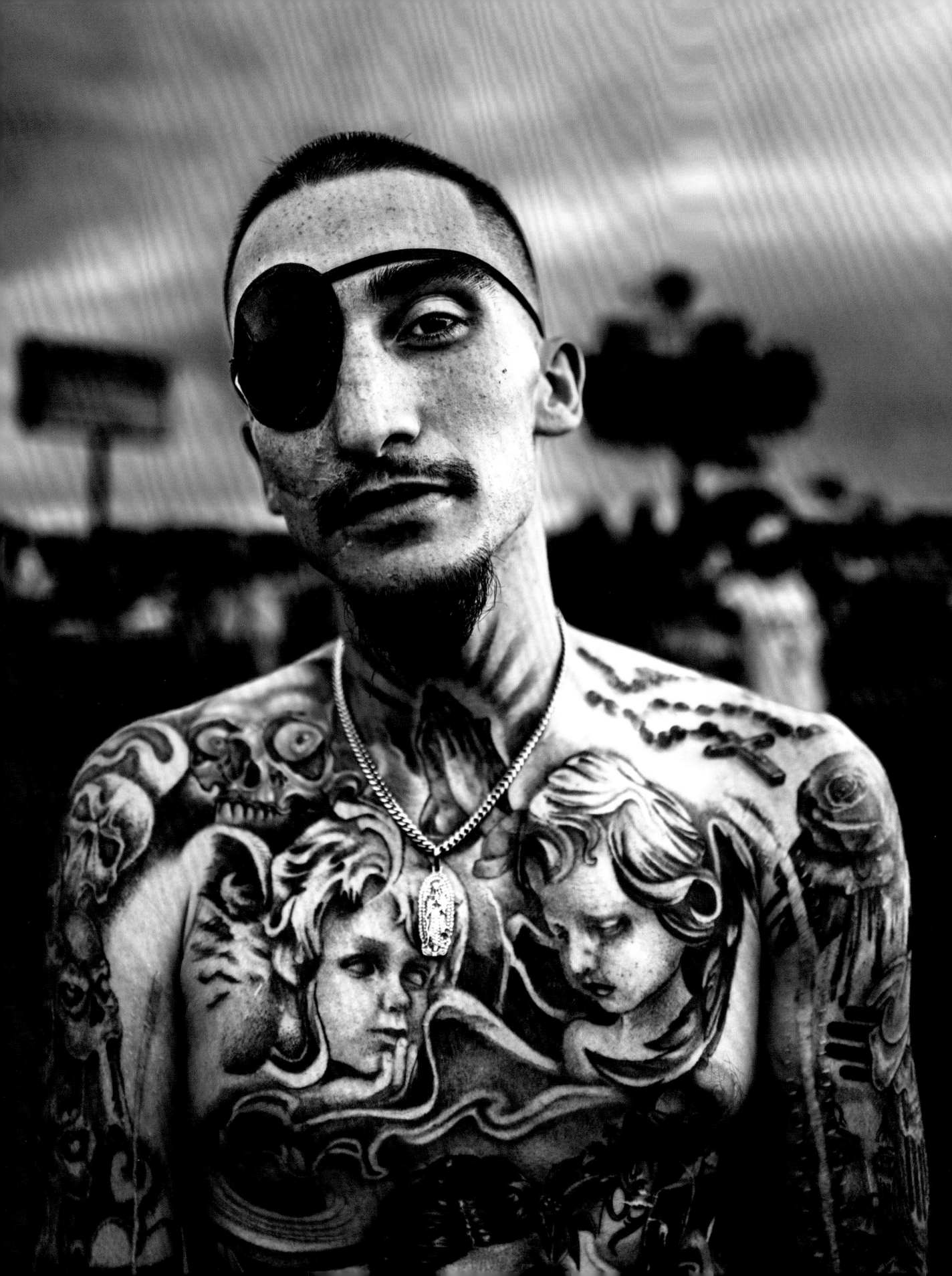

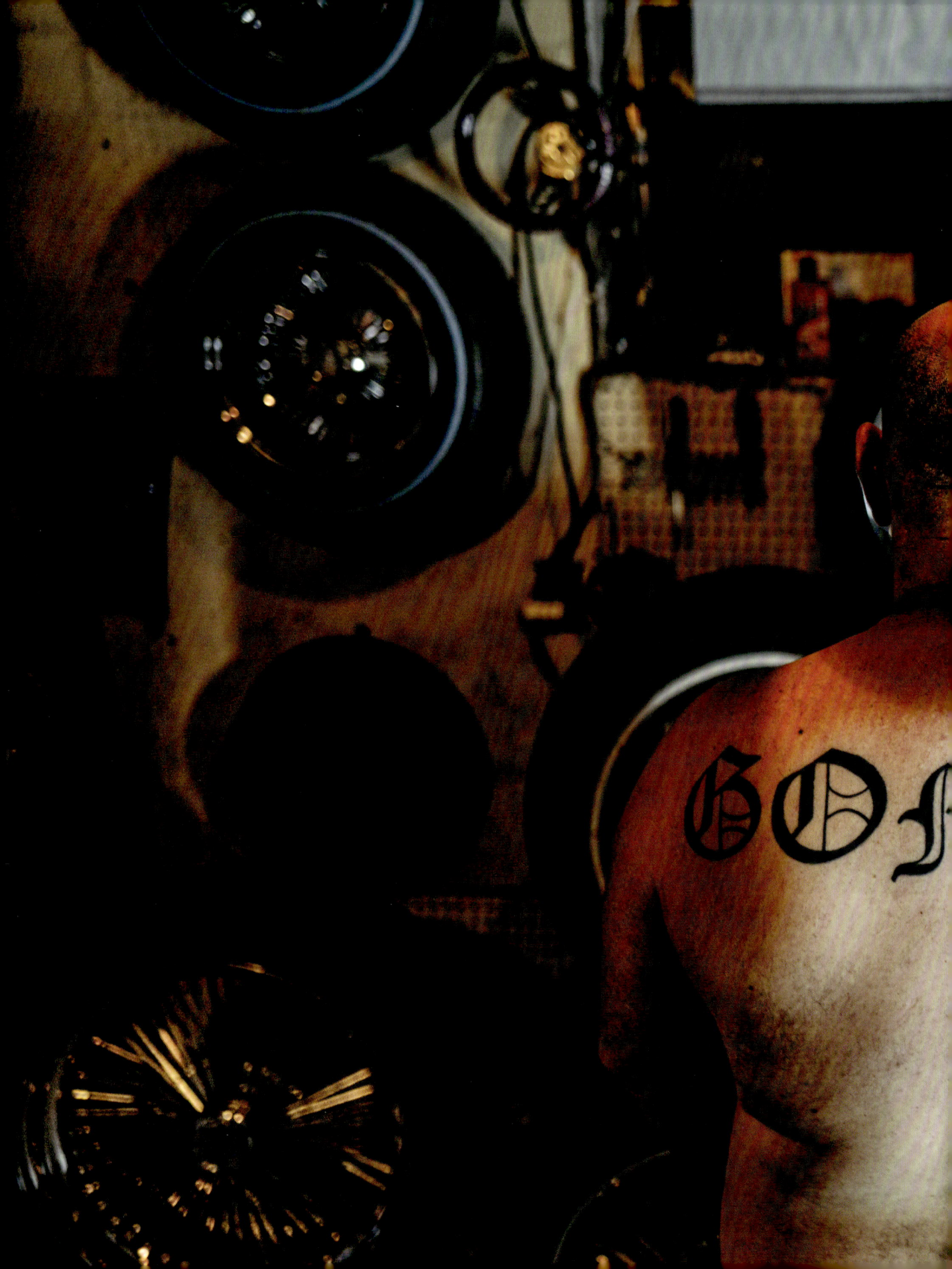

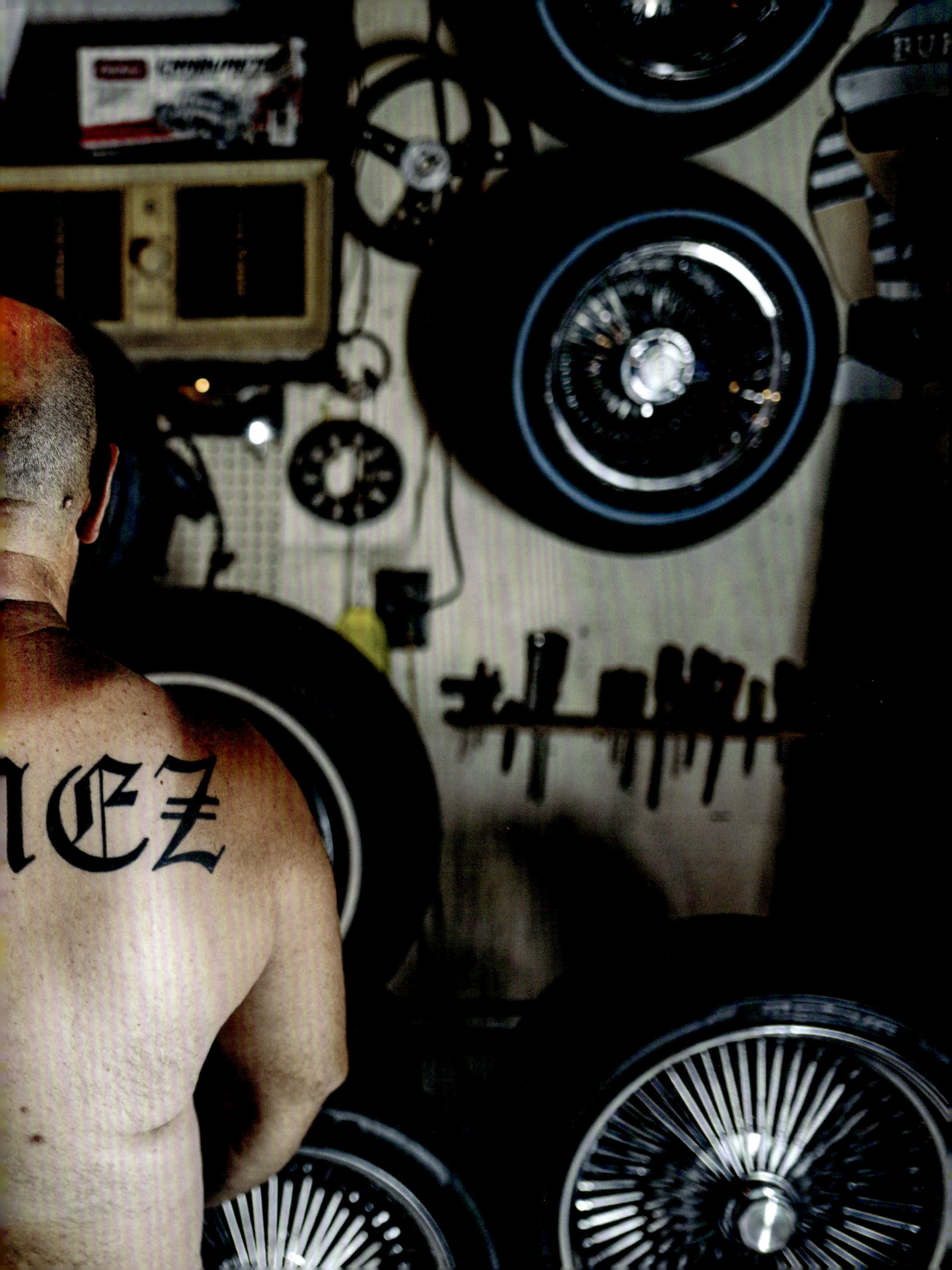

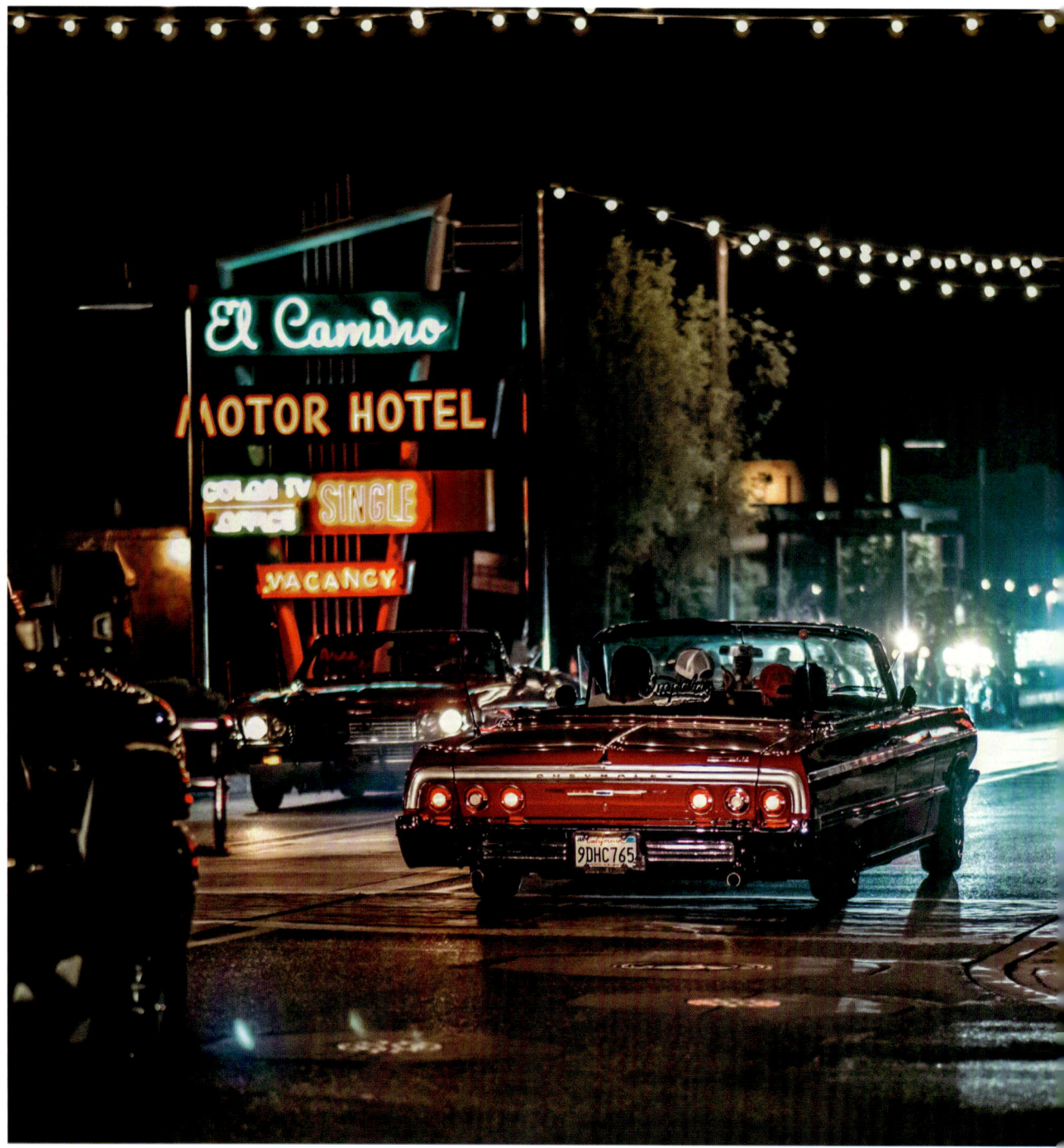

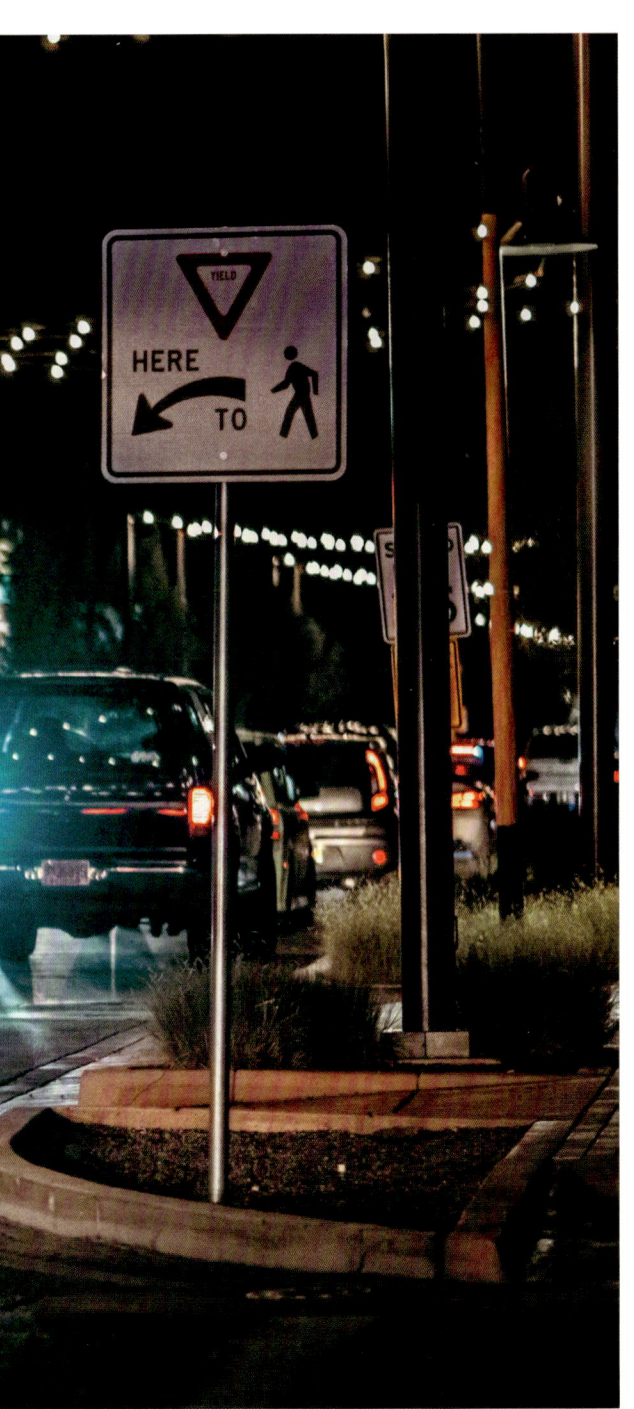

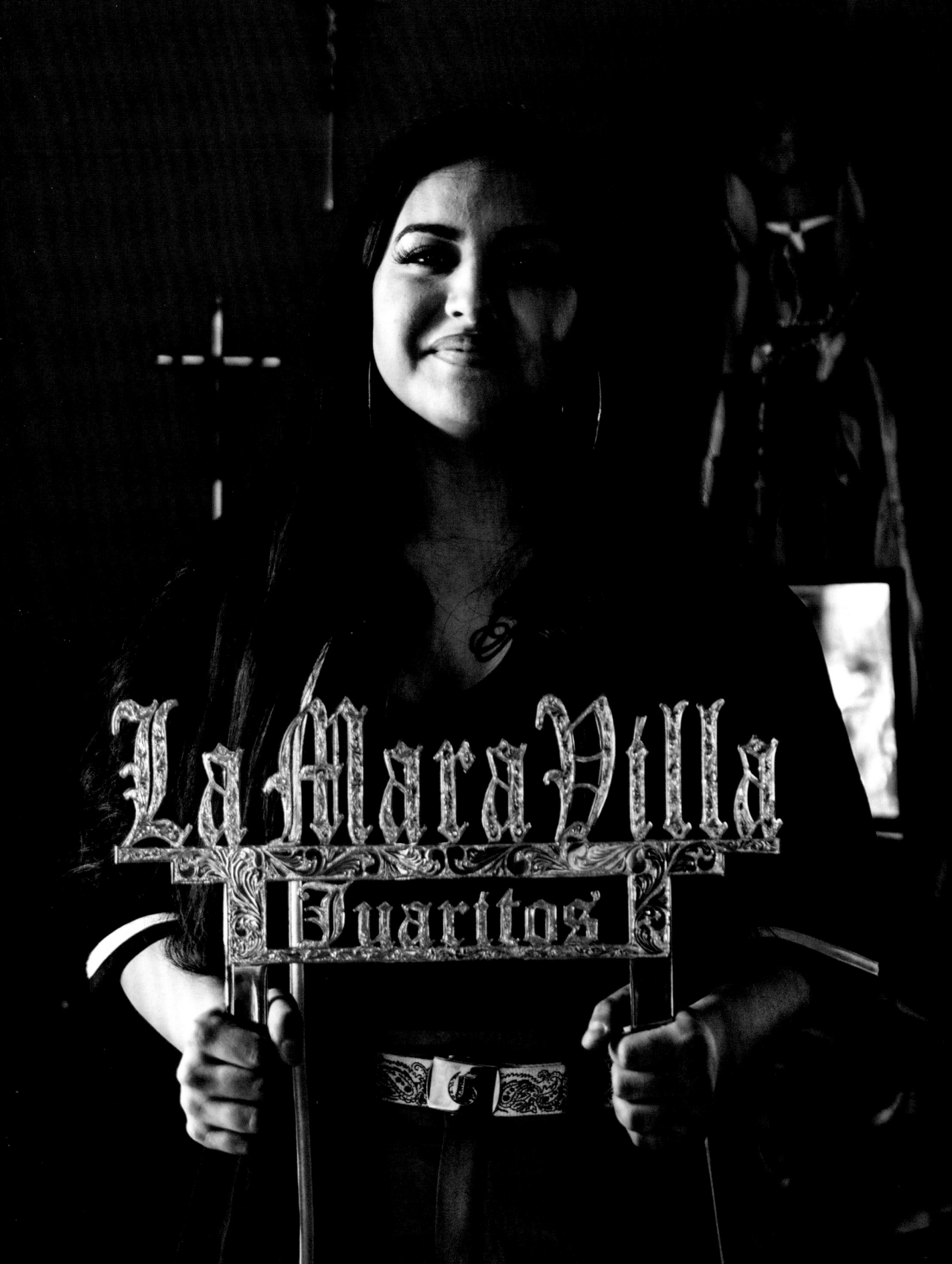

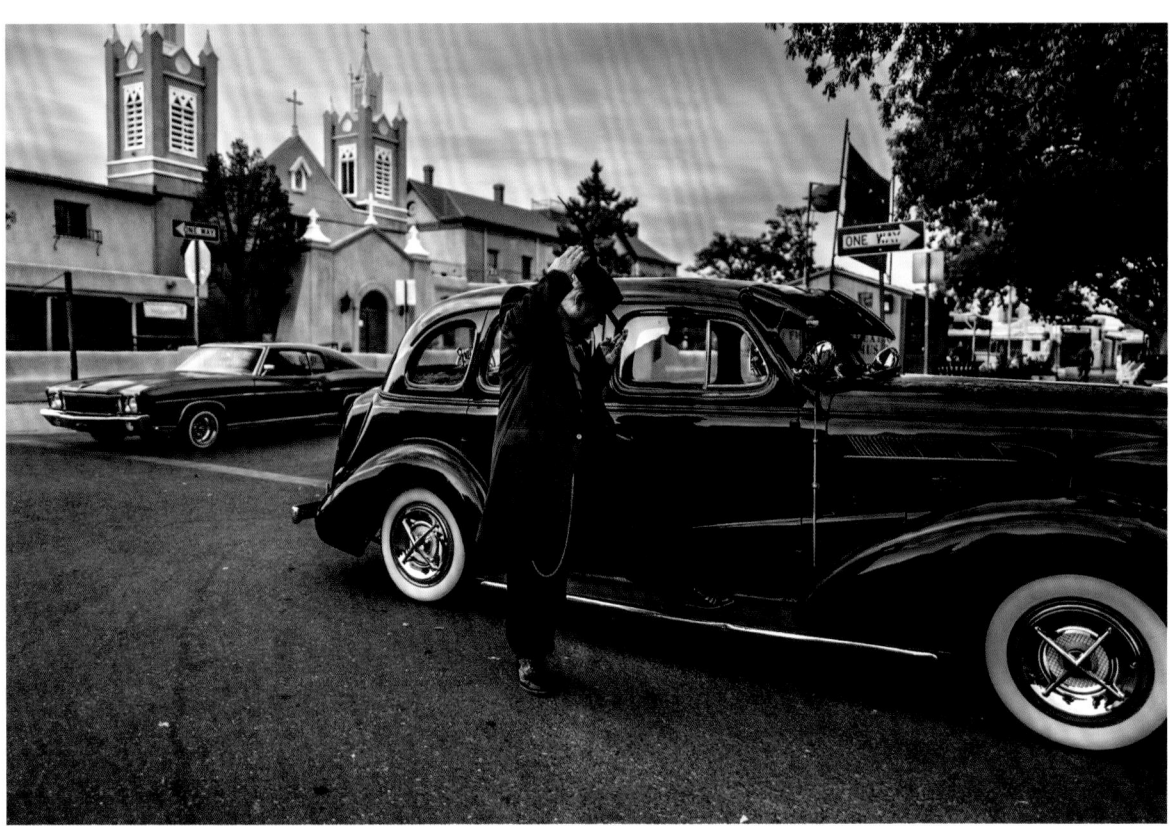

(*opposite page*) Icela Garcia, Barelas, Albuquerque, 2023.

Oldtown on a Sunday afternoon, Albuquerque, 2023.

(*following pages*) Día de Muertos, Downtown Albuquerque, 2022.

Portrait of Angela Valdez Lopez Blanco, Santa Fe, 2024.

Matthew Cordova tattoos his father in law, Albuquerque, 2023.

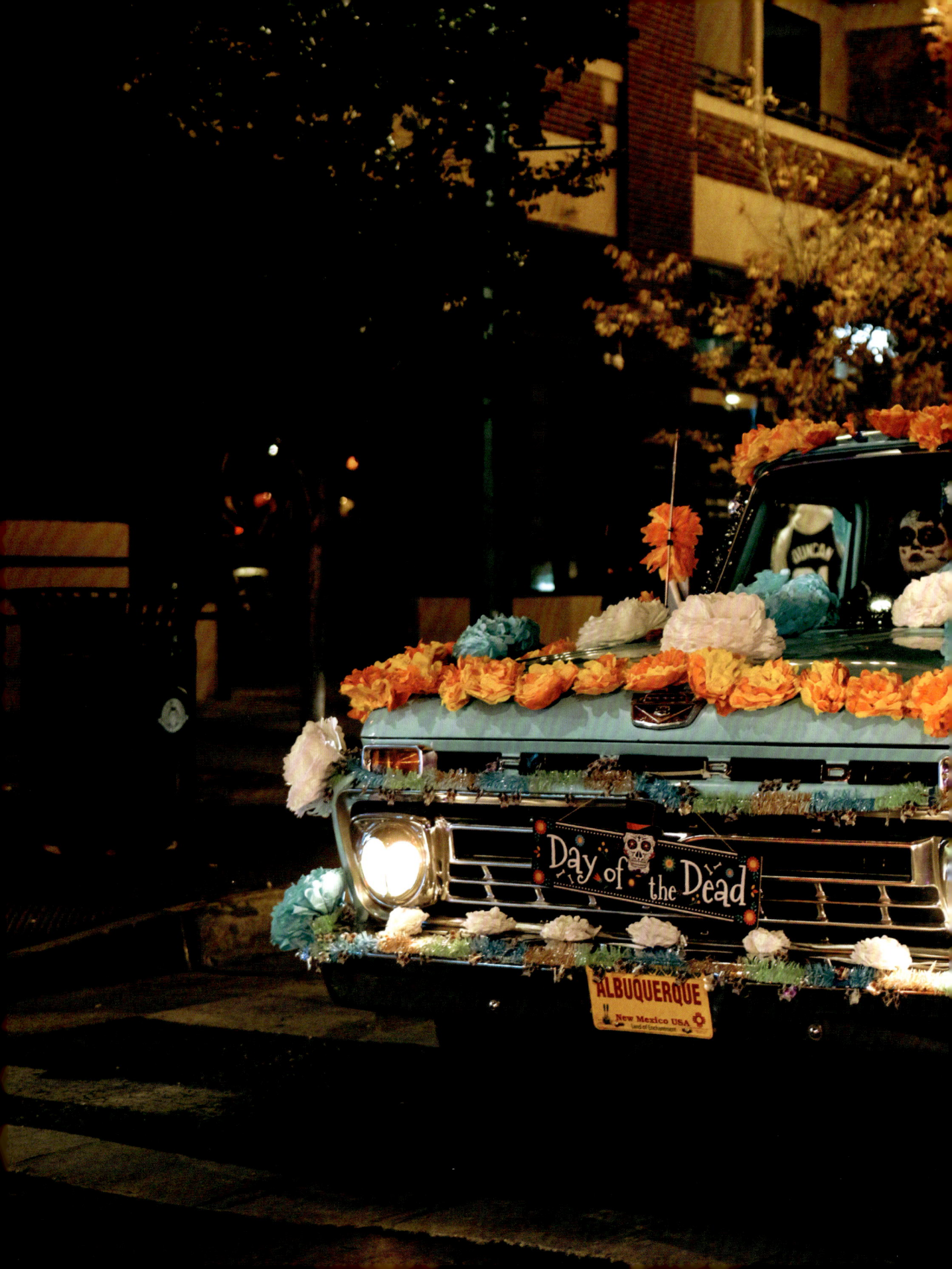

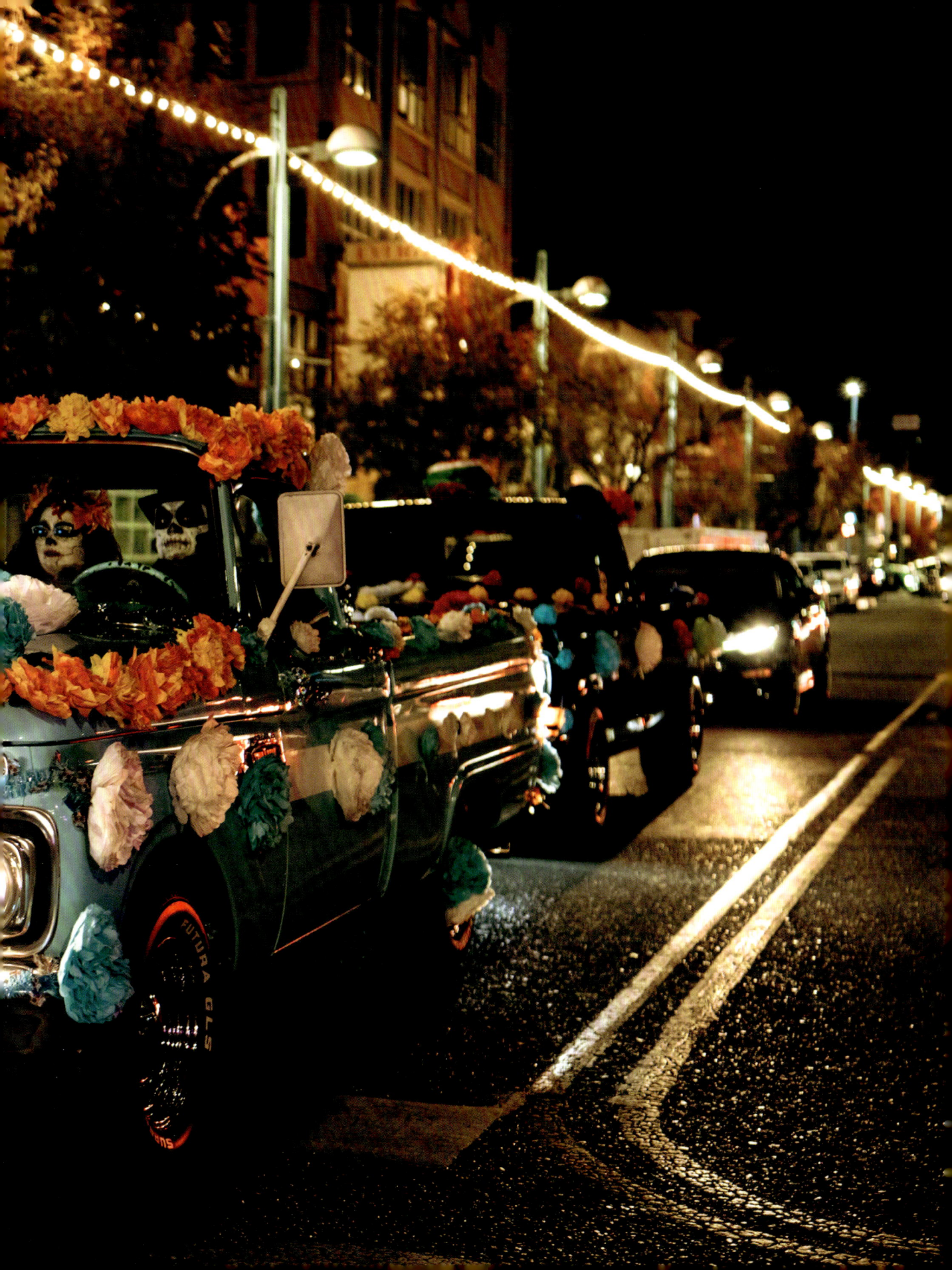

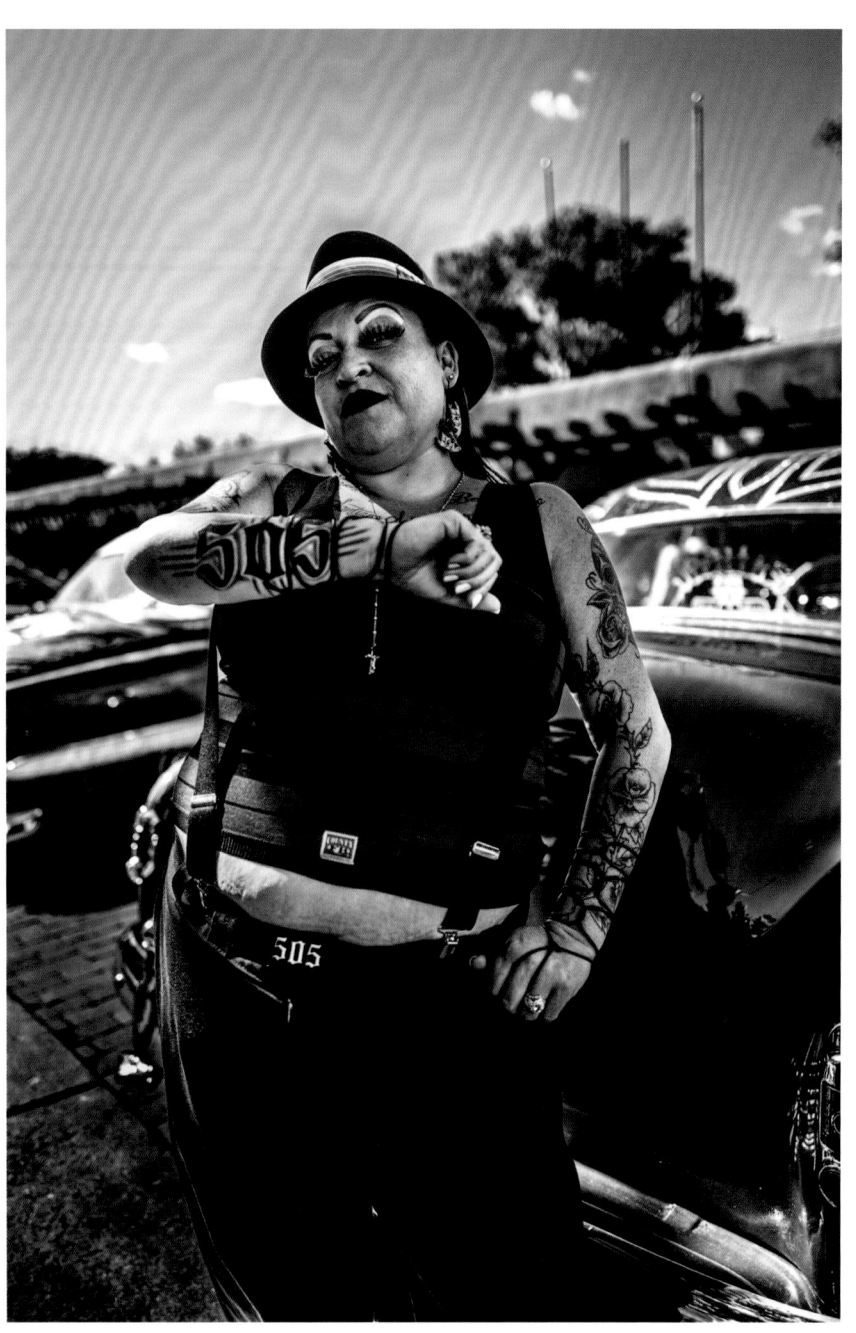

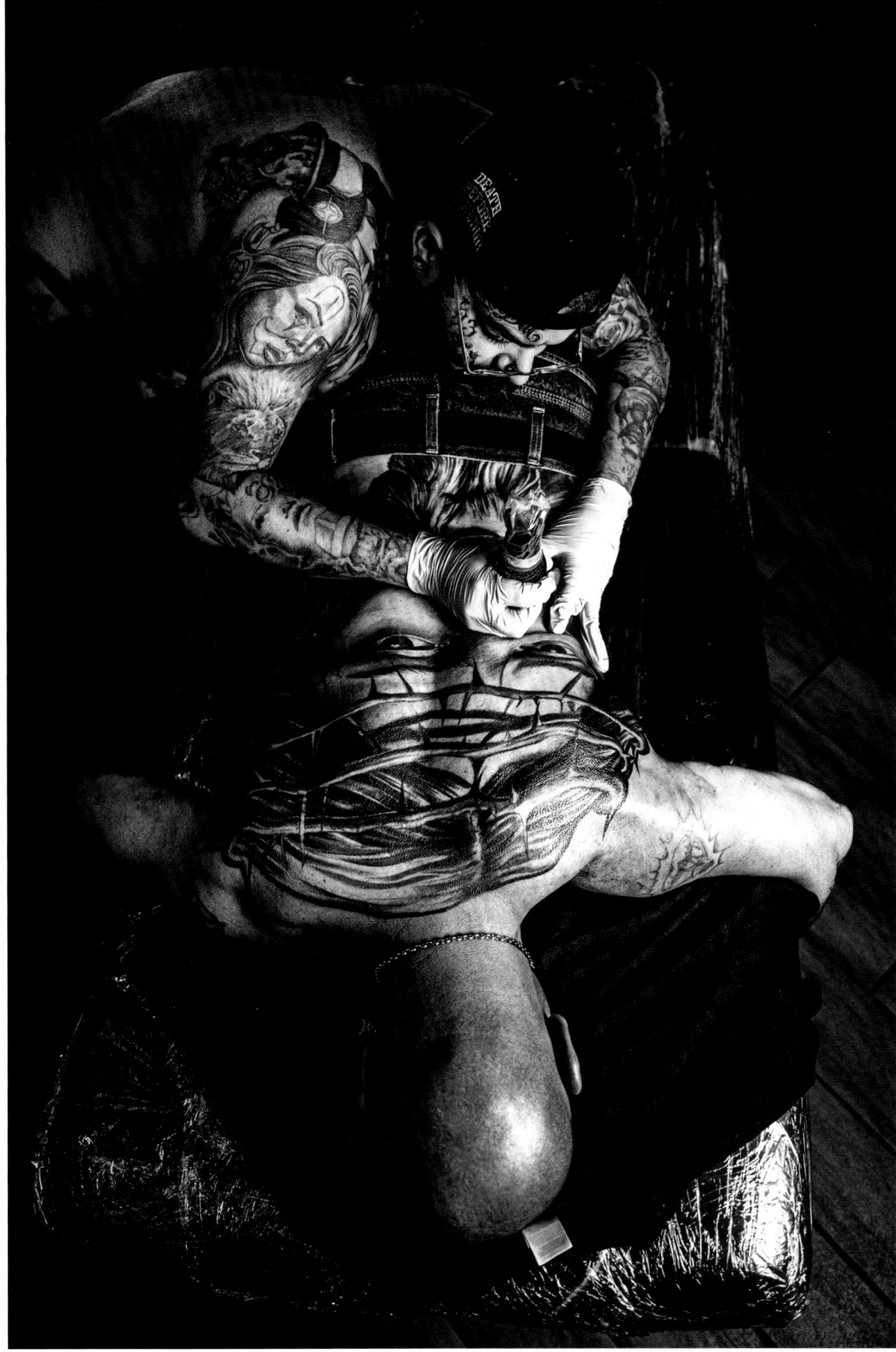

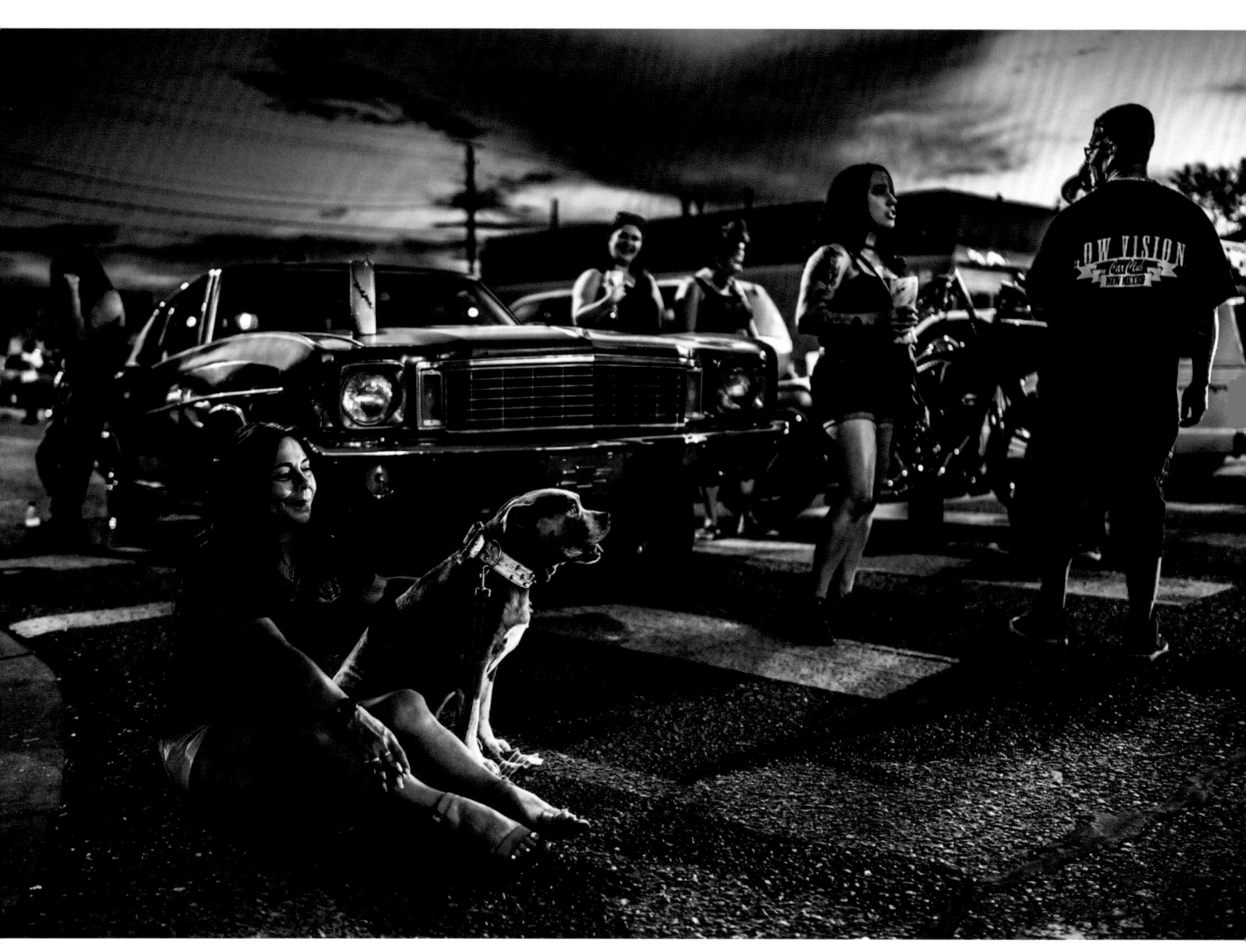

Seventh Street and Central Avenue, Downtown Albuquerque, 2022.

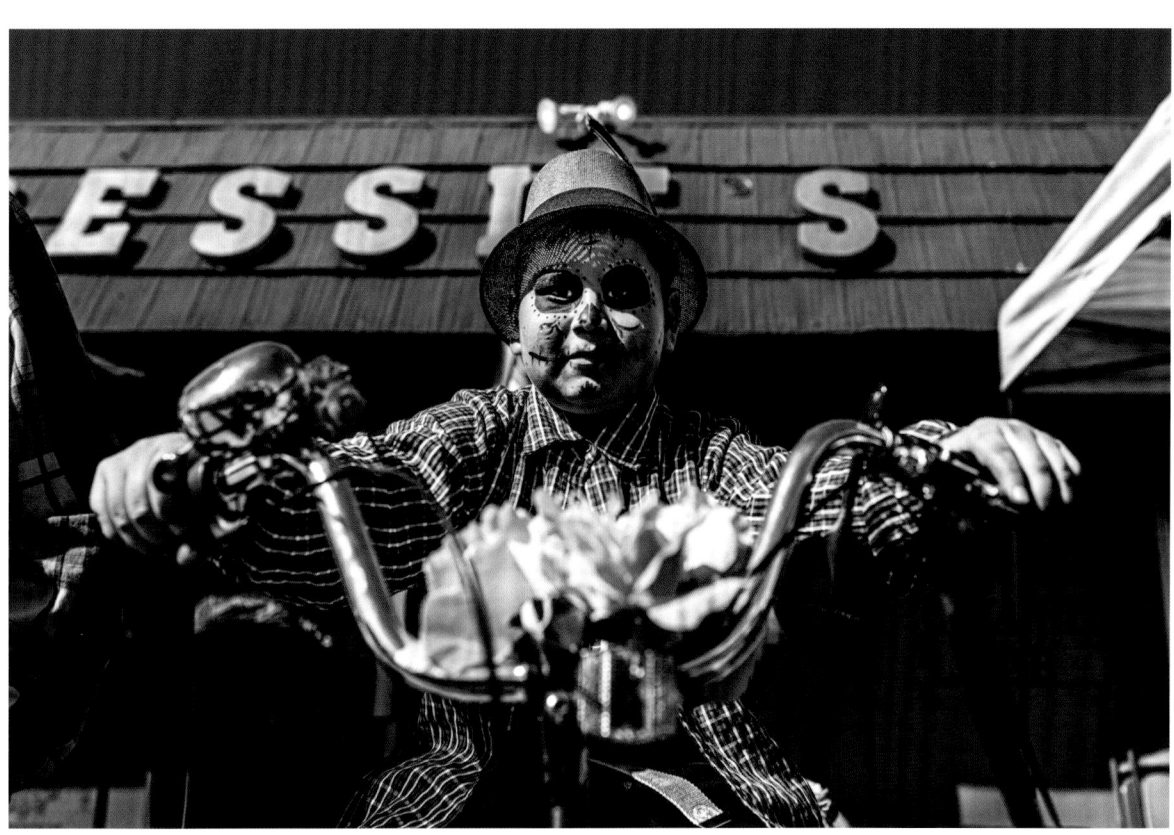

A boy on his lowrider bicycle, Día de los Muertos, South Valley, Albuquerque, 2023.

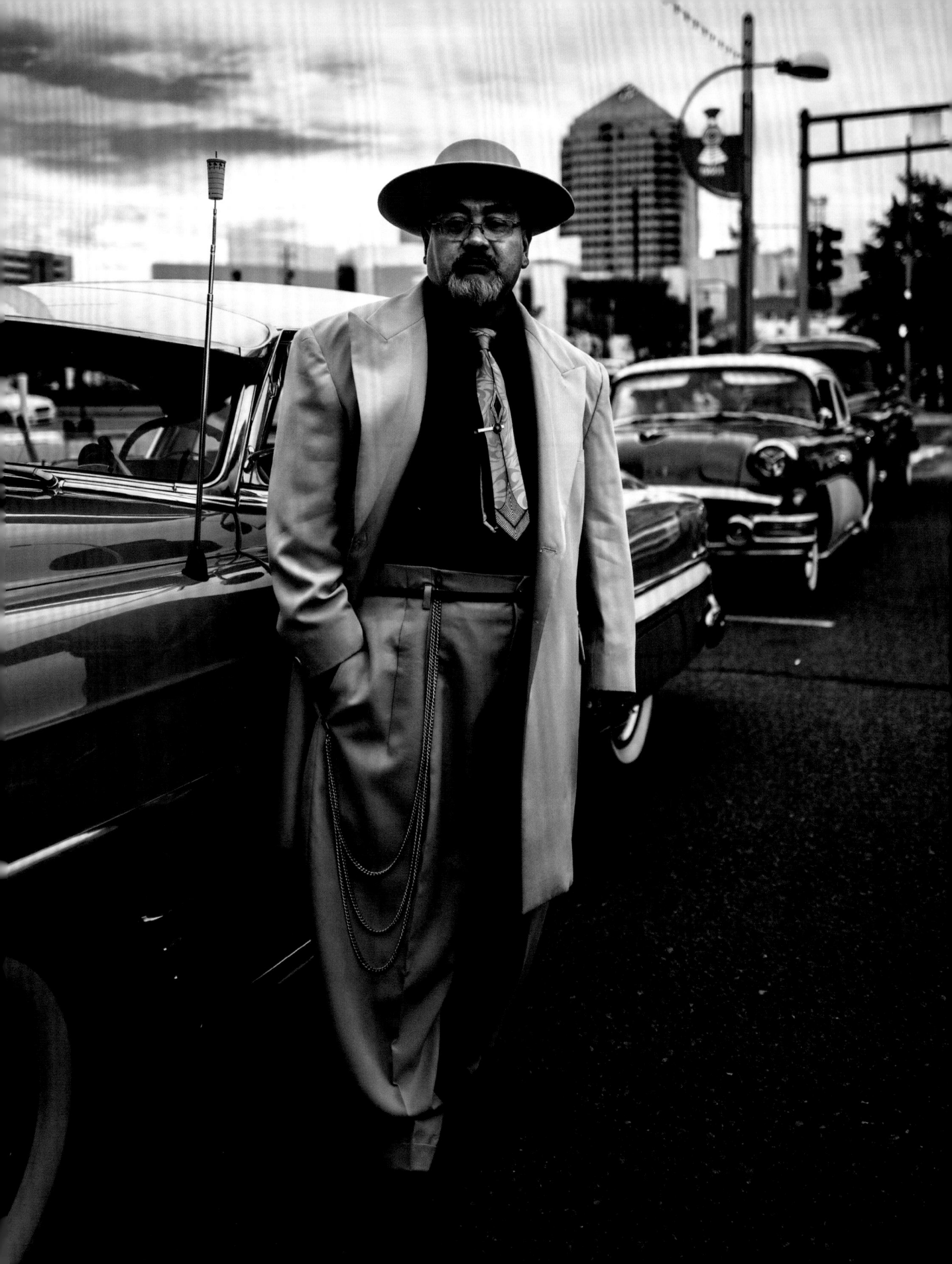

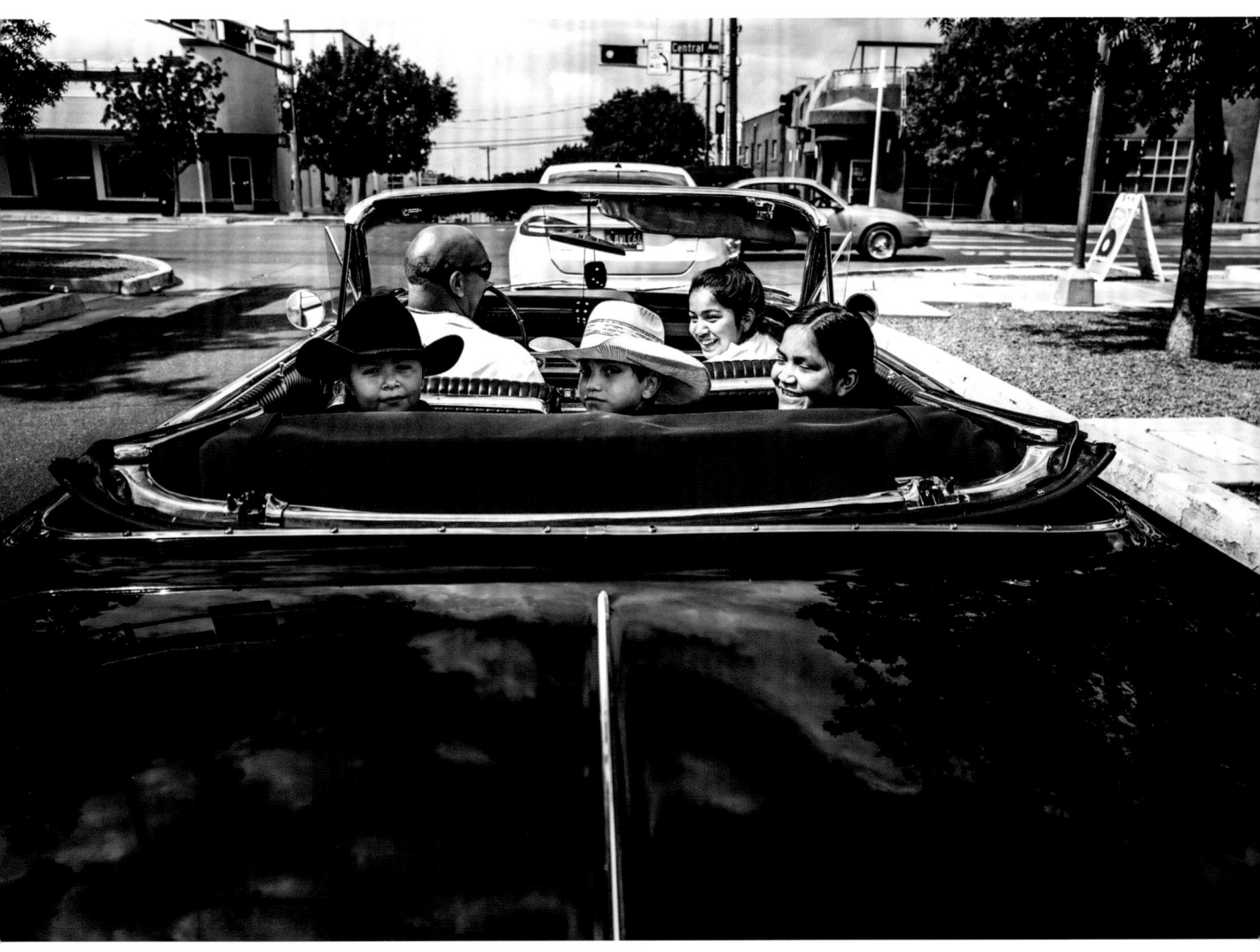

(*opposite page*) A man in a zoot suit, Downtown Albuquerque, 2021.

Family out for a Sunday cruise, Nob Hill, Albuquerque, 2021.

(*following pages*) A Chevrolet El Camino drives past the San Felipe de Neri Parish, Oldtown, 2021.

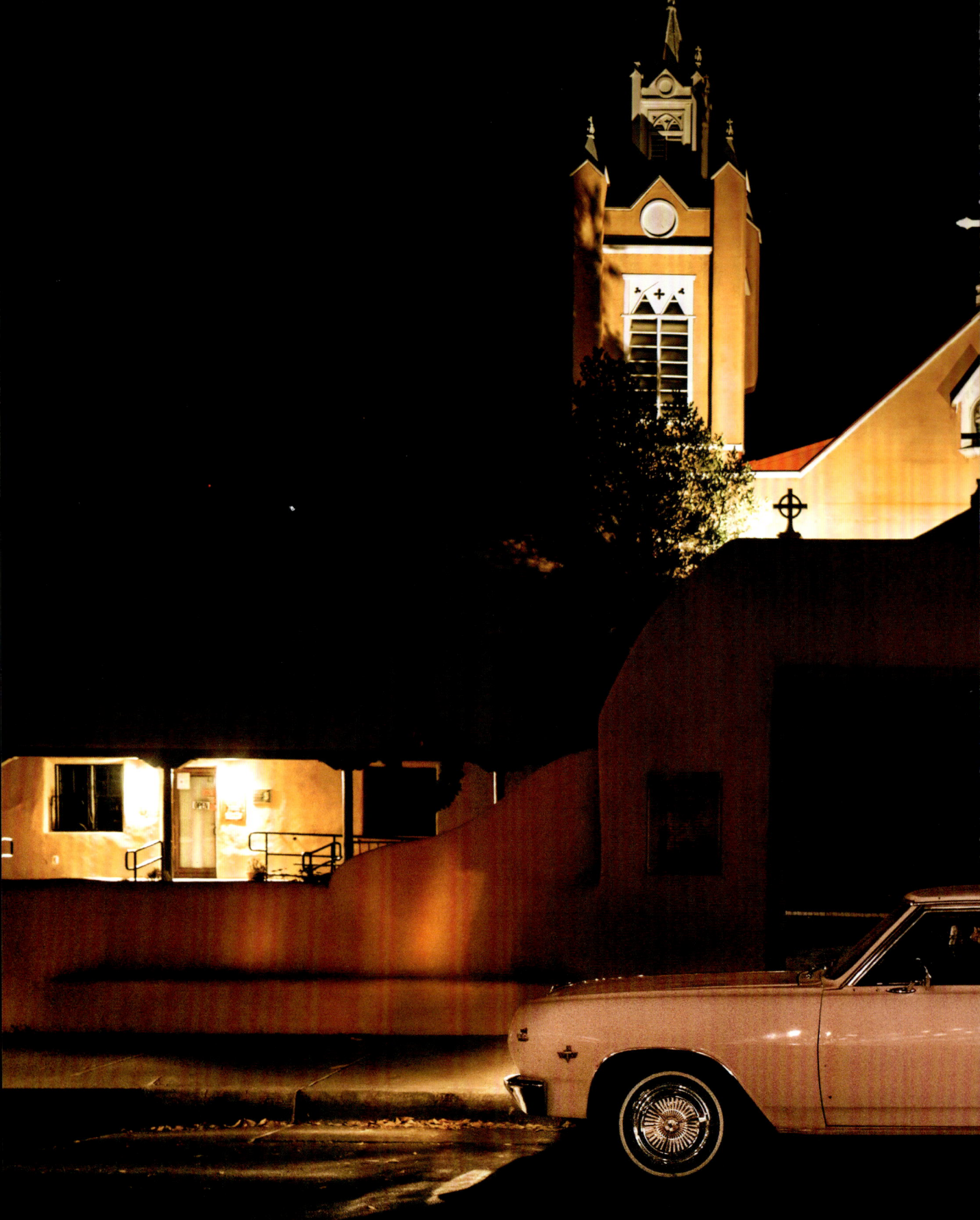

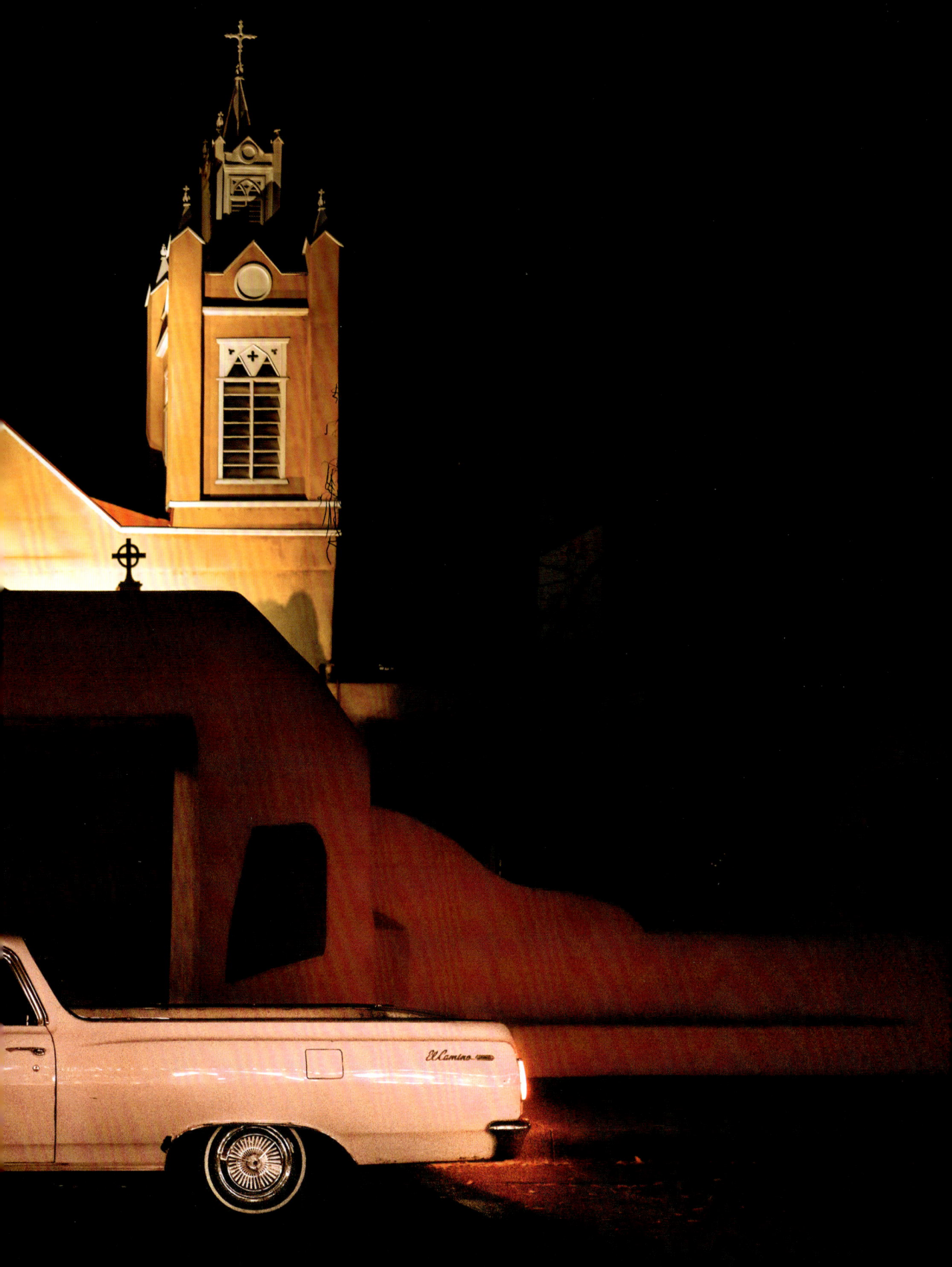

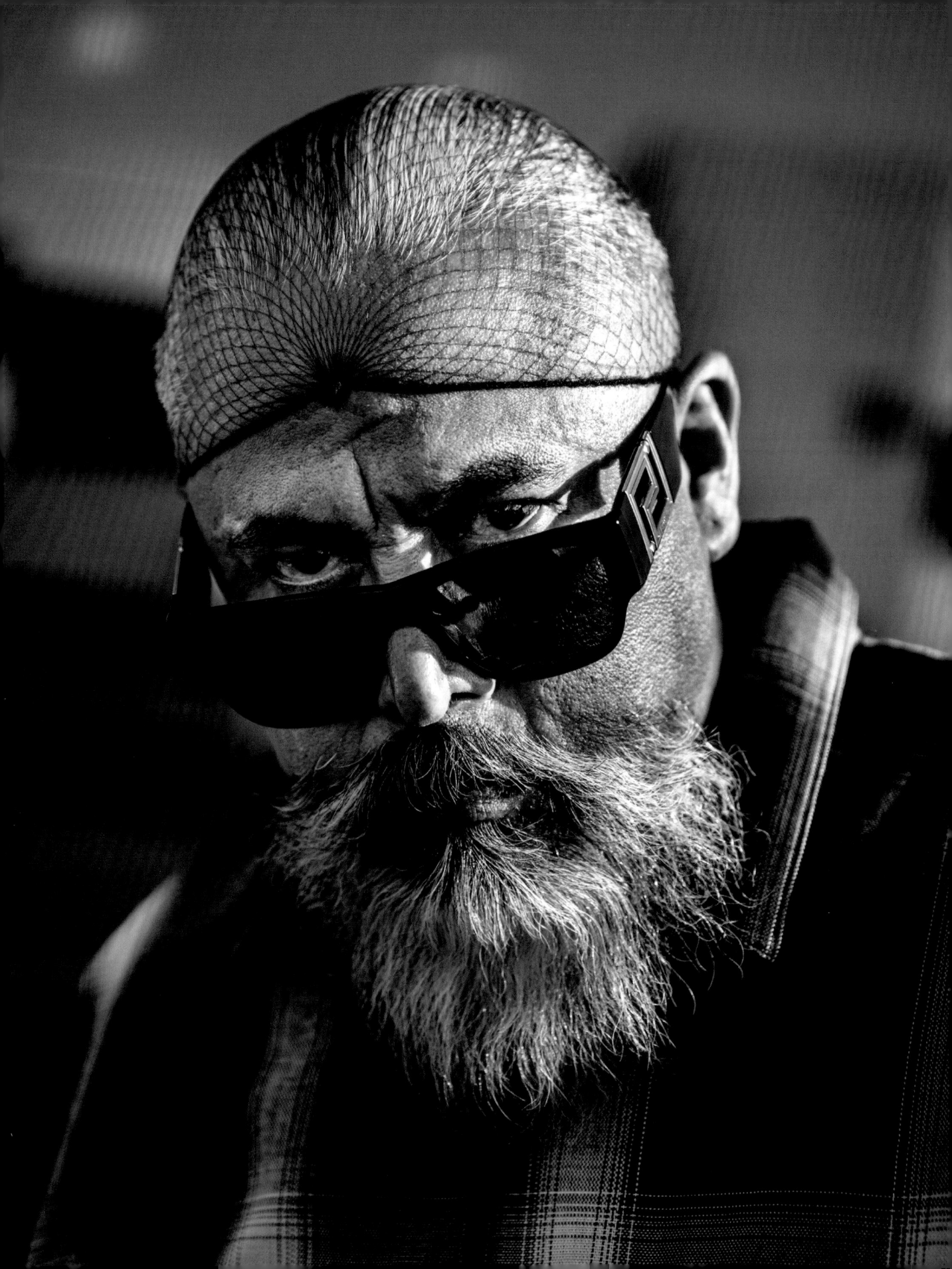

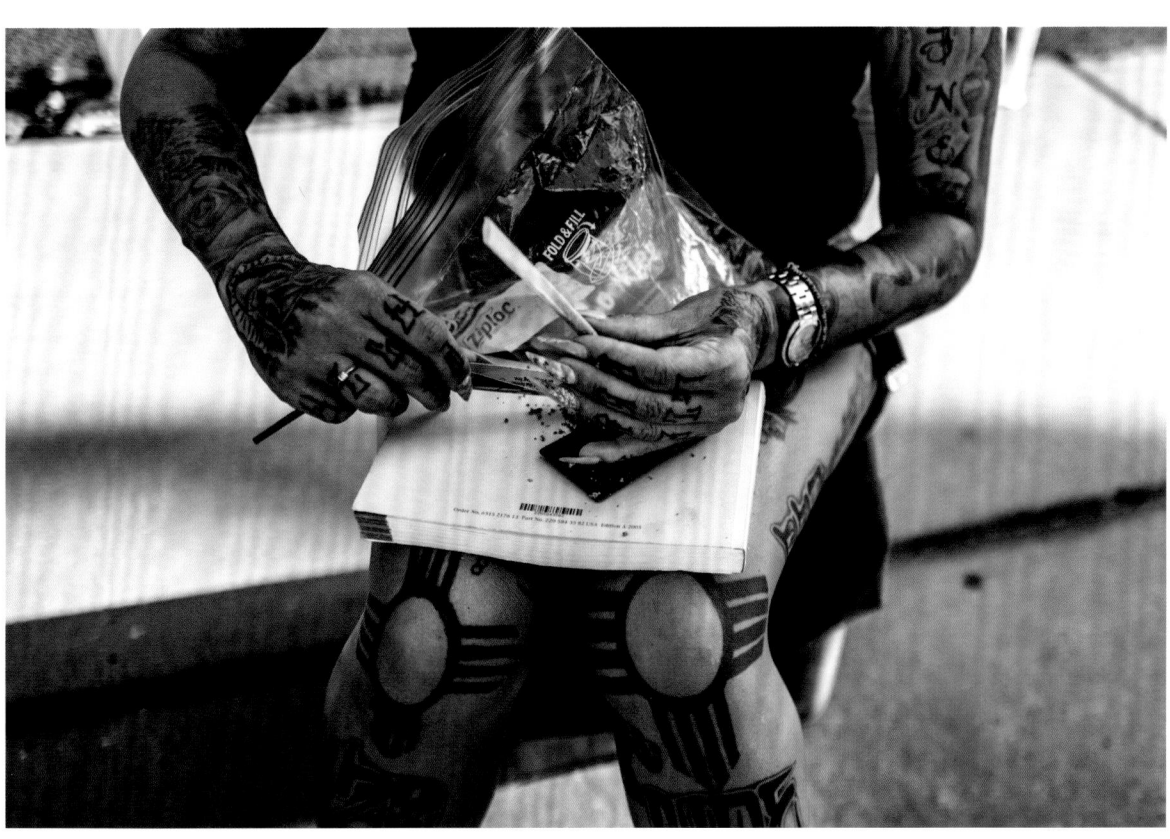

(*opposite page*) Oscar Guzman, Albuquerque, 2024.

Sharky Loca, Downtown Albuquerque, 2024.

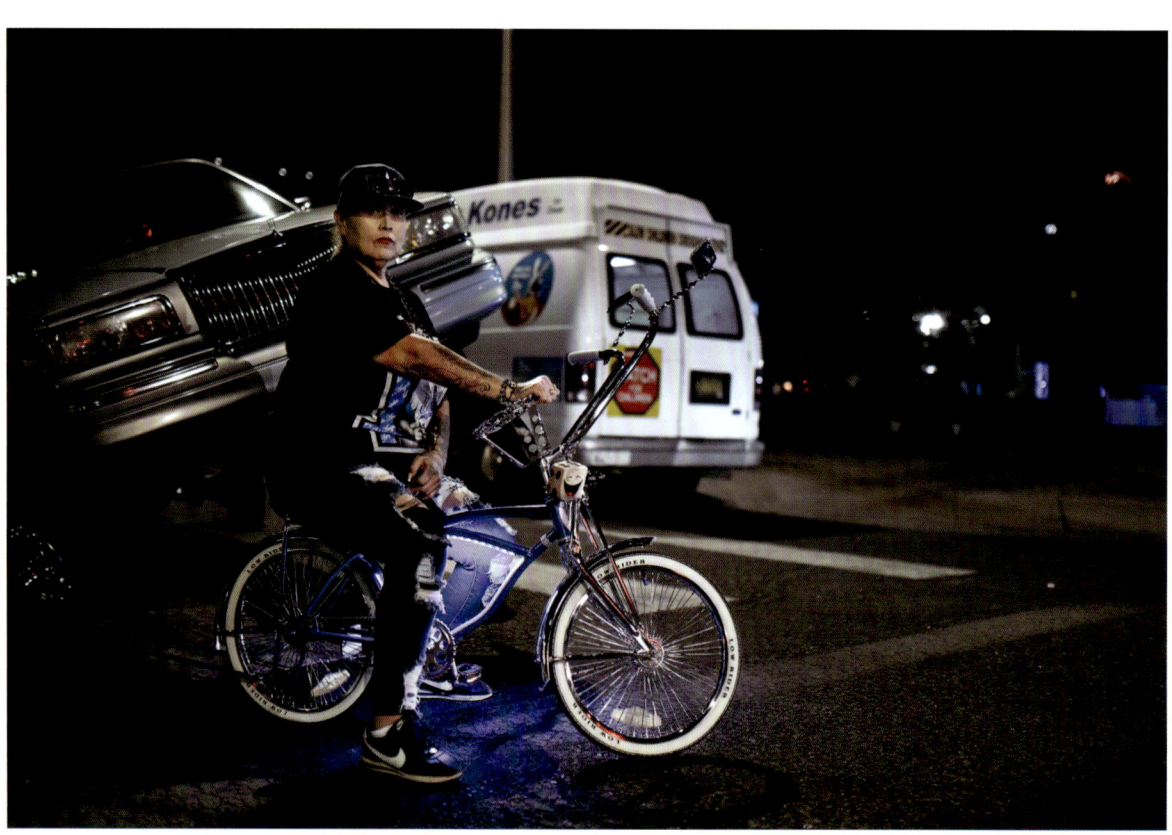

Patricia Ochoa on her lowrider bike, Downtown Albuquerque, 2023.

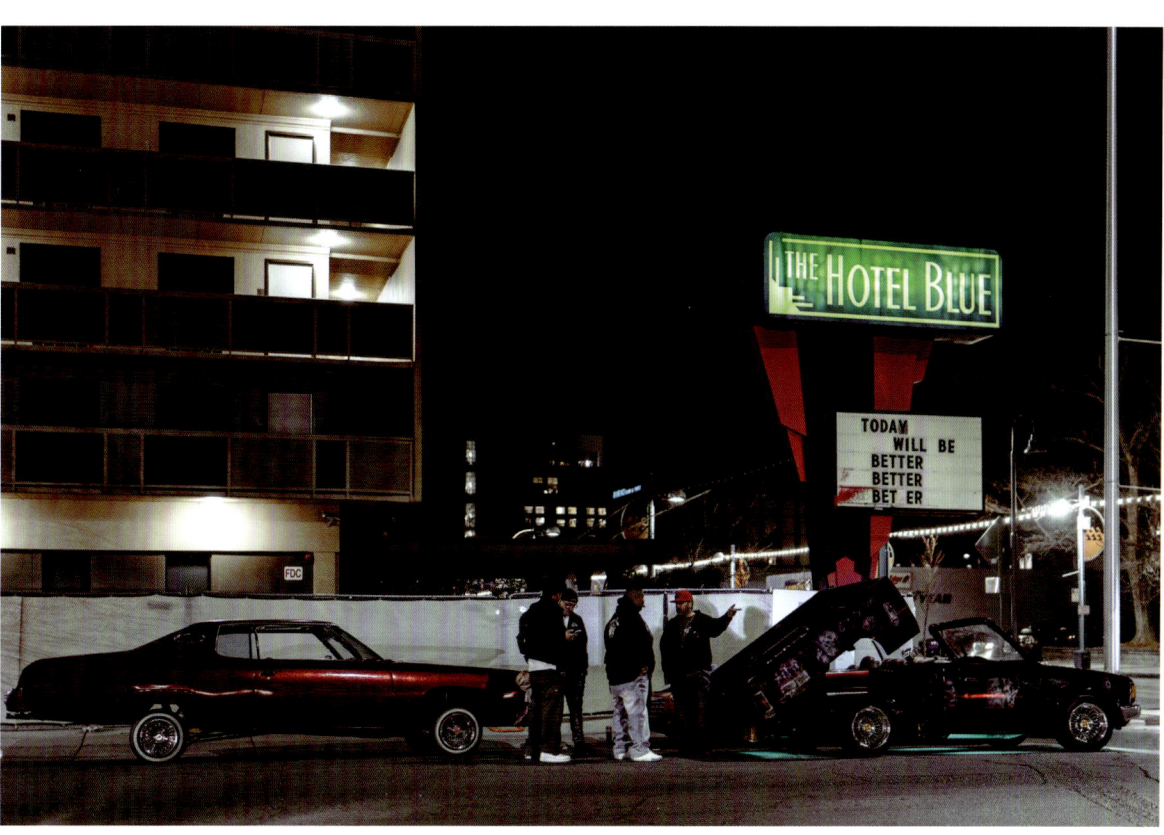

Friends hang out on a Sunday night, Downtown Albuquerque, 2022.

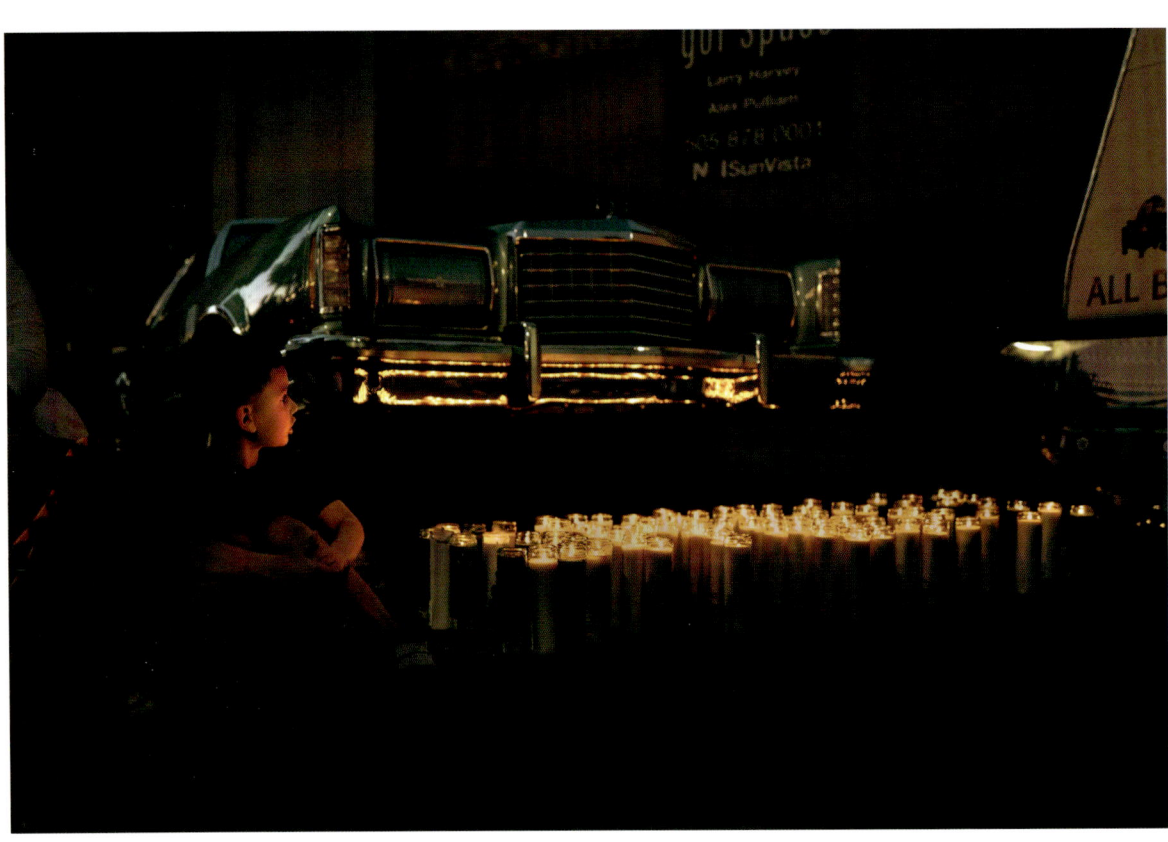

Memorial for Steven "Sparky" Gomez, Downtown Albuquerque, 2021.

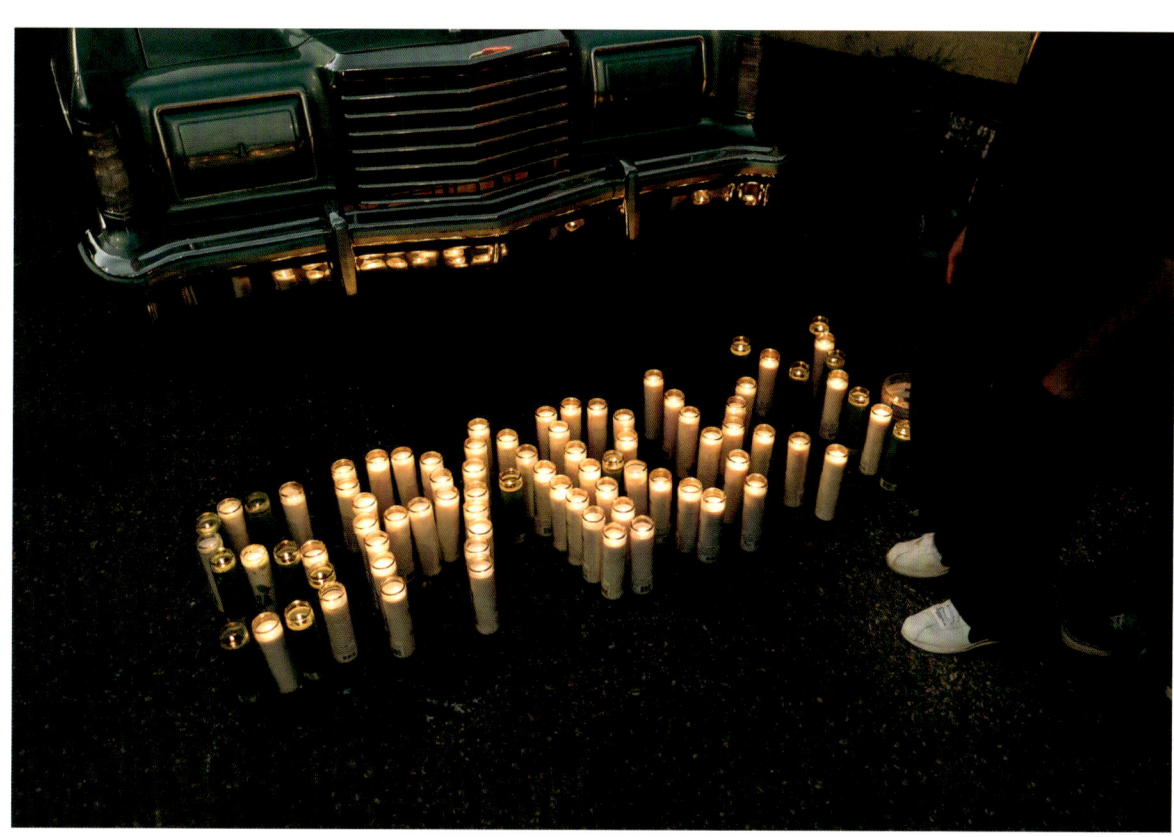

A man rides his lowrider bike down Fourth Street, Barelas, Albuquerque, 2023.

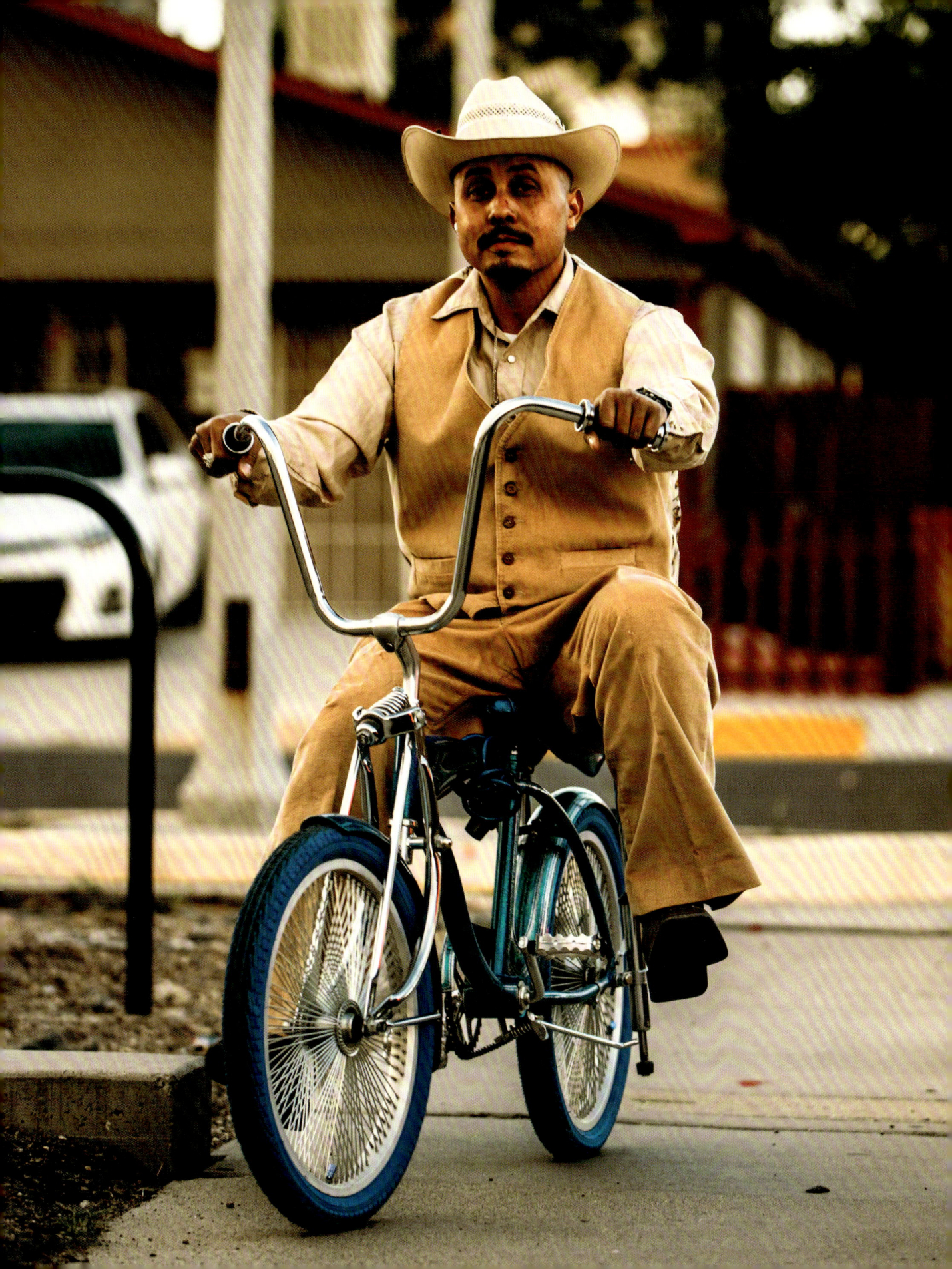

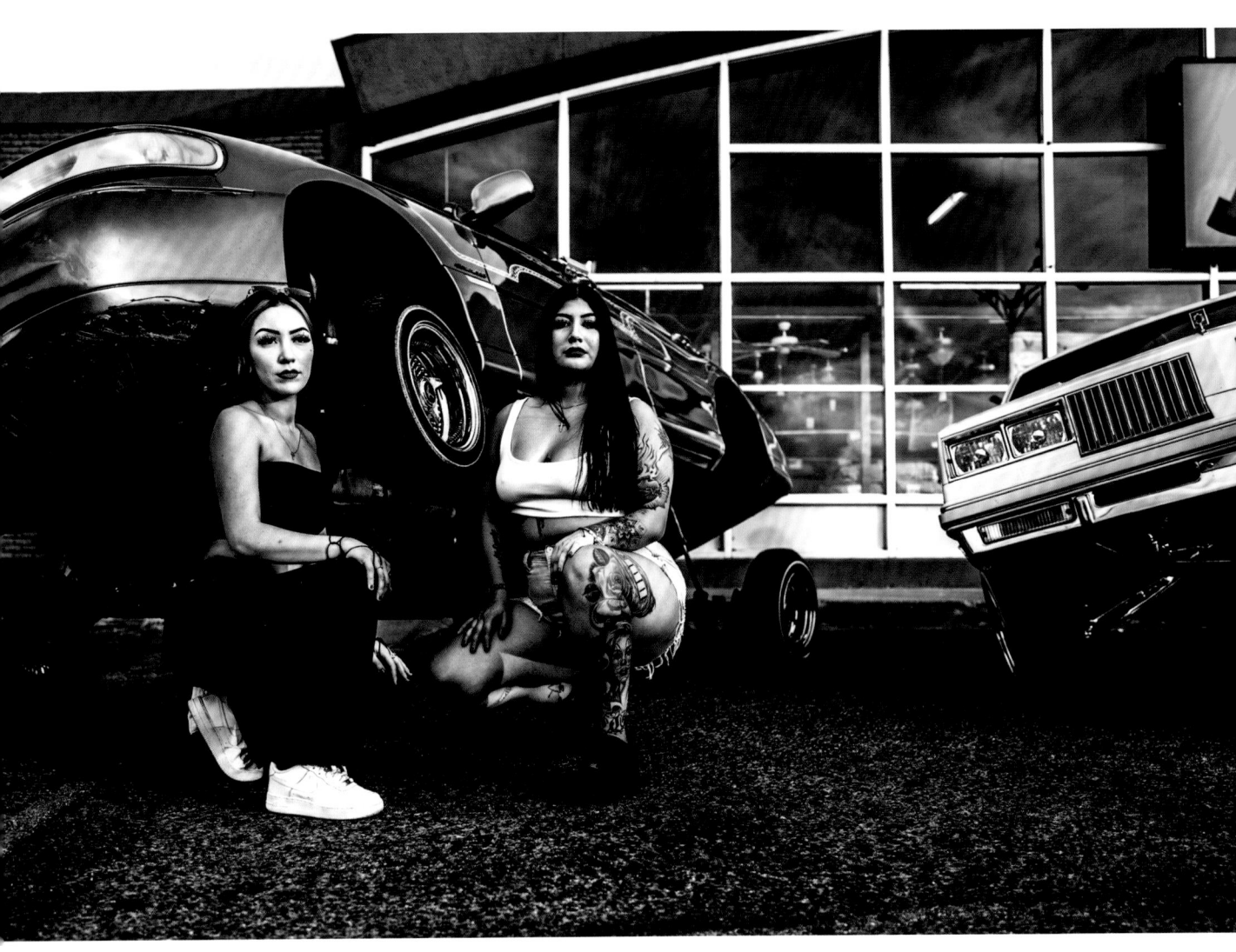

Soniah Martinez Silas (*right*) and friend, Albuquerque, 2021.

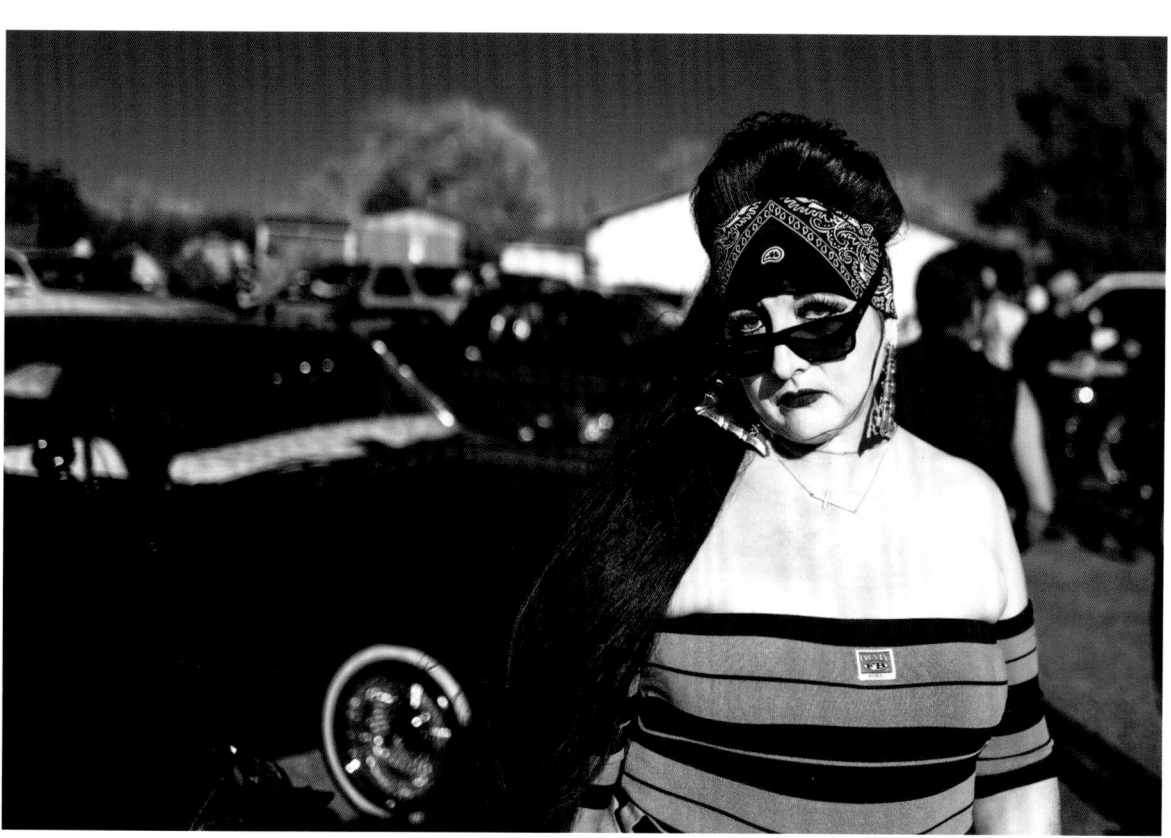

Good Friday, Española, New Mexico, 2022.

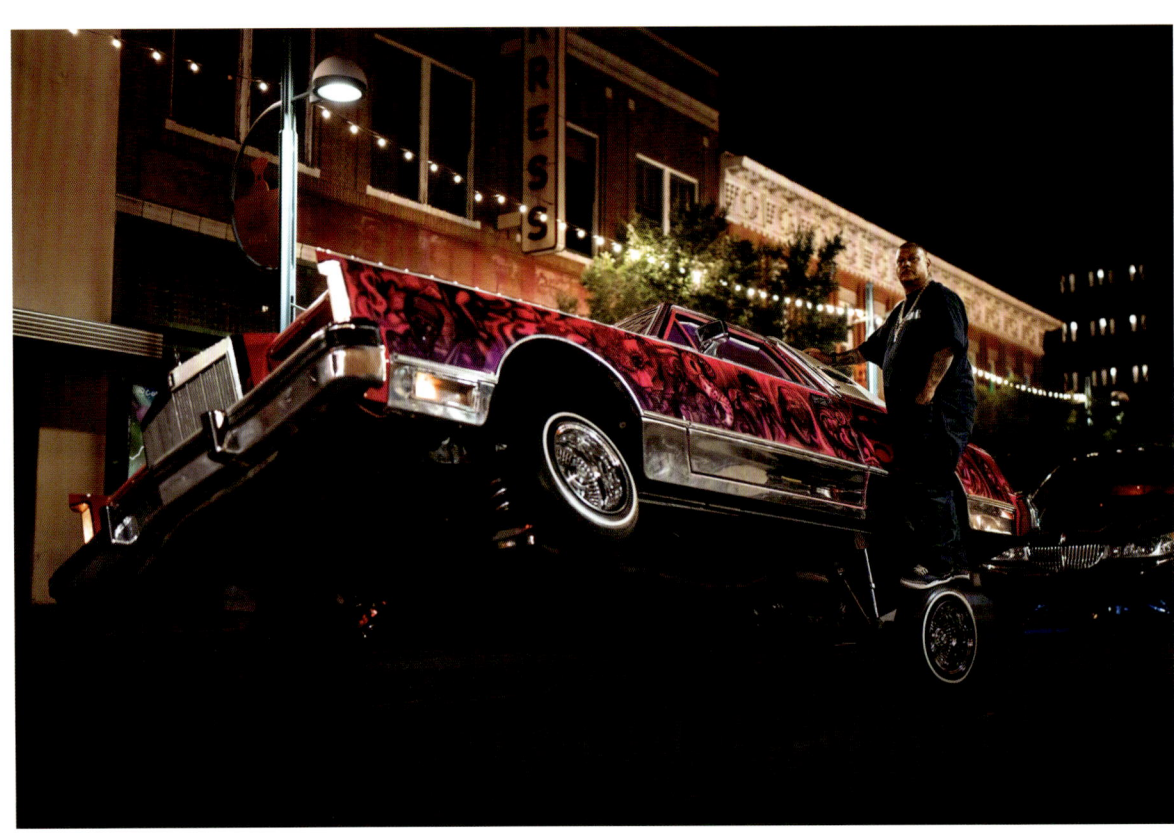

Eddie Miramonte, Downtown Albuquerque, 2022.

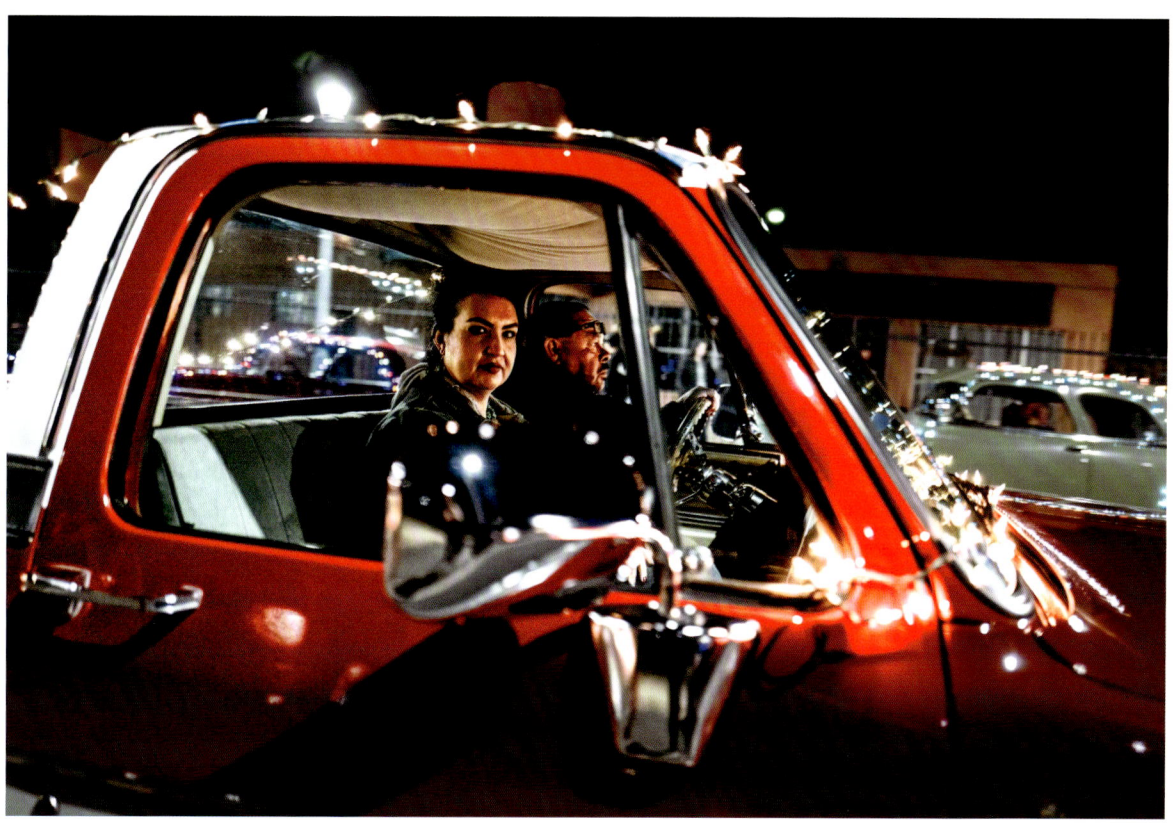

Cruising on Fourth Street, Barelas, Albuquerque, 2021.

(*following pages*) Kiana's Guadalupe tattoo, La Joya, New Mexico, 2023.

Bianca Sanchez, Guadalupe tattoo, Albuquerque, 2021.

Emma in her Quinceañera dress, Barelas, Albuquerque, 2024.

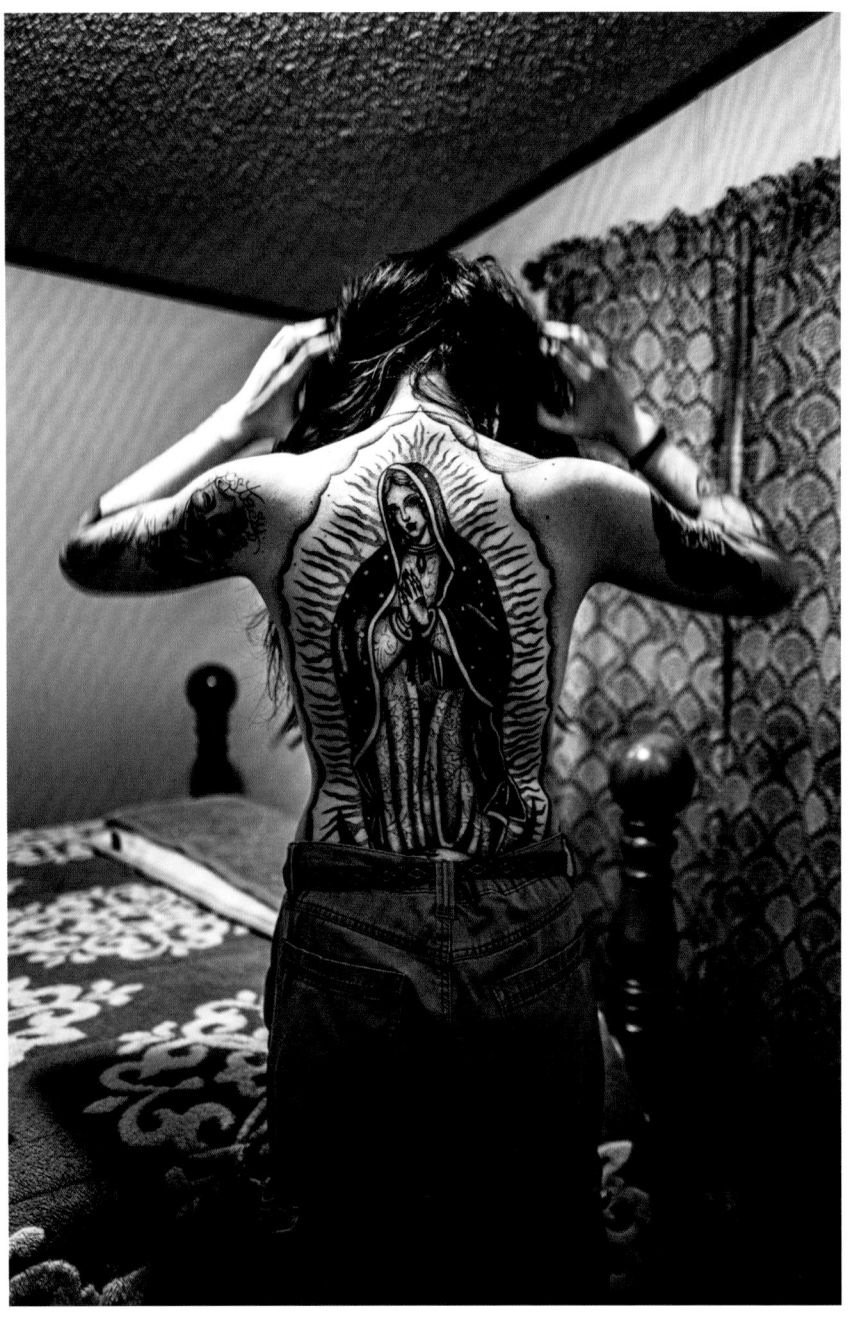

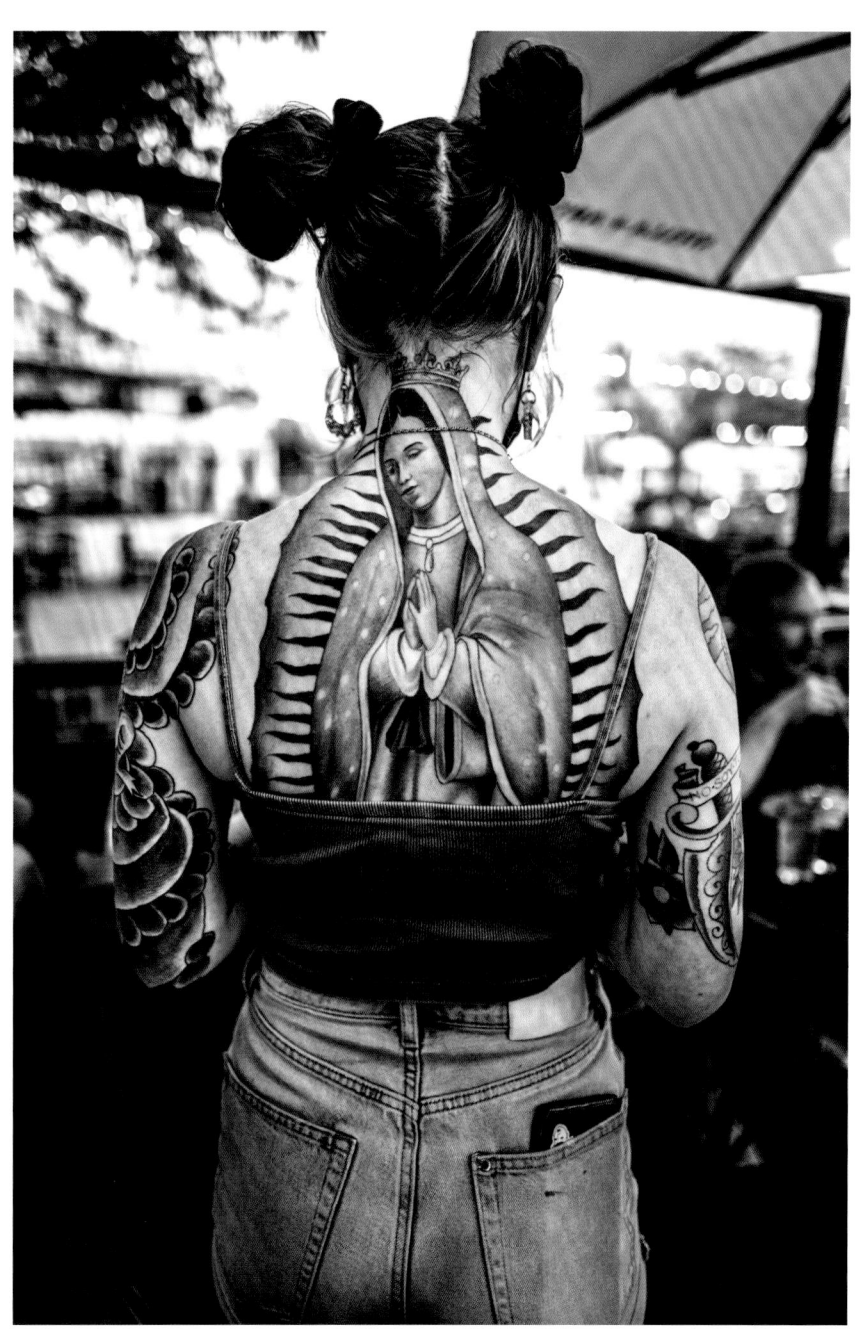

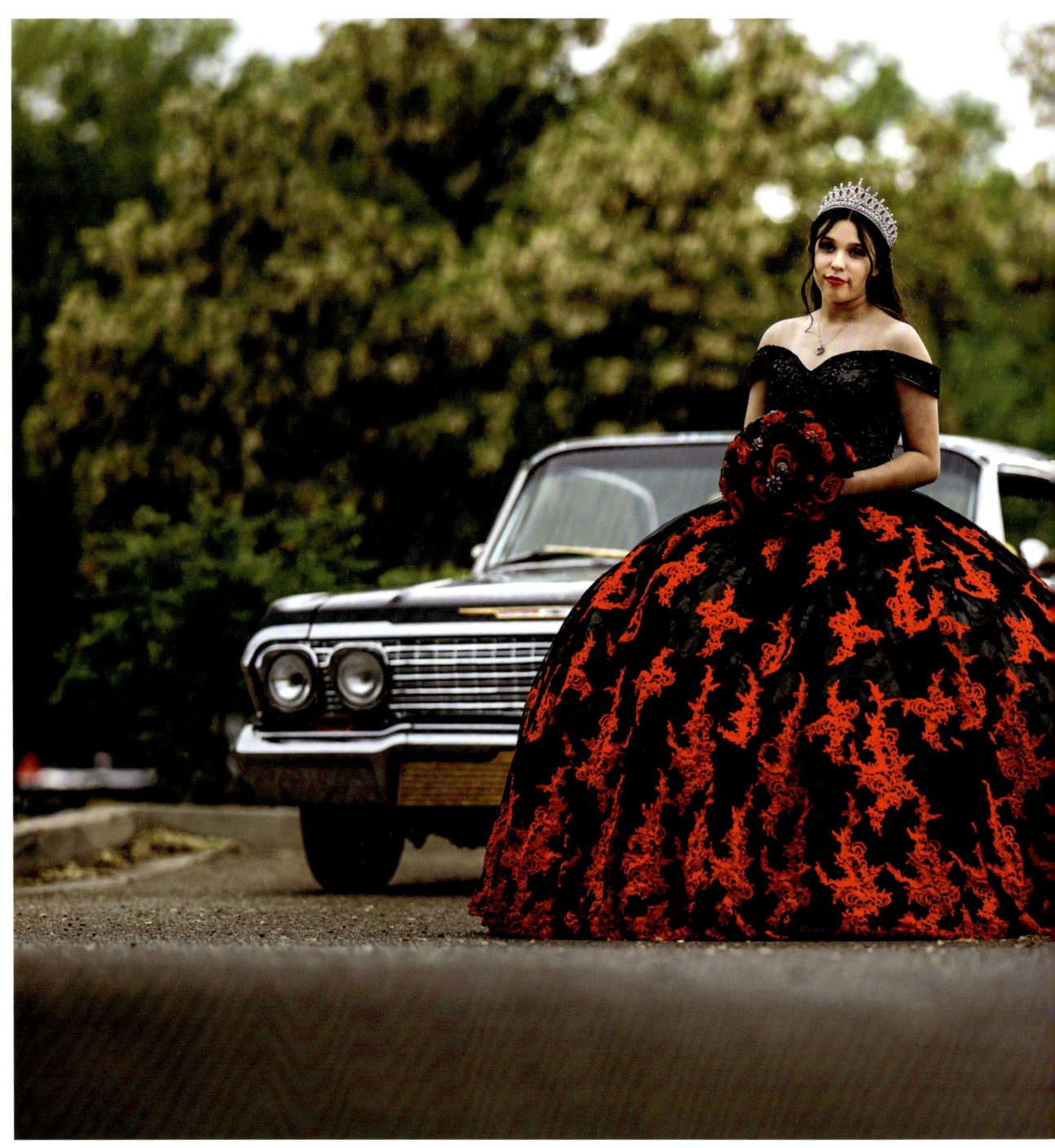

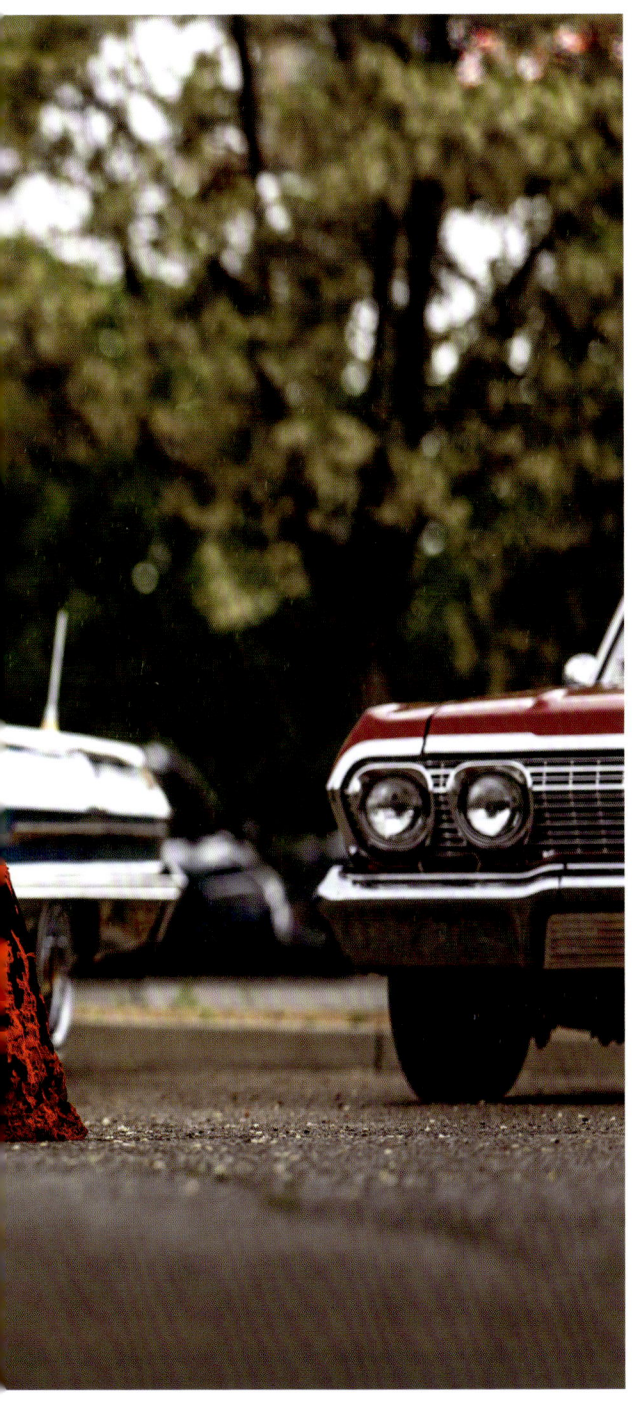

Downtown Albuquerque, 2021.

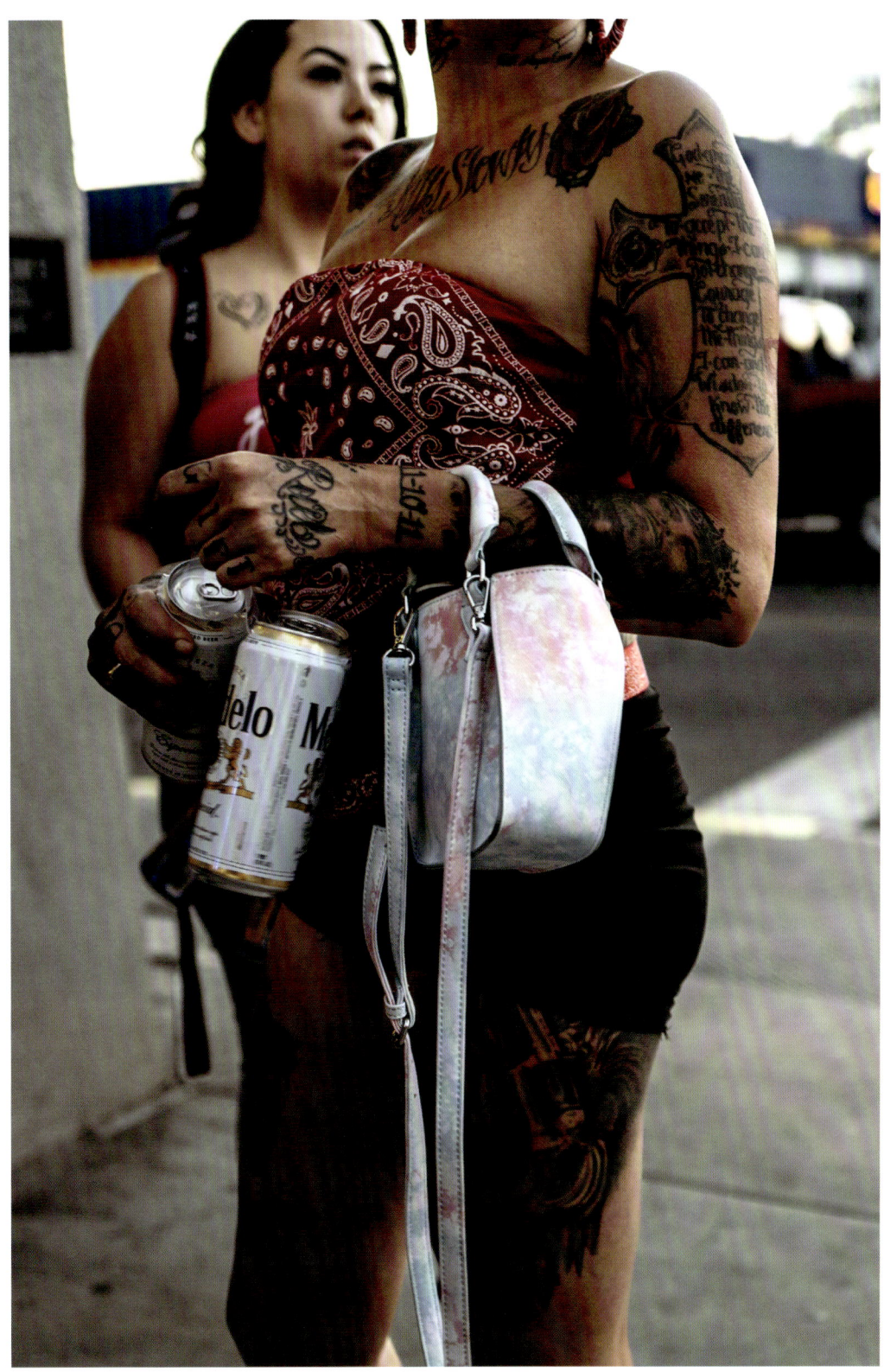

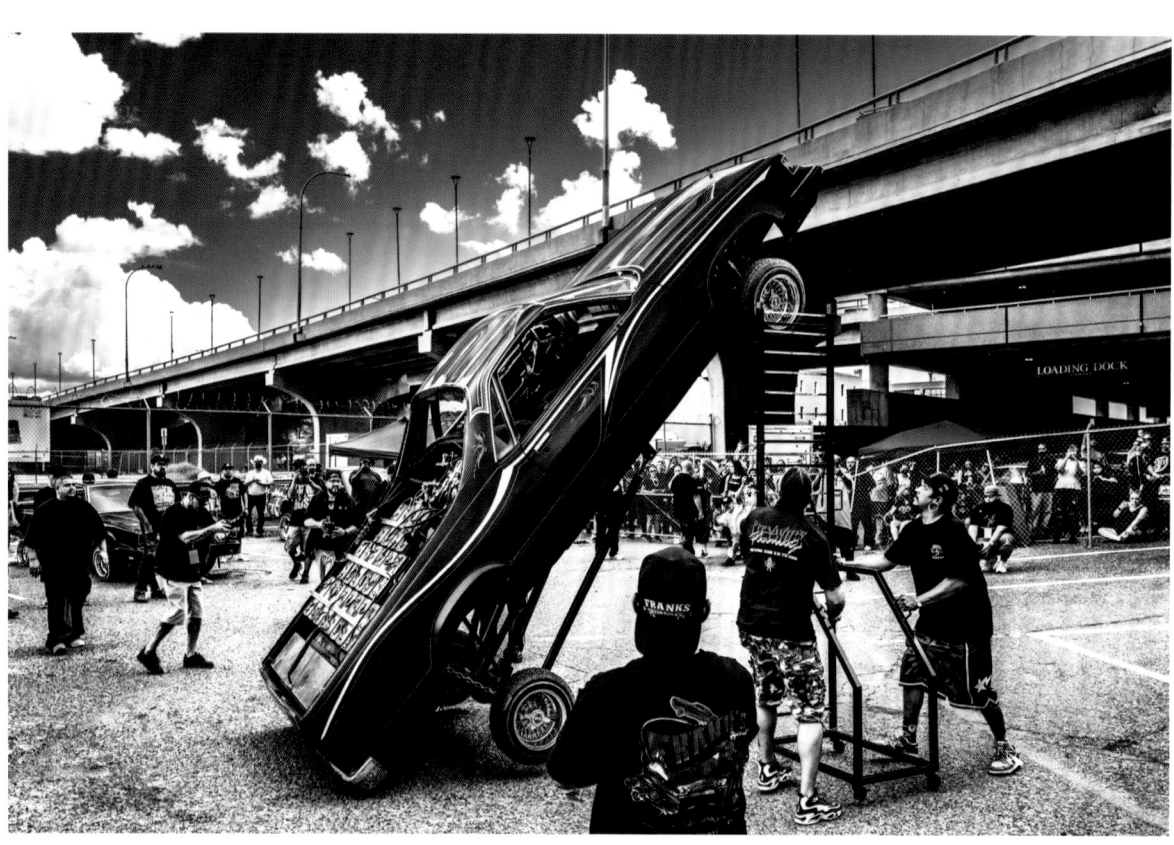

Lowrider Super Show, Downtown Albuquerque, 2021.

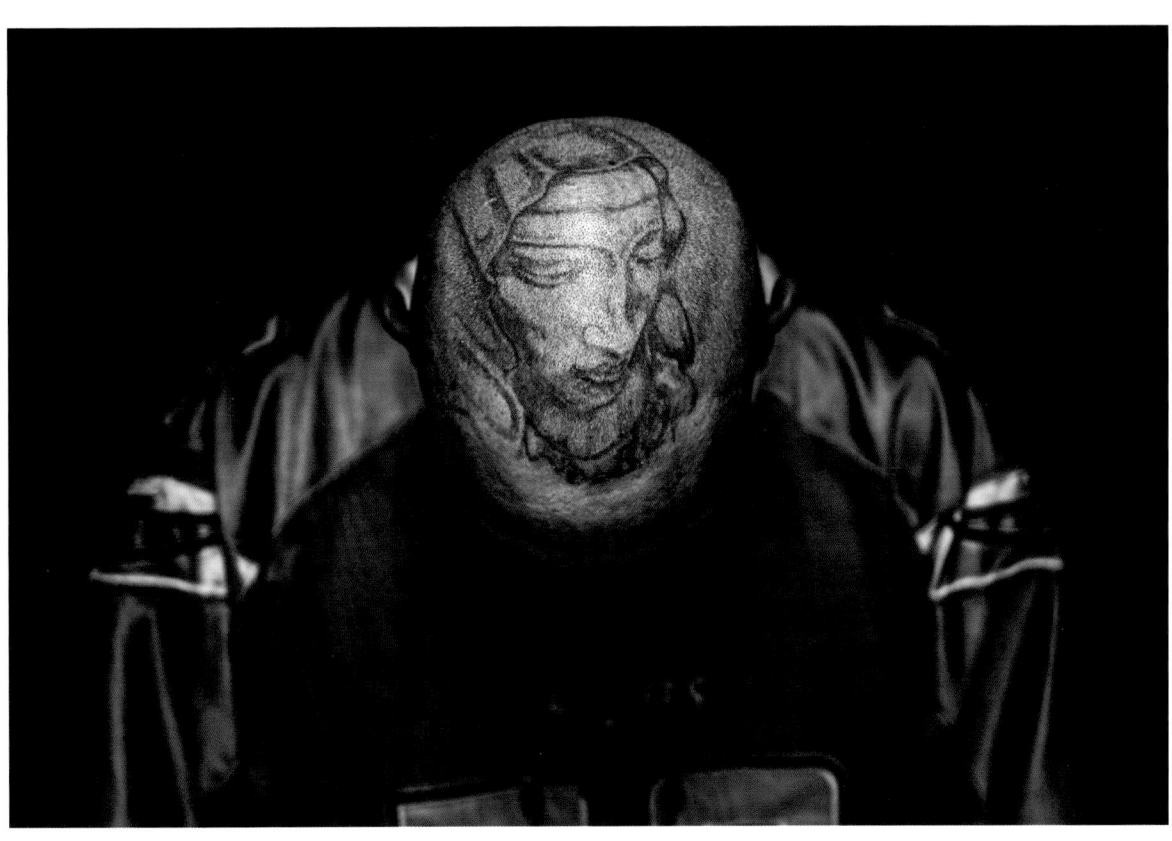

Crook shows his head tattoo, Barelas, Albuquerque, 2023.

(*following pages*) A group of dog breeders, Albuquerque, 2021.

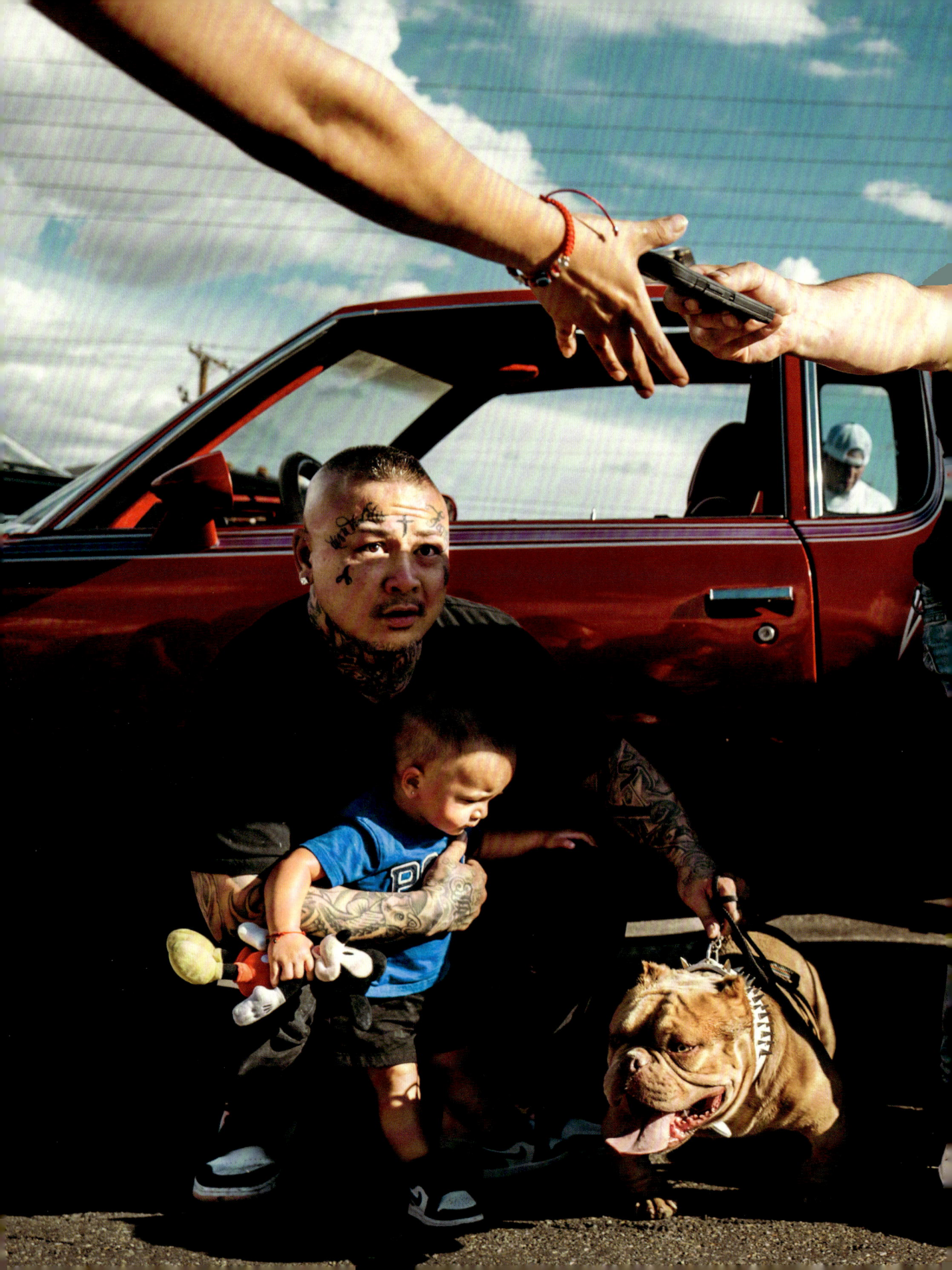

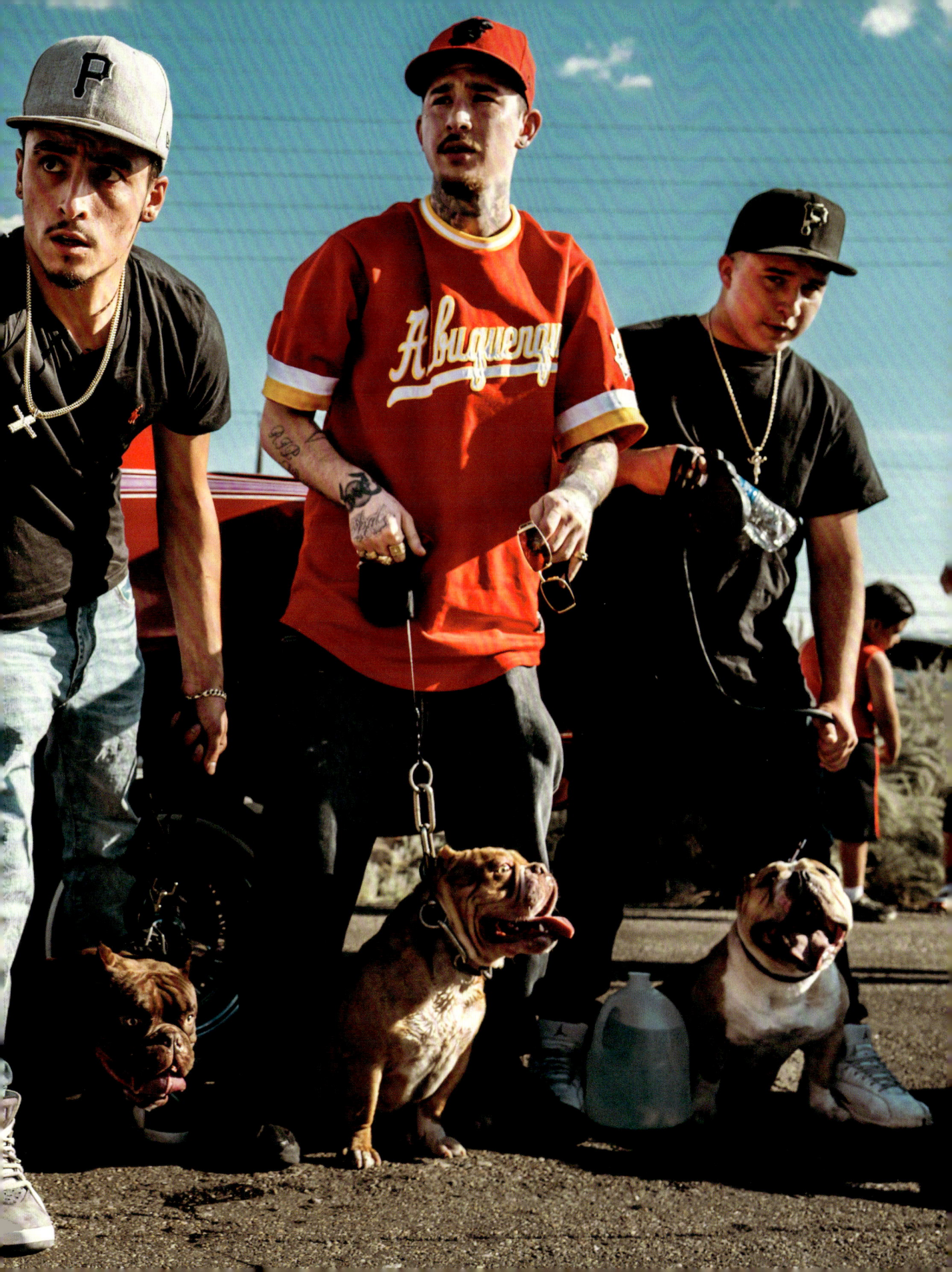

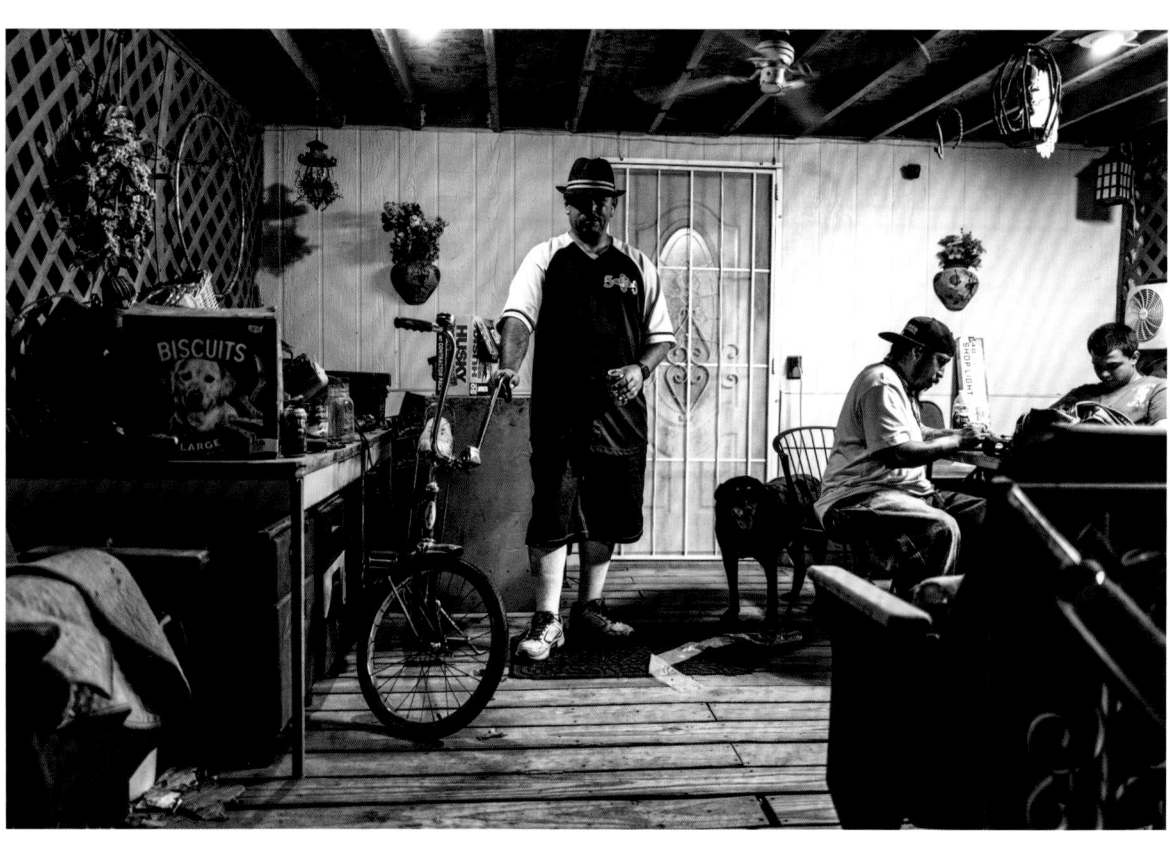

Jason Gomez at home, South Valley, Albuquerque, 2024.

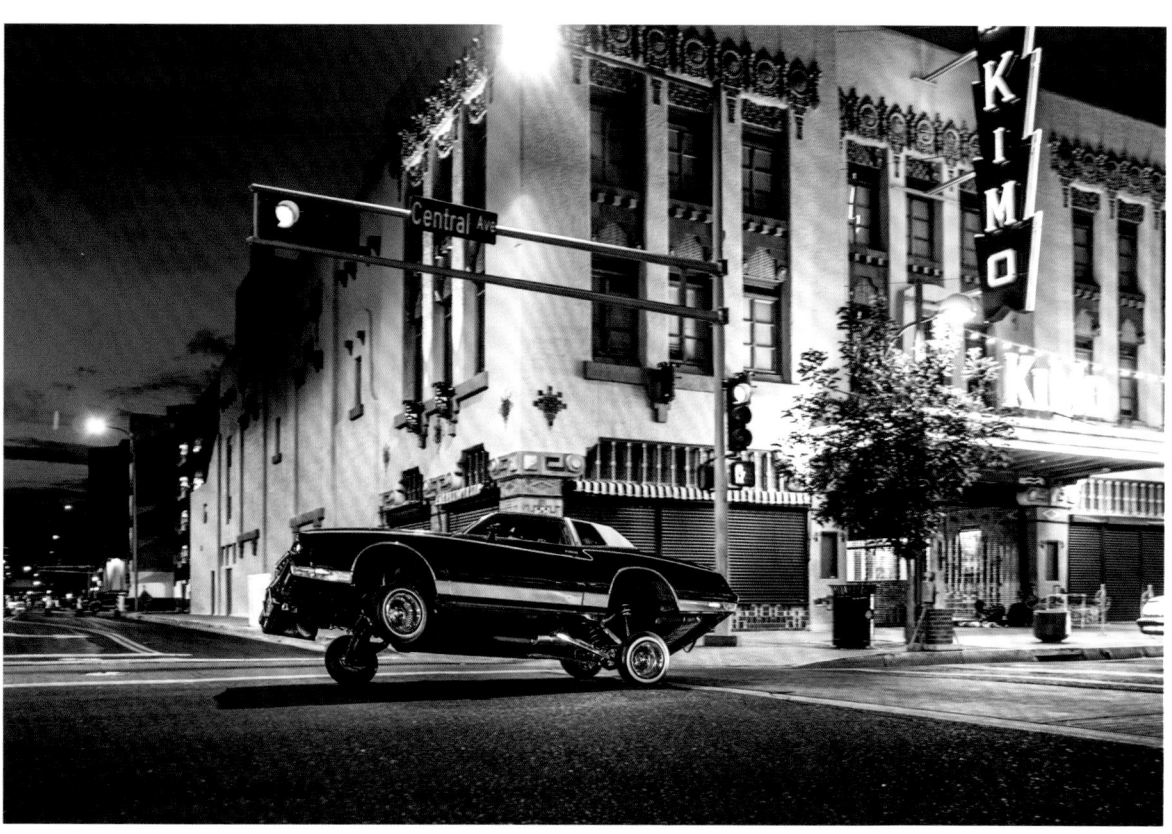

Lowrider riding on three wheels past the Kimo Theatre, Downtown Albuquerque, 2021.

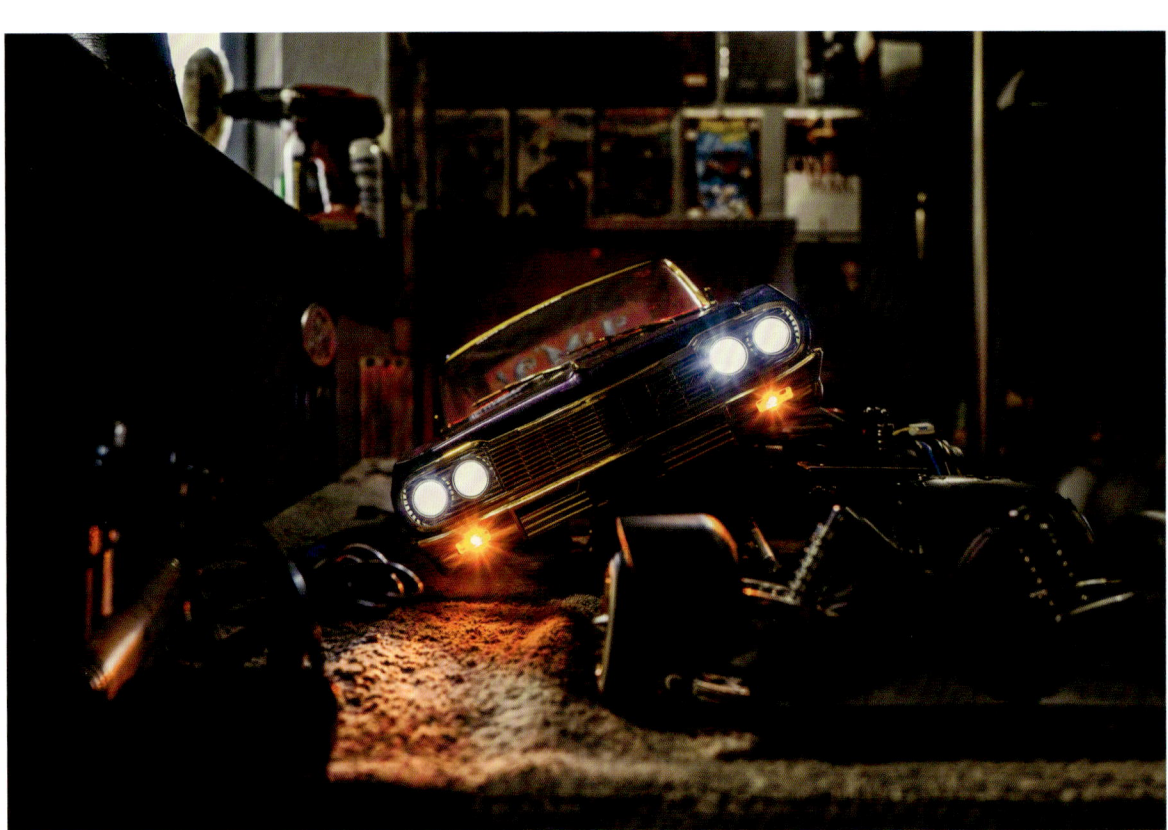

Flacos's remote control lowrider, Barelas, Albuquerque, 2024.

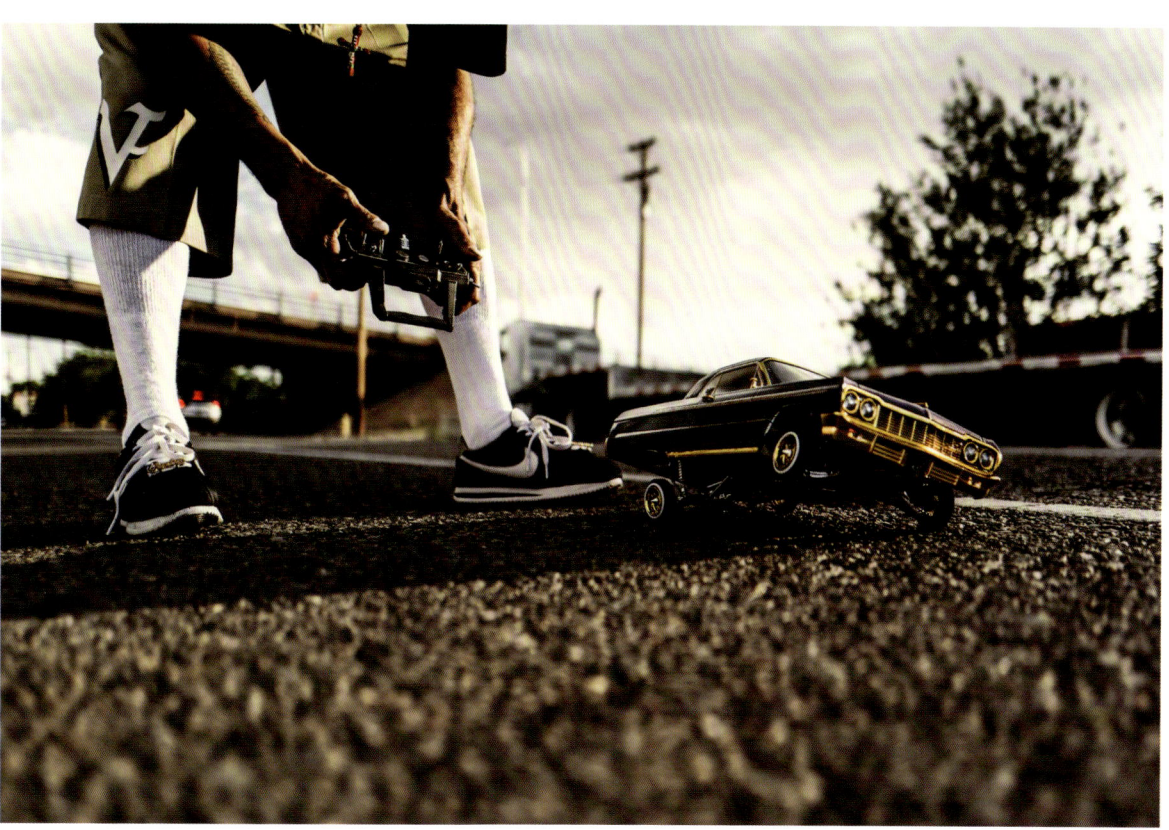

Flaco and his remote control lowrider, Barelas, Albuquerque, 2024.

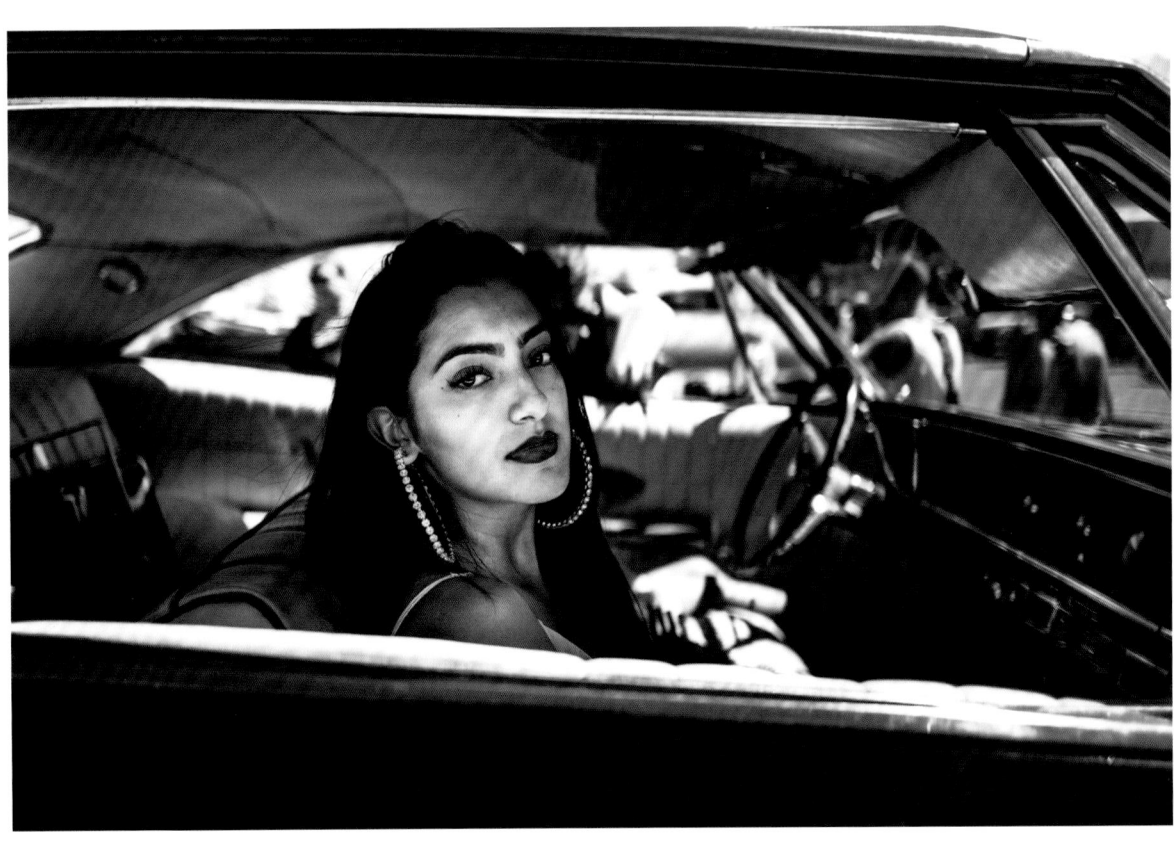

Unique Lovato sits in her father Fritoso's Impala, Albuquerque, 2021.

(*opposite page*) Portrait of Bo Paul, Downtown Albuquerque, 2021.

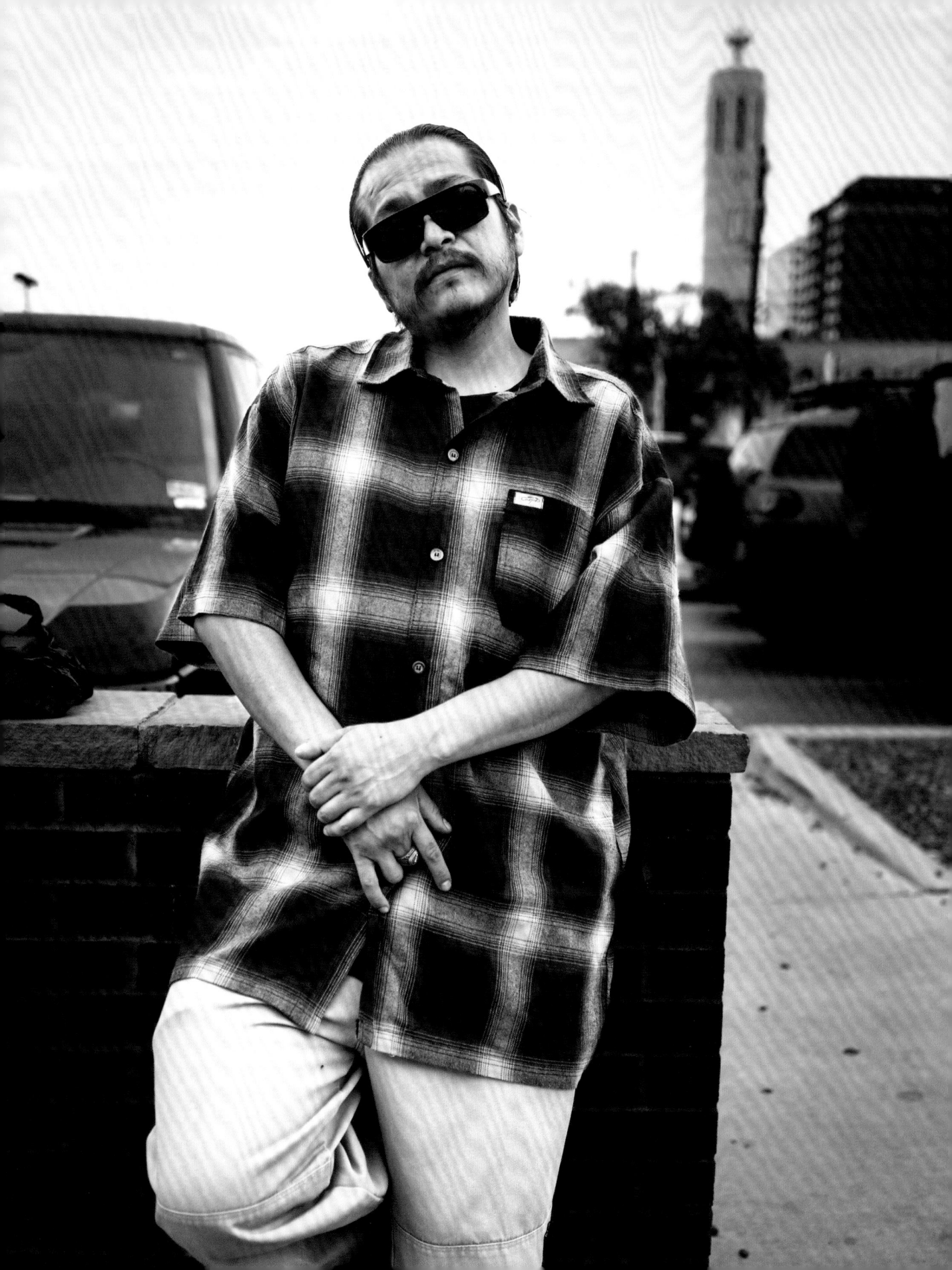

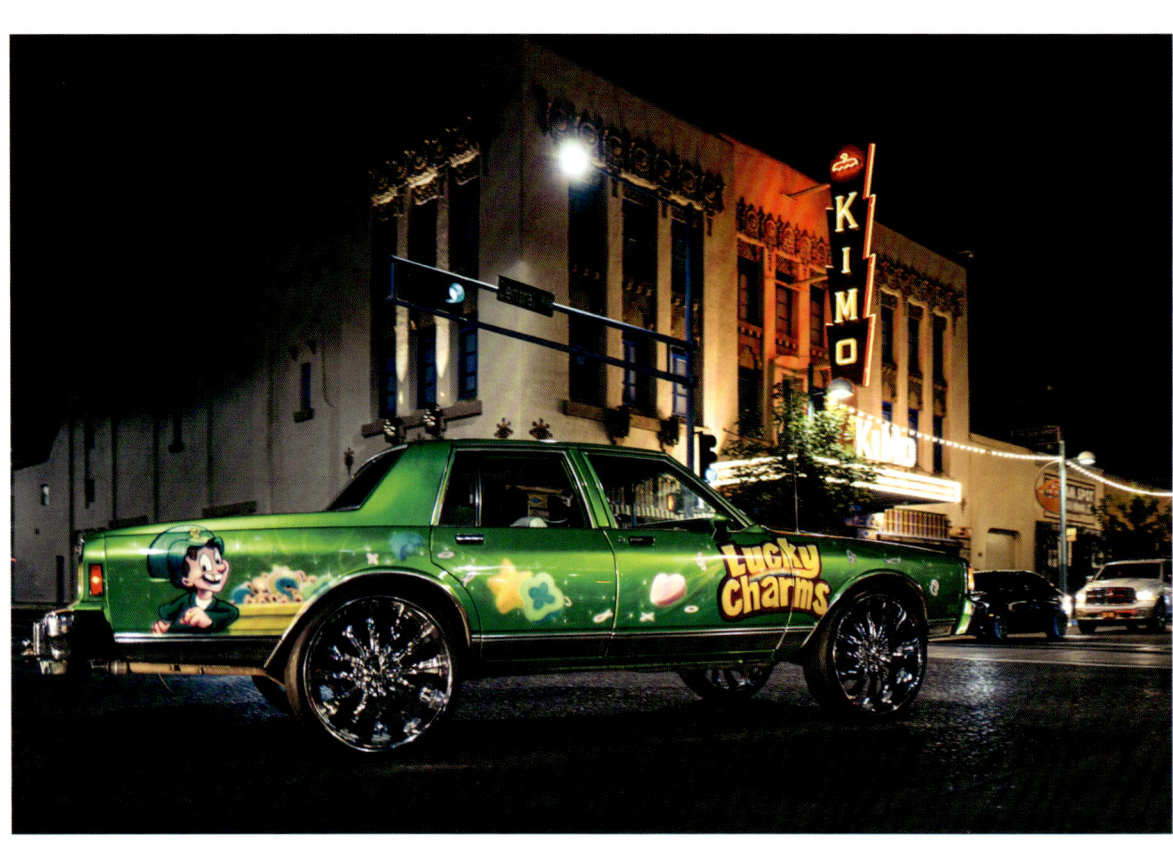

Kimo Theatre, Downtown Albuquerque, 2021.

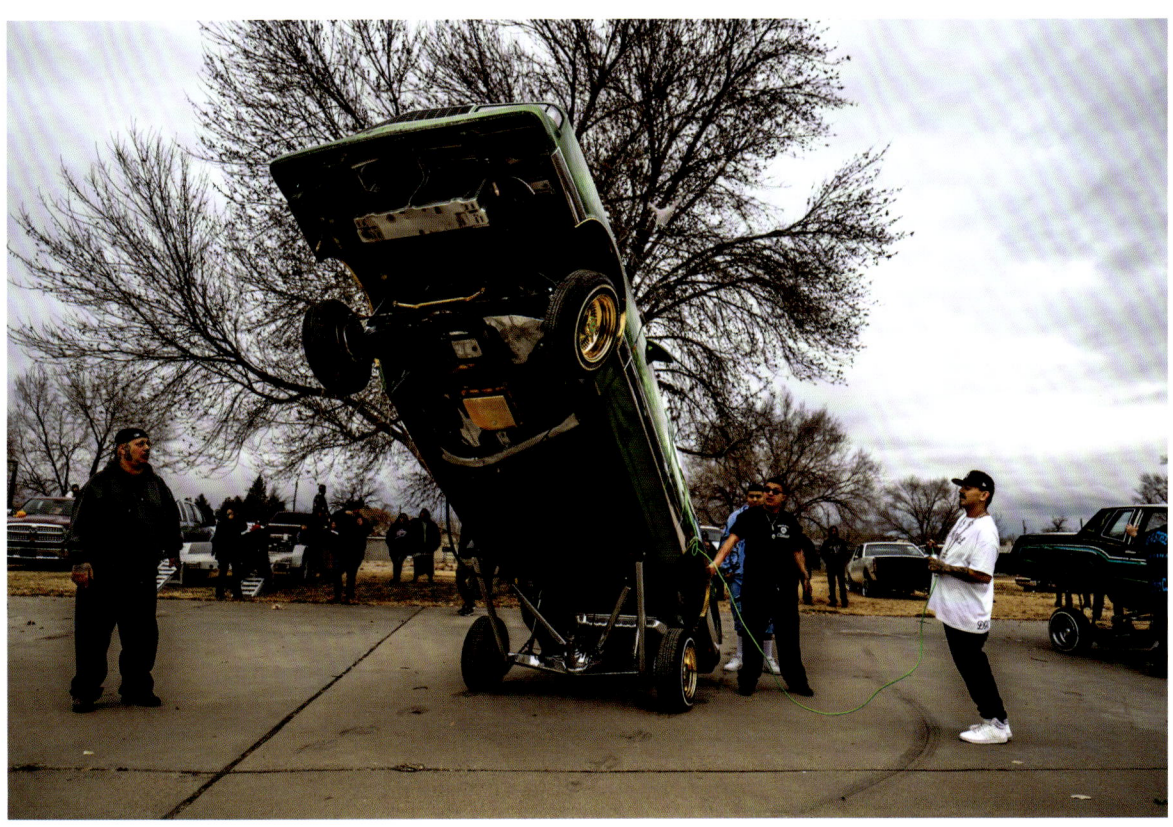

Anthony Maldonado hops his car at a memorial for his brother, South San Jose Park, Albuquerque, 2024.

(*following pages*) Sonny leans out of his car to record video, Downtown Albuquerque, 2021.

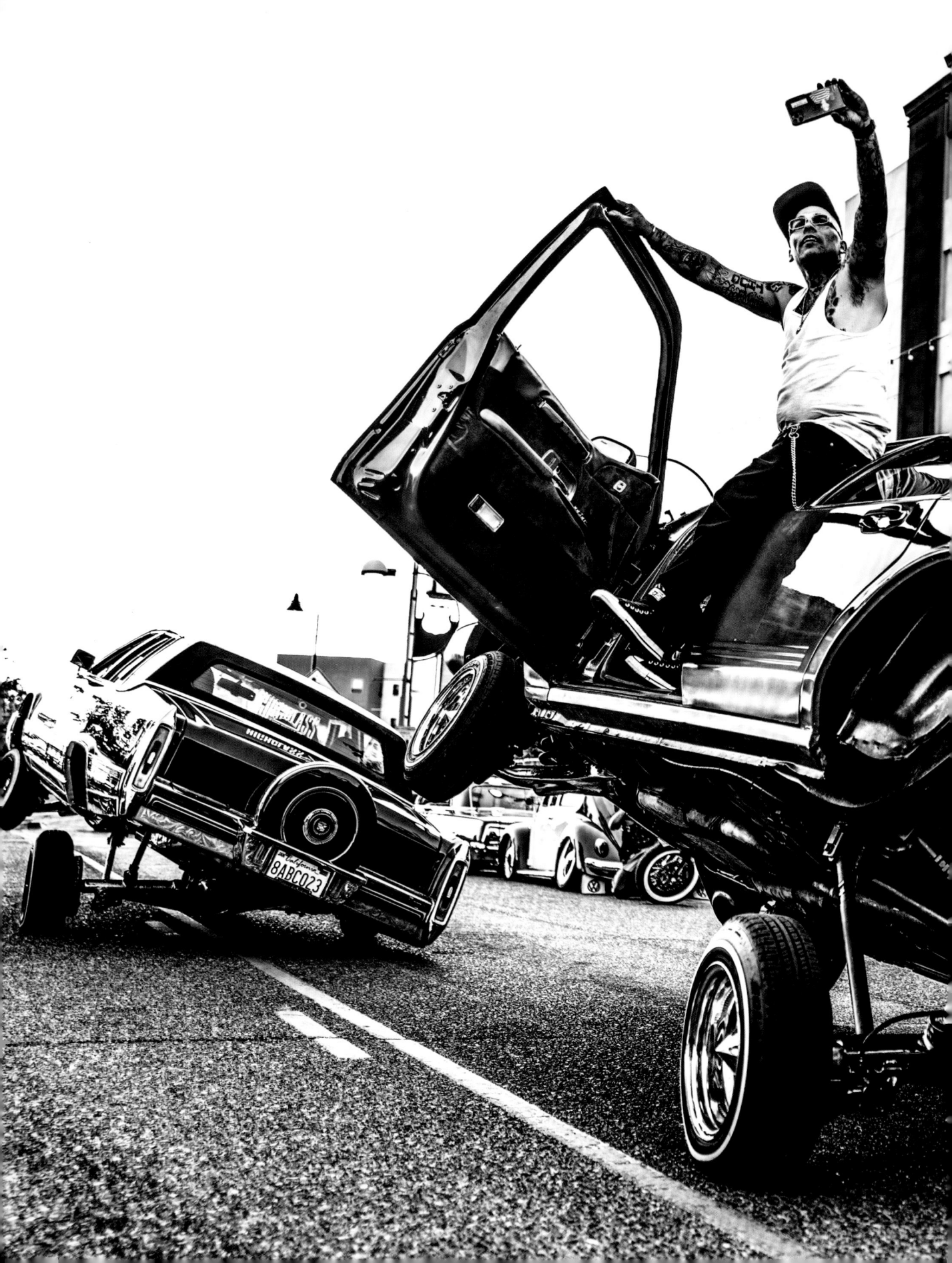

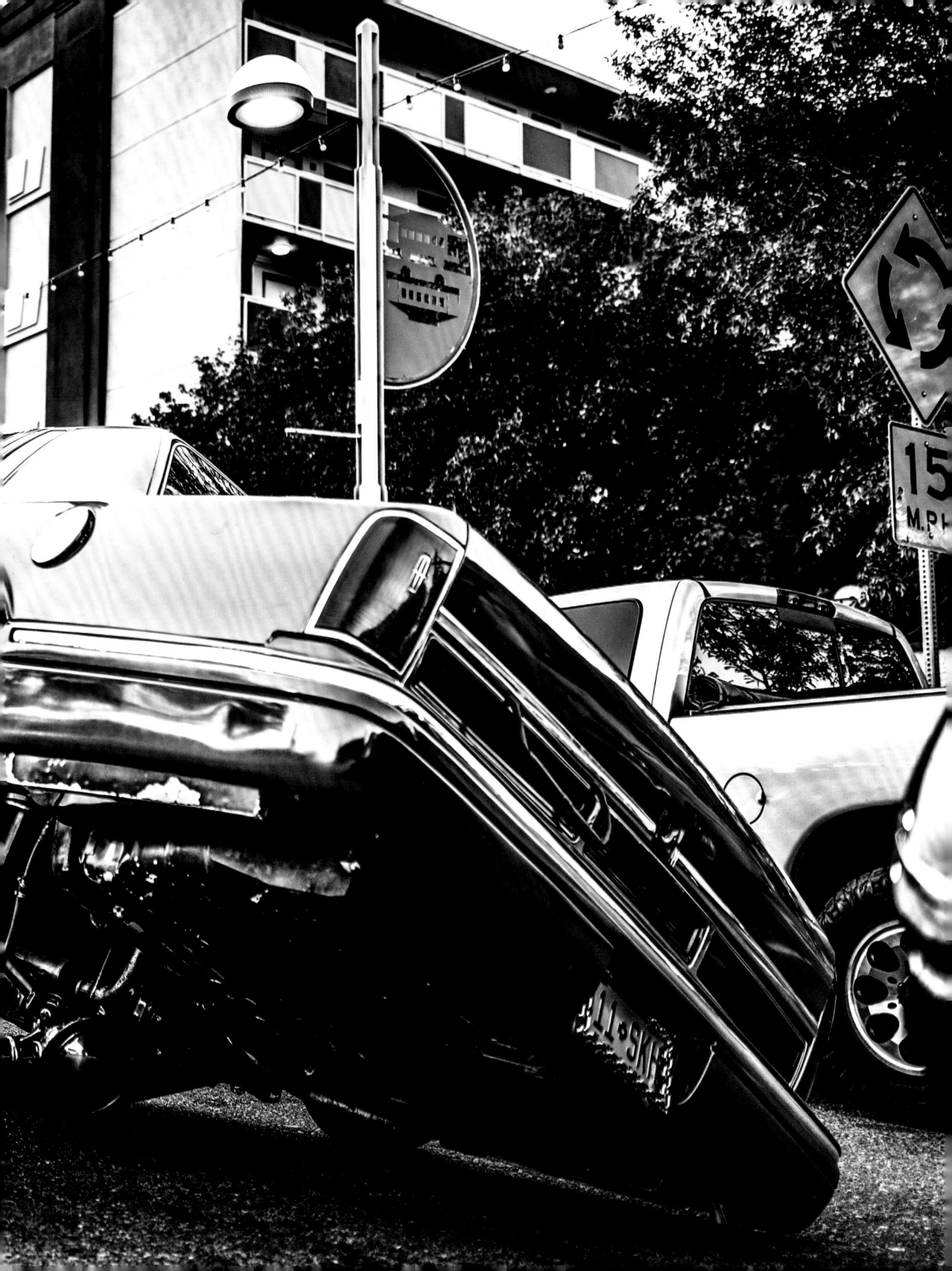

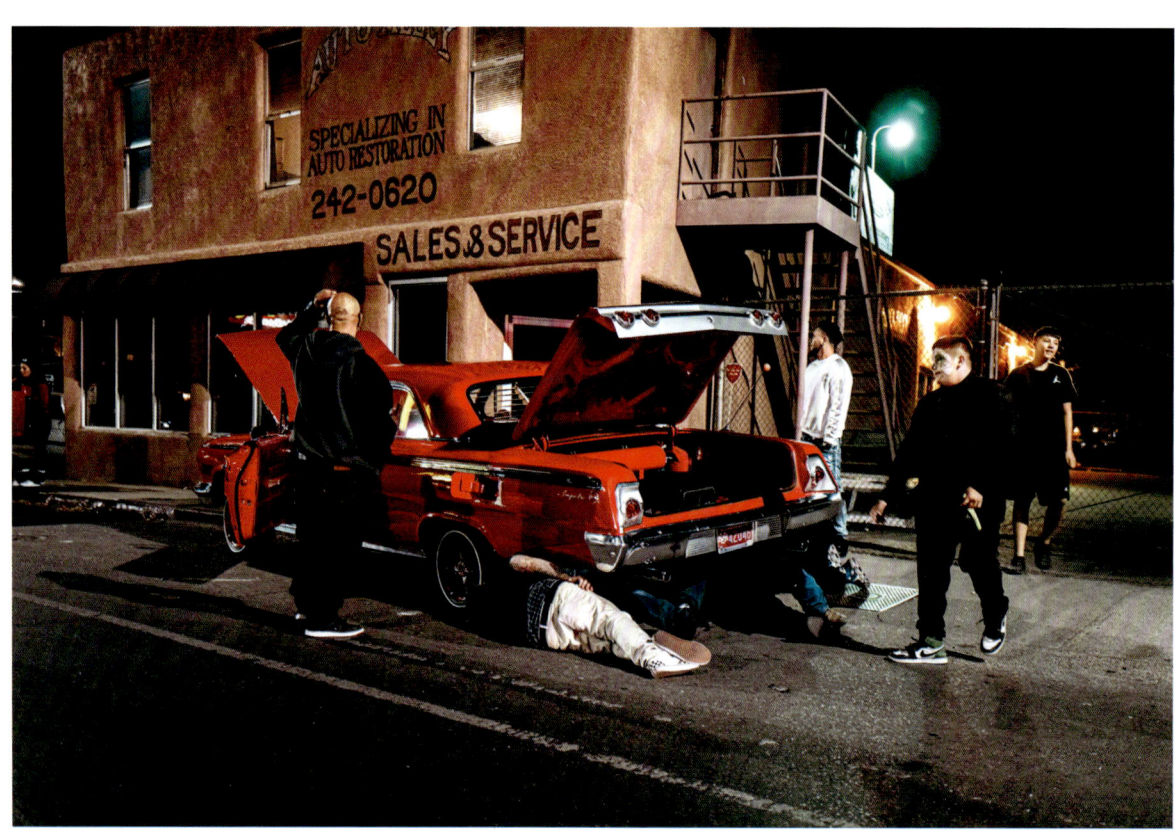

The community comes together to repair a car, Barelas, Albuquerque, 2023.

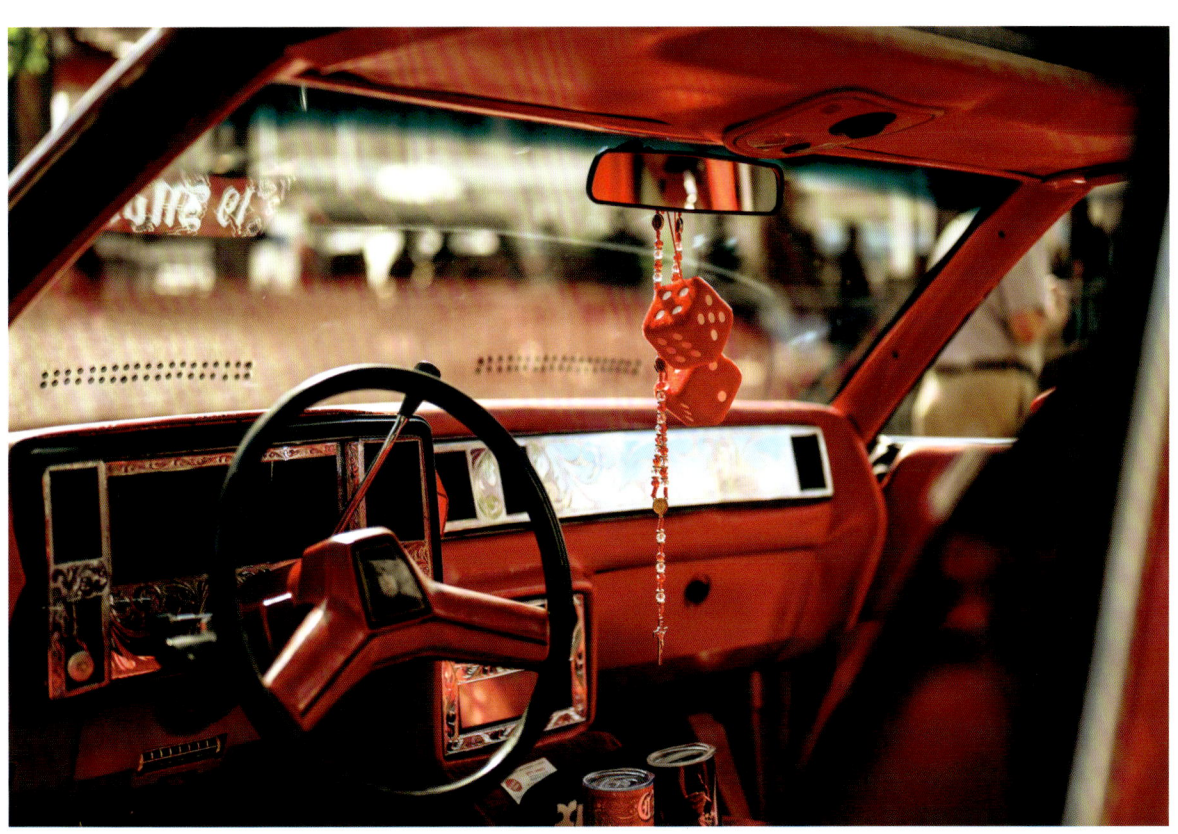

Interior of Francisco's Chevorlet Monte Carlo, Downtown Albuquerque, 2024.

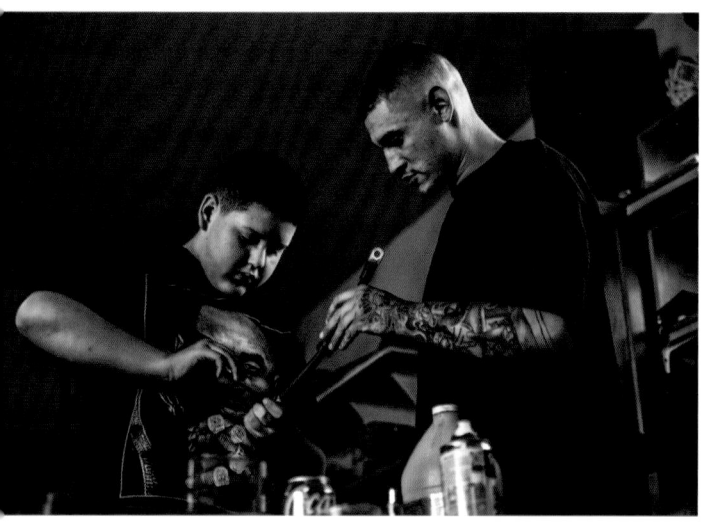
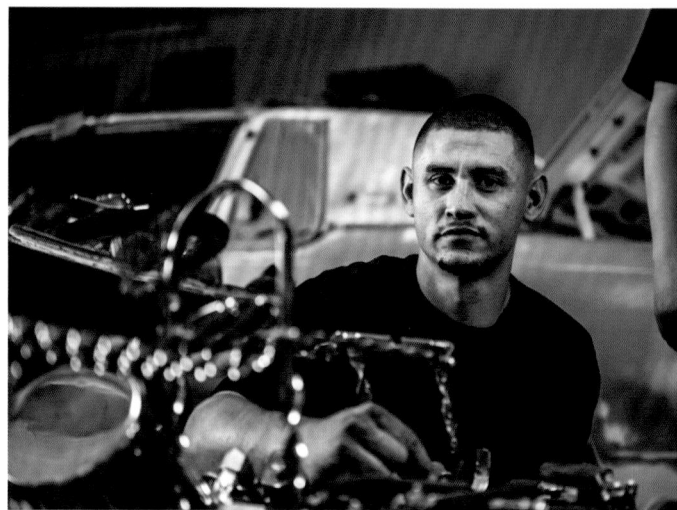
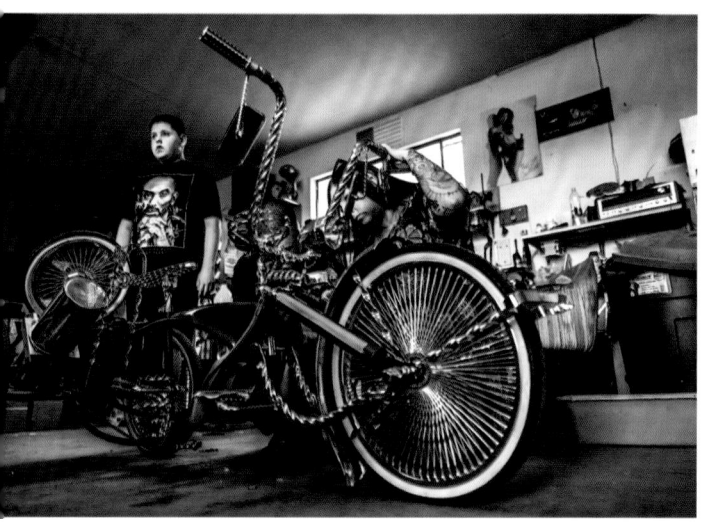
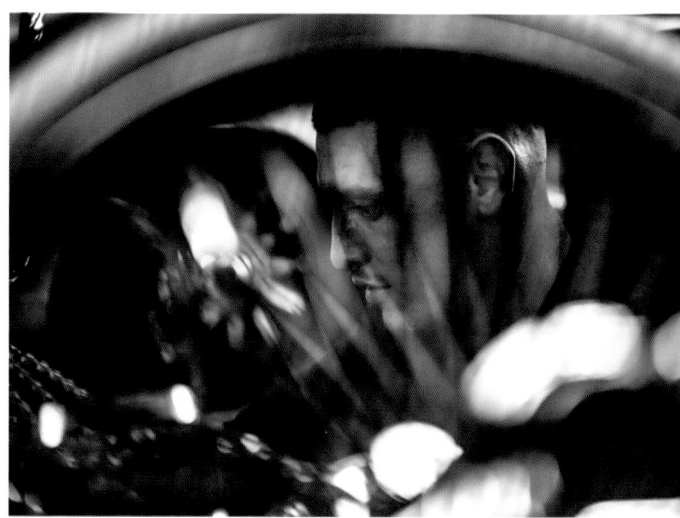

Joel Leon and Si working on a lowrider bike, Albuquerque, 2024.

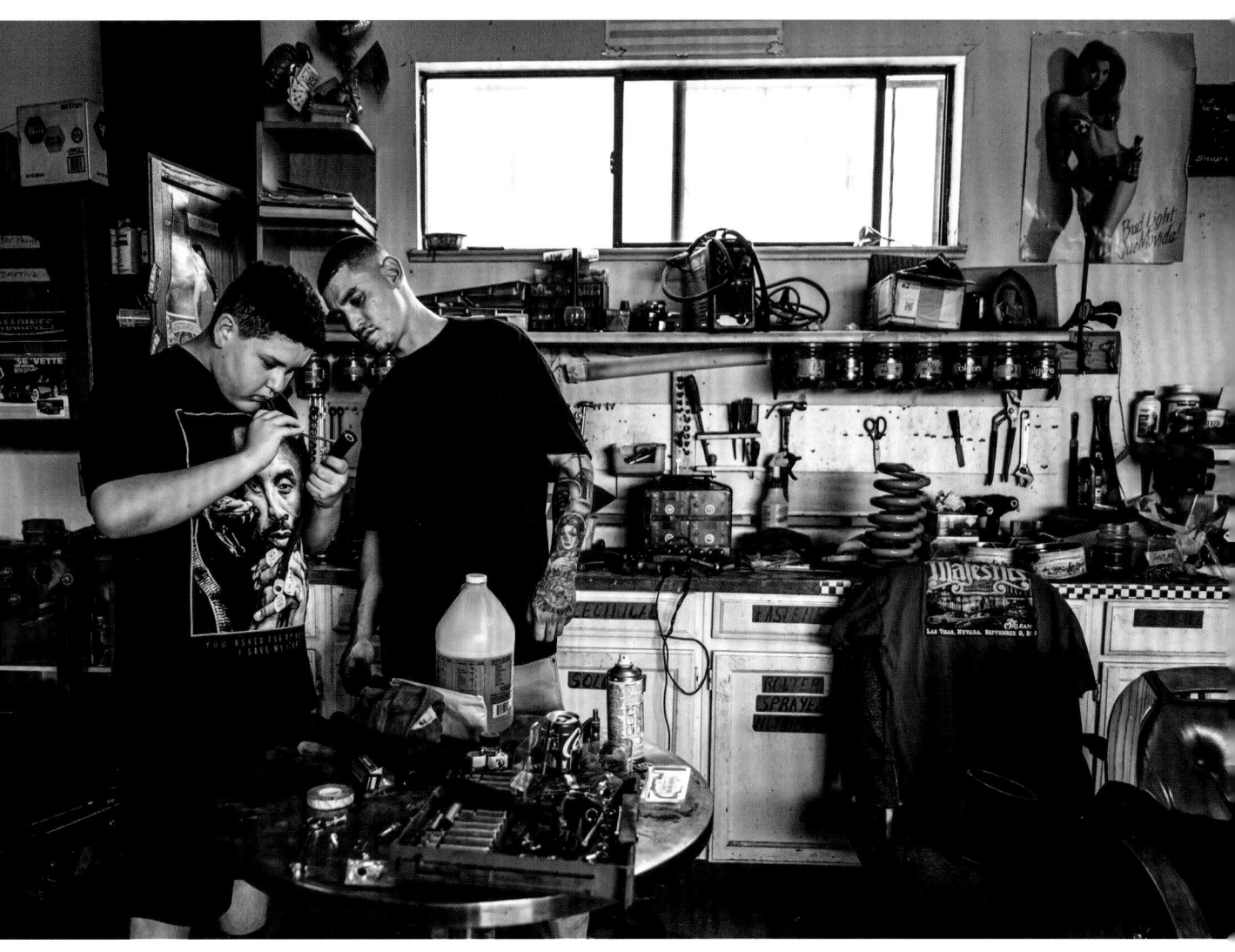

Joel Leon teaching Si how to use a tool, Albuquerque, 2024.

(*following pages*) Crook and his daughter, Barelas, Albuquerque, 2023.

Jeremy Salas, Seventh Street and Central Avenue, Downtown Albuquerque, 2021.

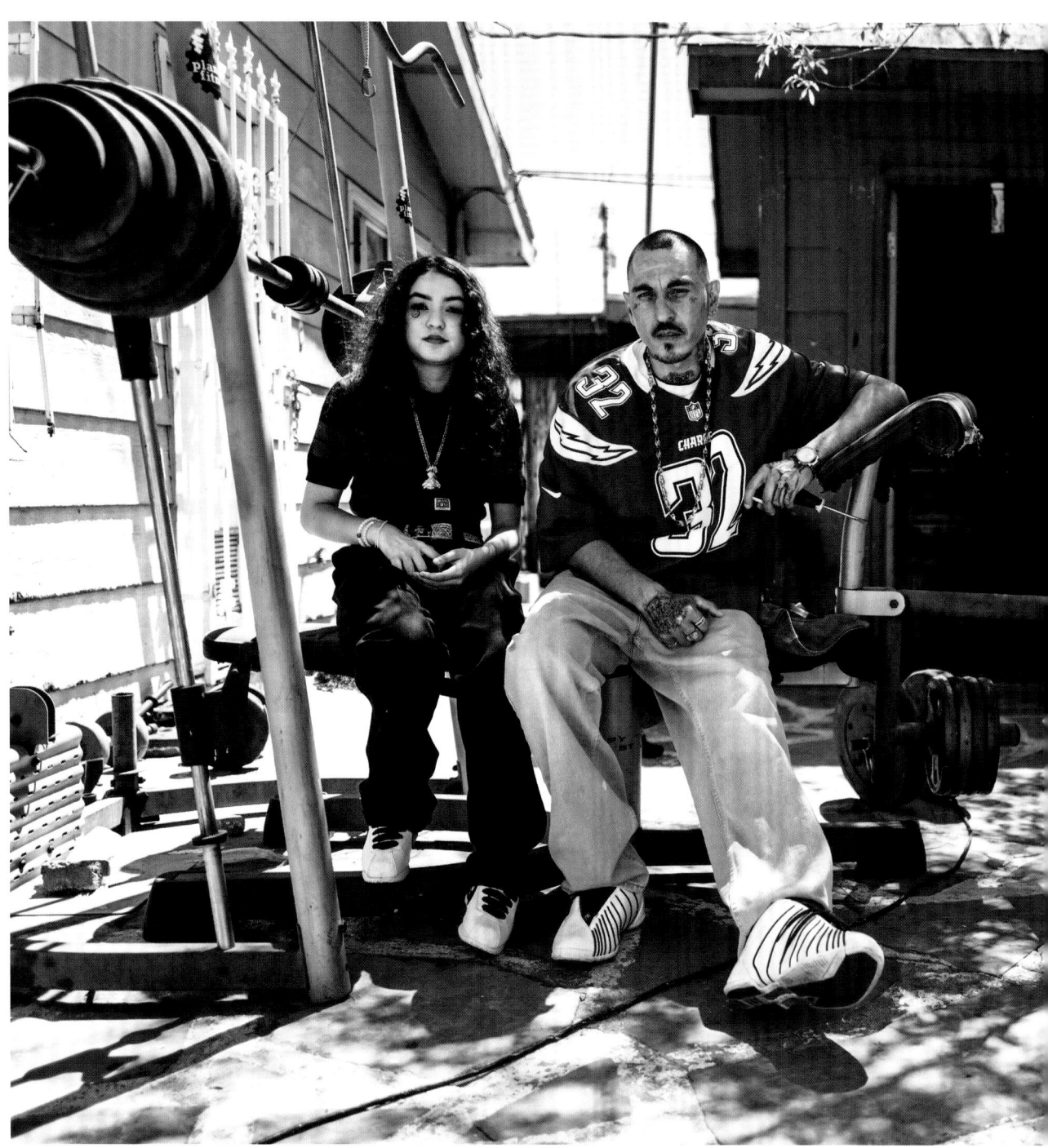

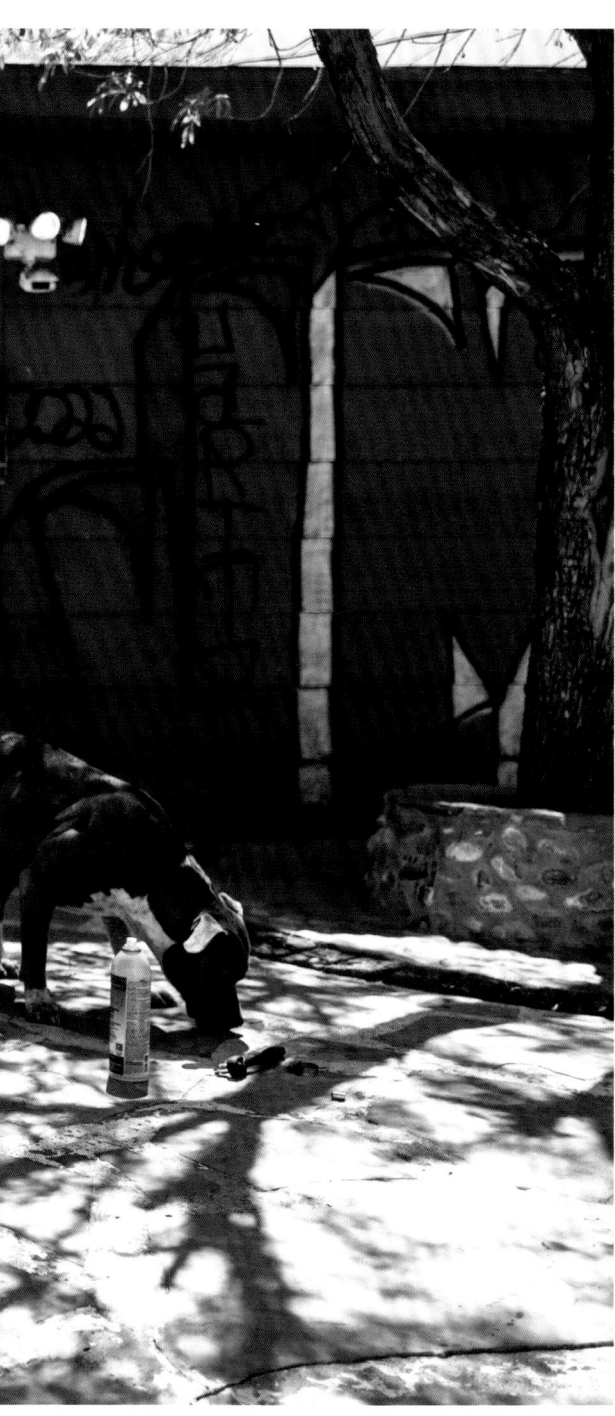

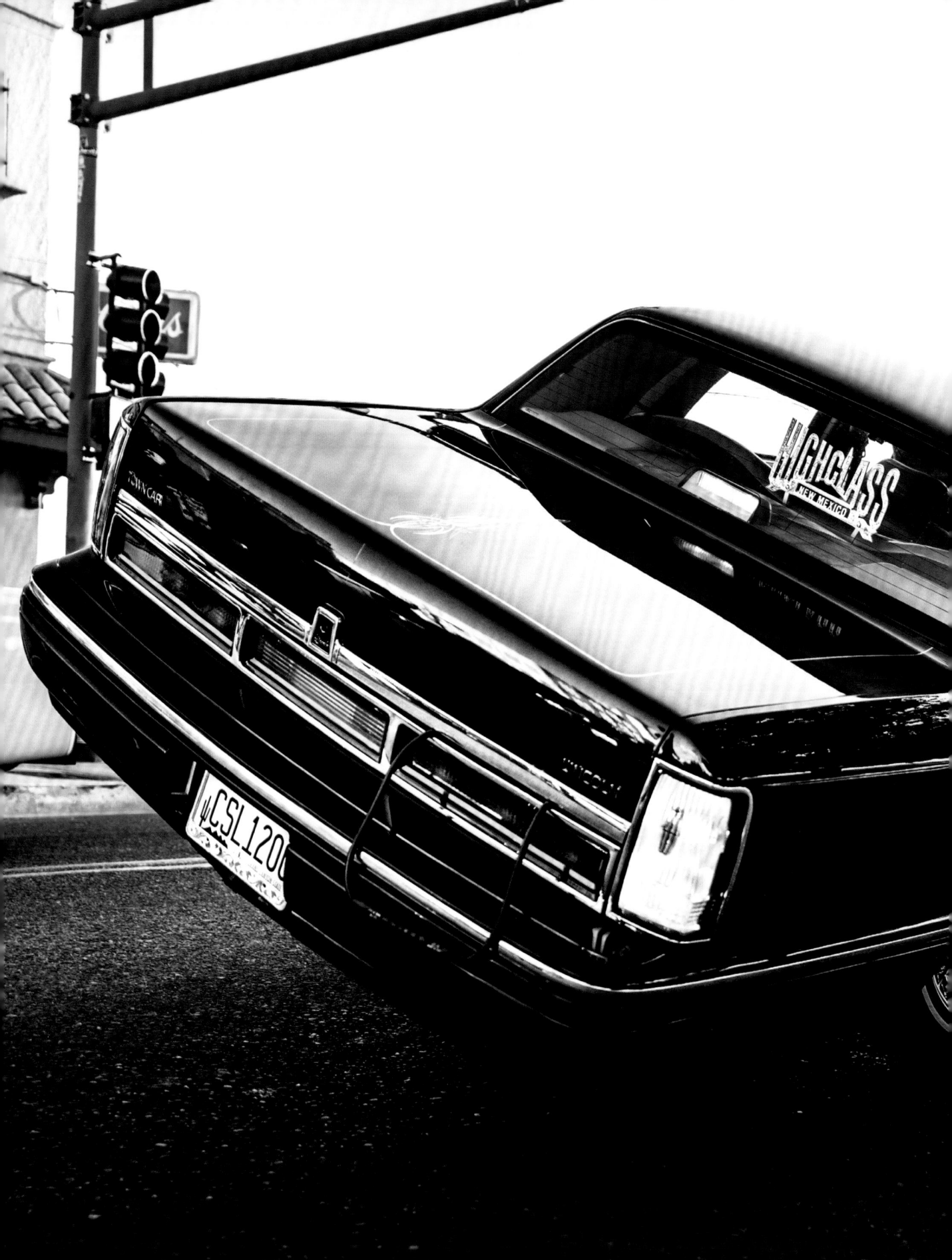

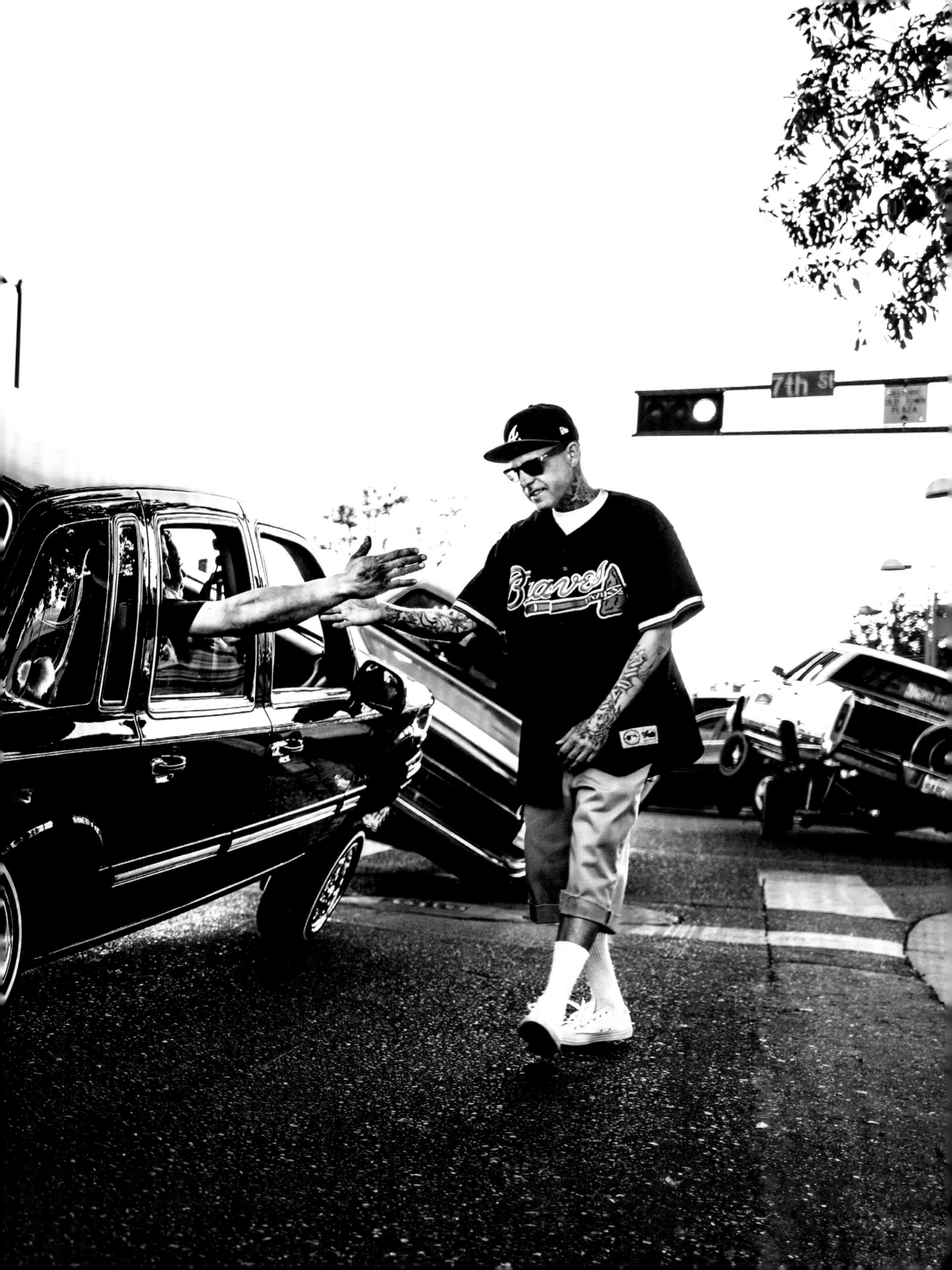

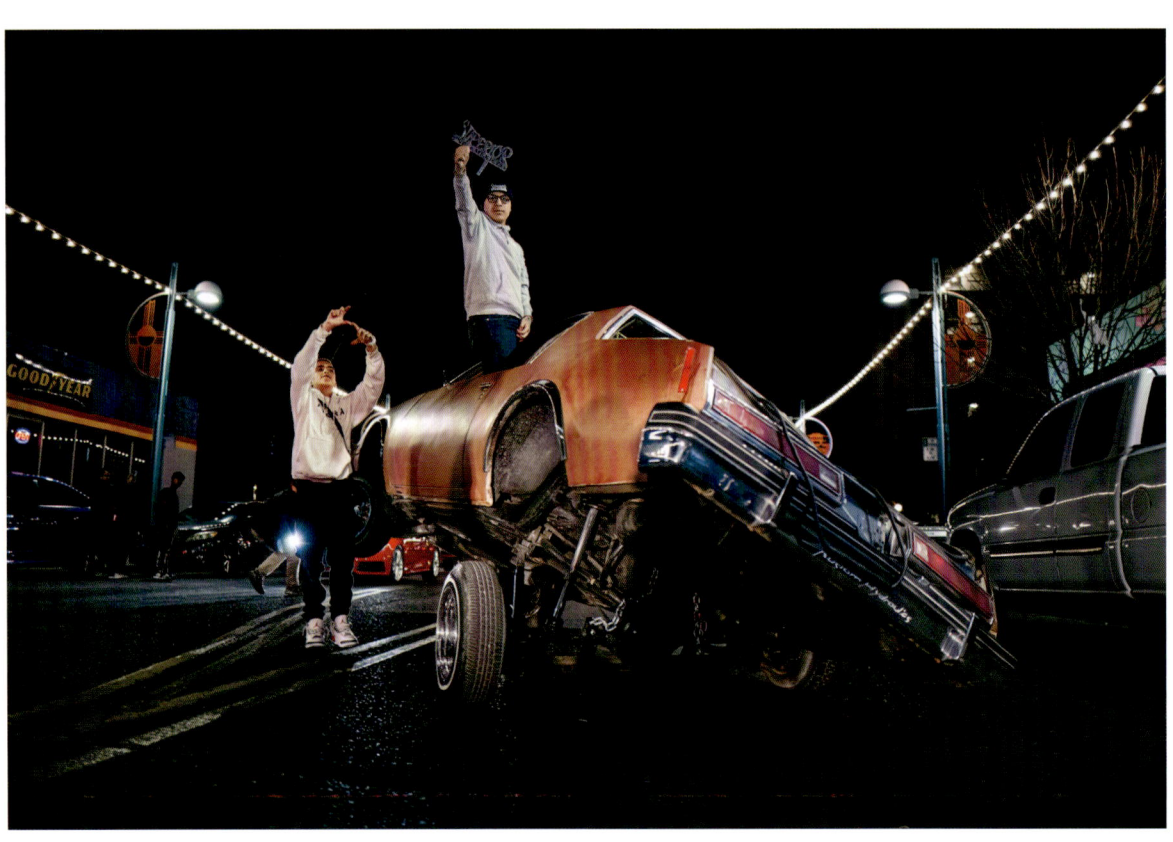

Superior Car Club, Downtown Albuquerque, 2023.

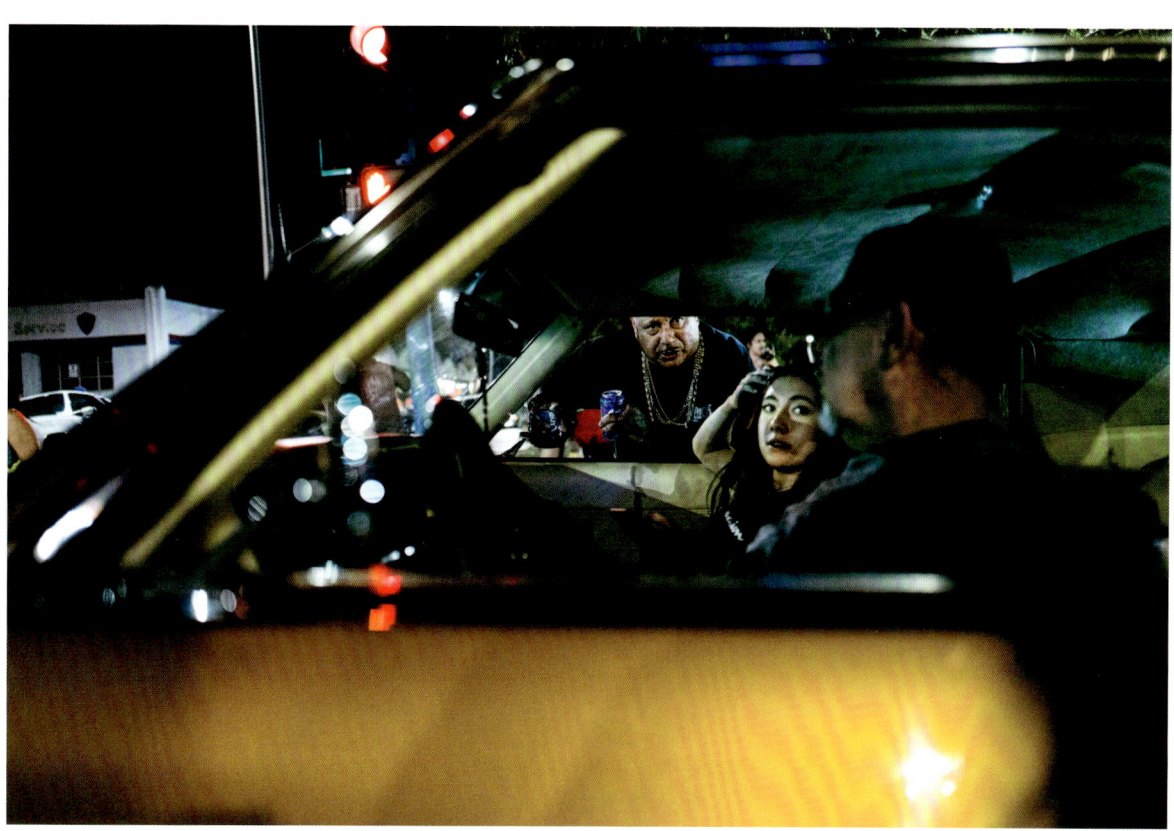

Roadside conversation, Downtown Albuquerque, 2022.

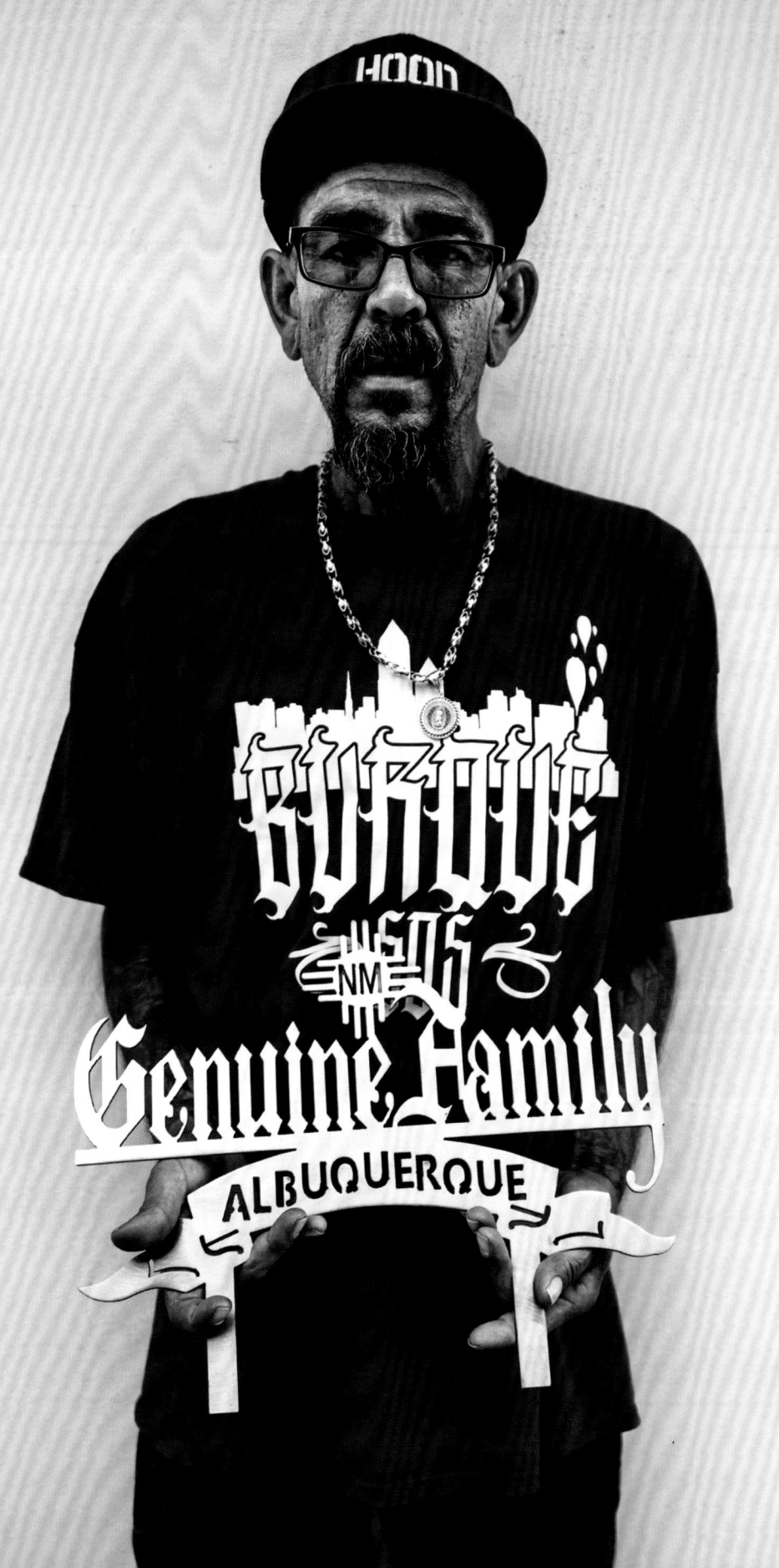

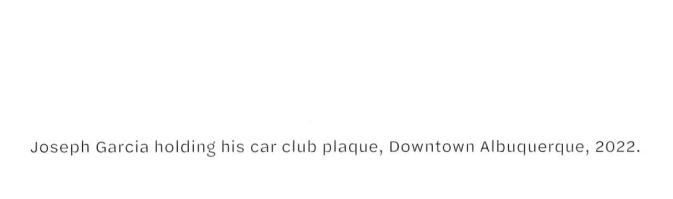

Joseph Garcia holding his car club plaque, Downtown Albuquerque, 2022.

Amor Bustamante, Downtown Albuquerque, 2023.

(*following pages*) Día de Muertos, Downtown Albuquerque, 2022.

El Camino Motor Hotel, Los Ranchos de Albuquerque, 2021.

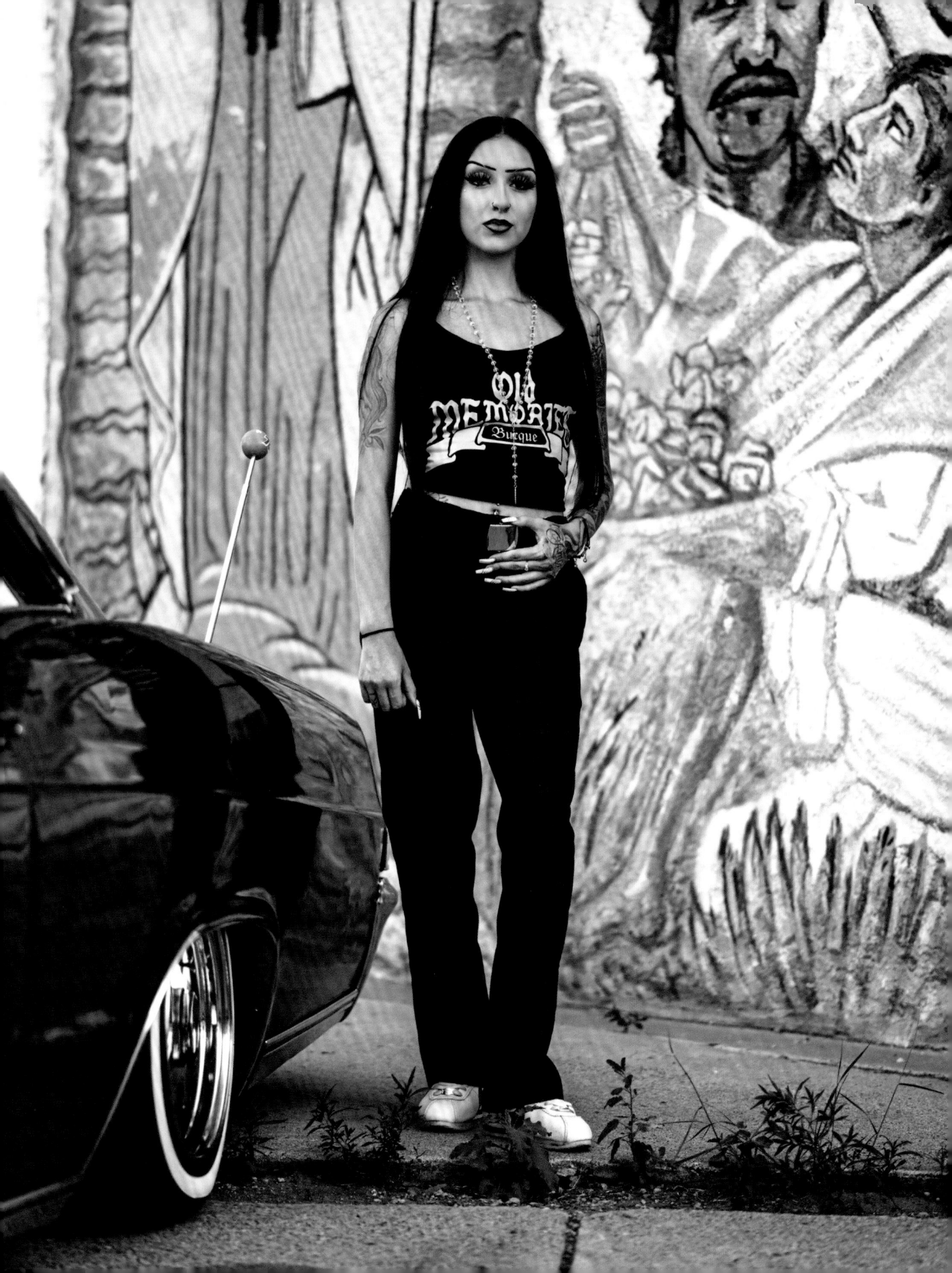

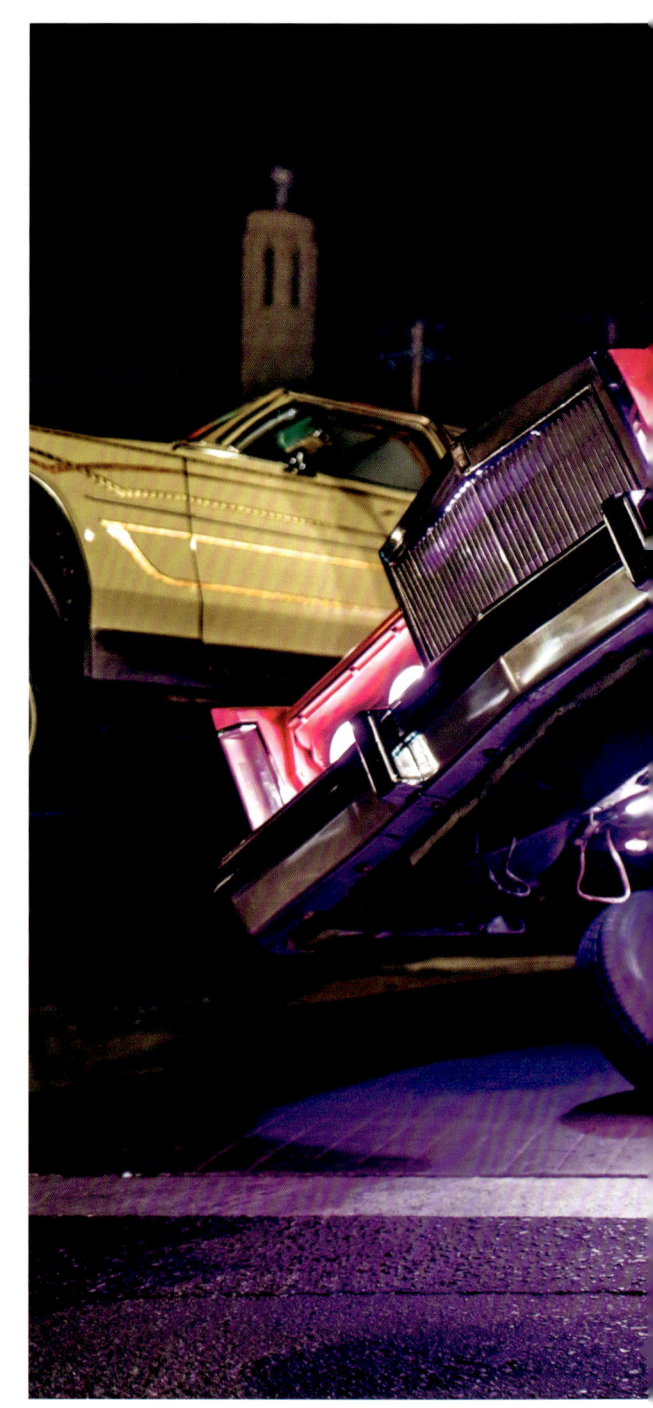

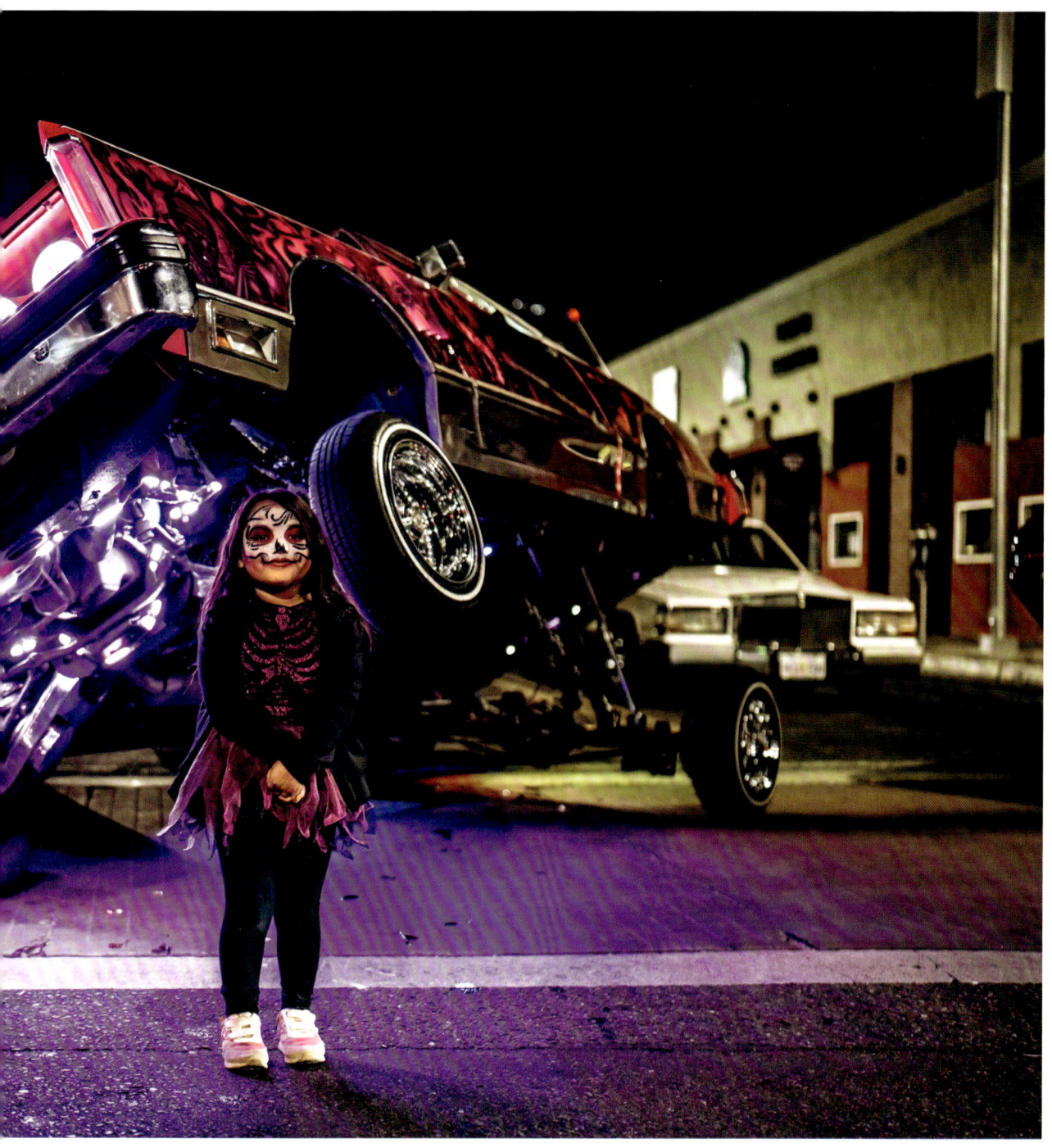

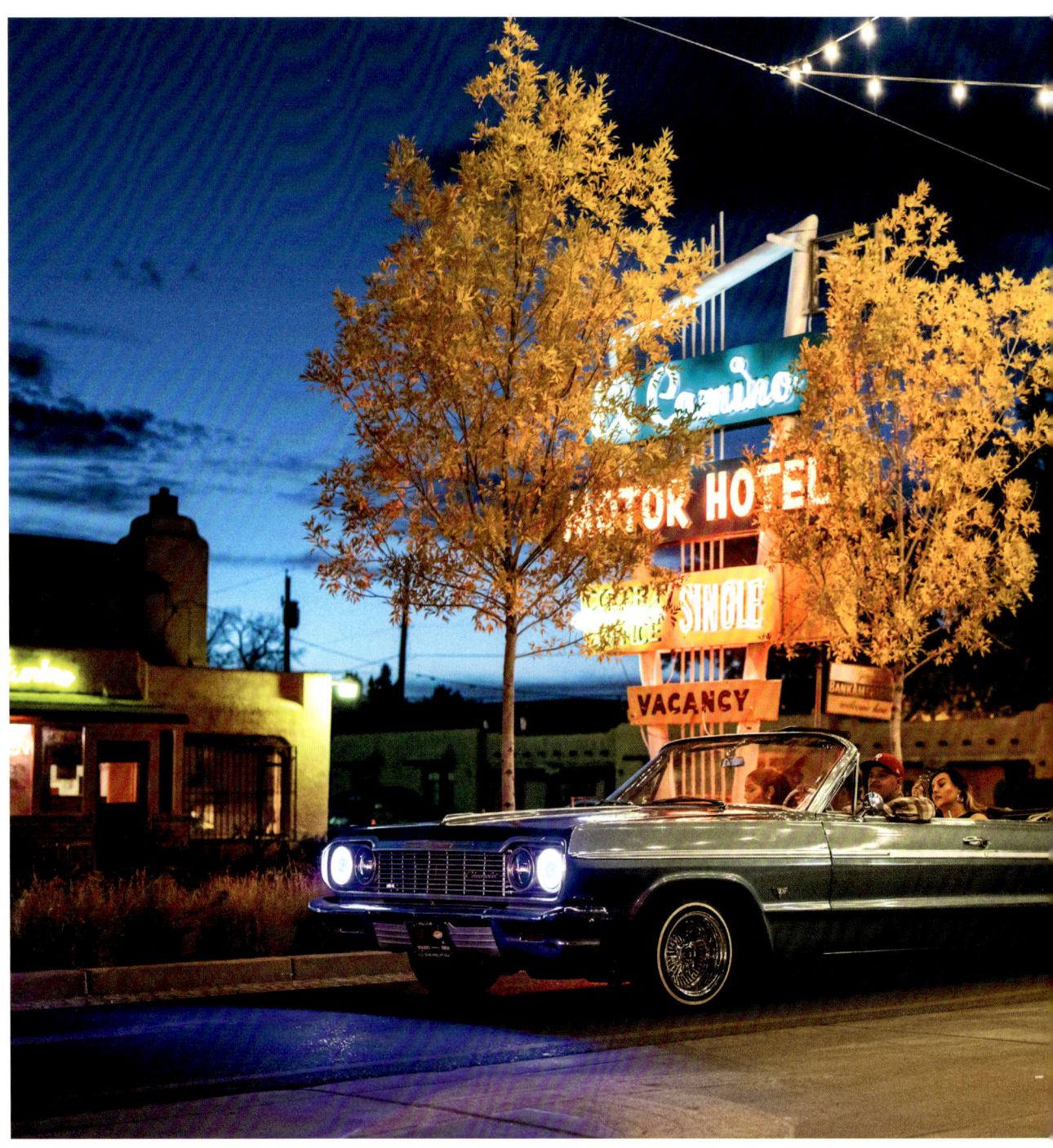

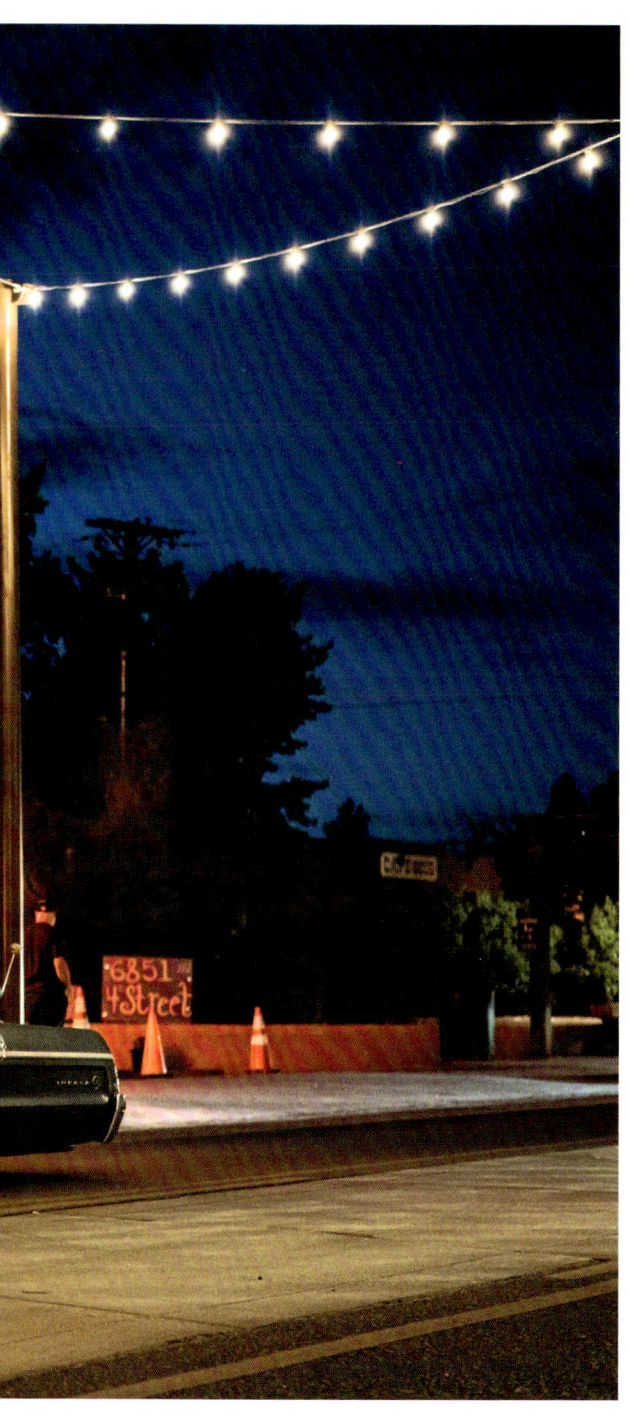

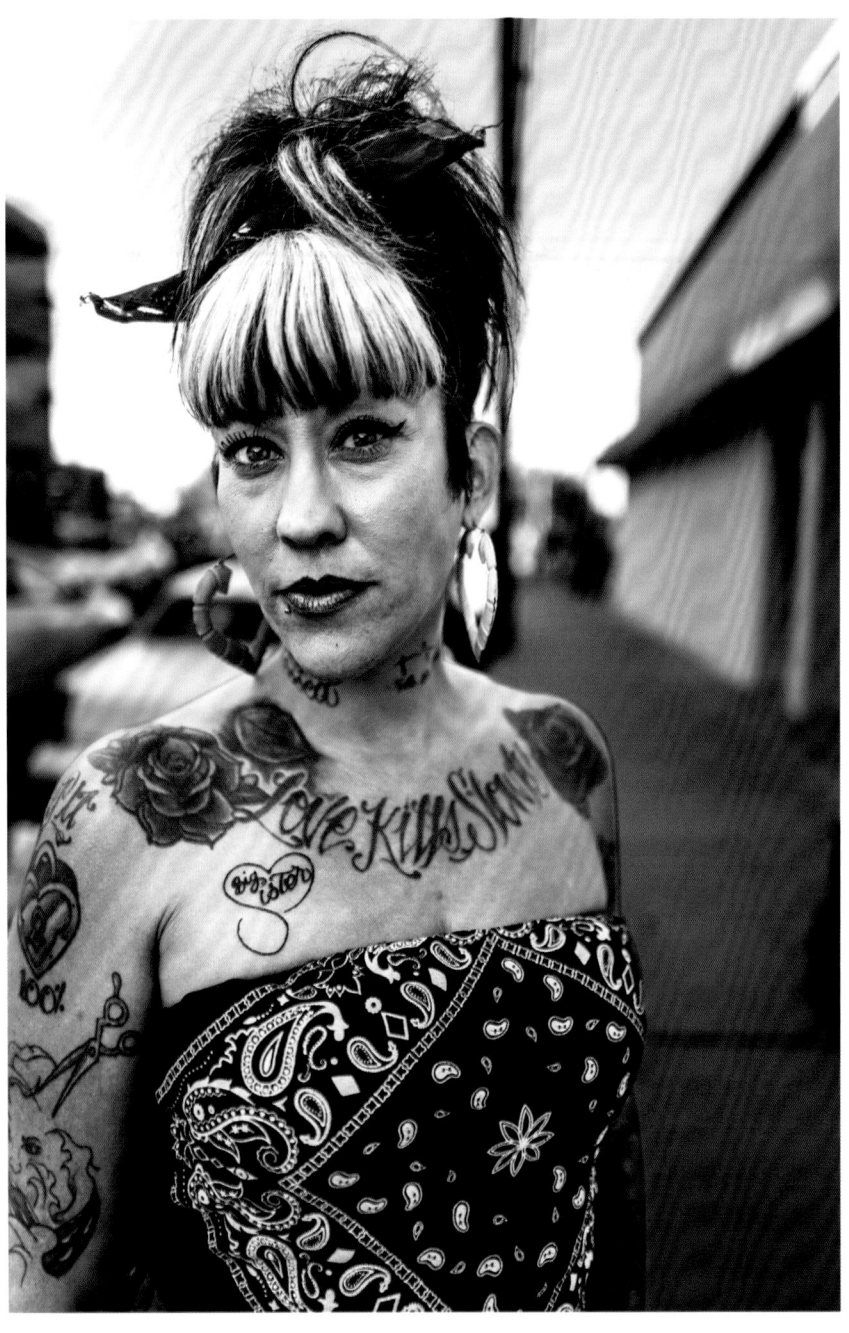

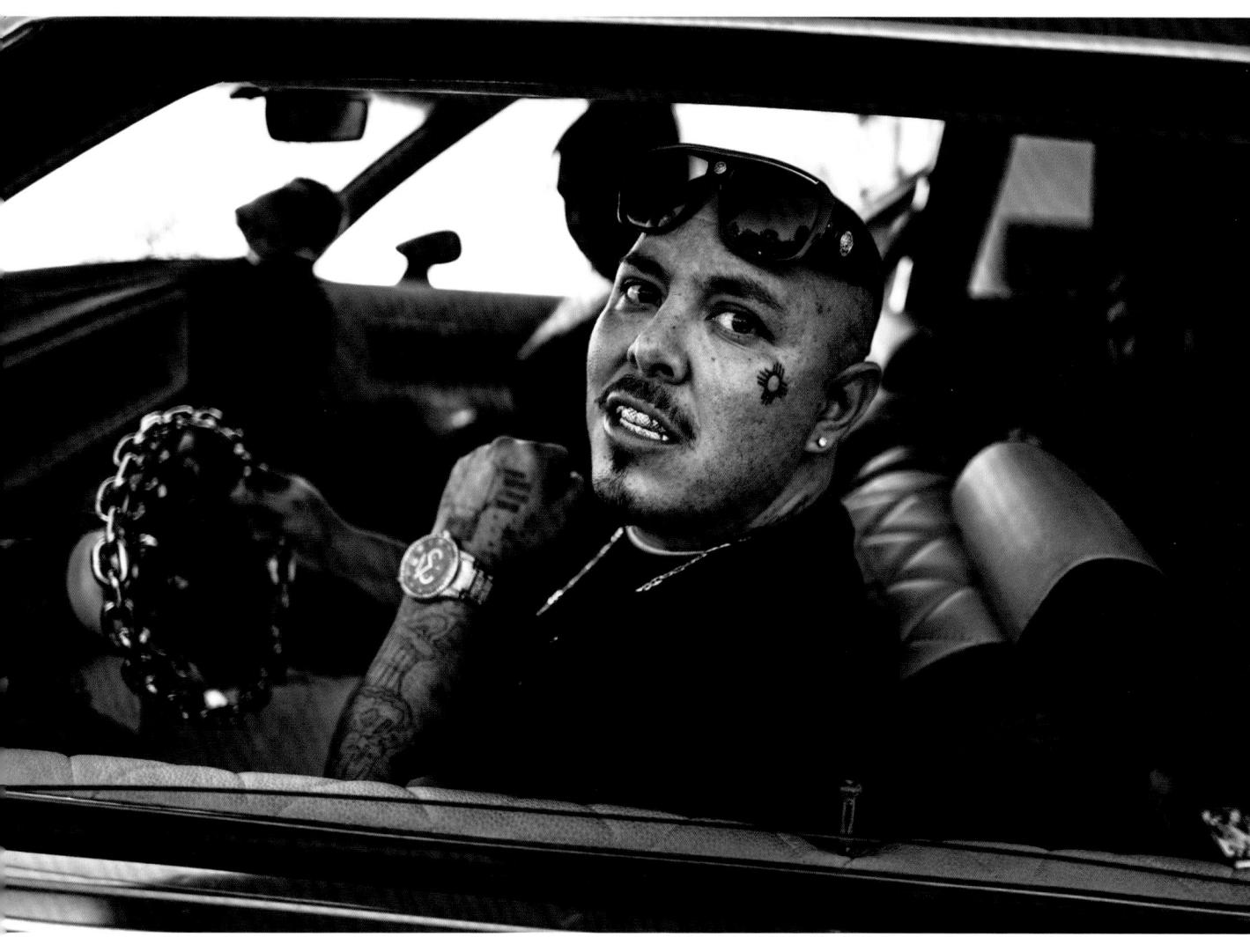

(*opposite page*) Angelita Sena, Downtown Albuquerque, 2021.

Cruising on Fourth Street, Barelas, Albuquerque, 2023.

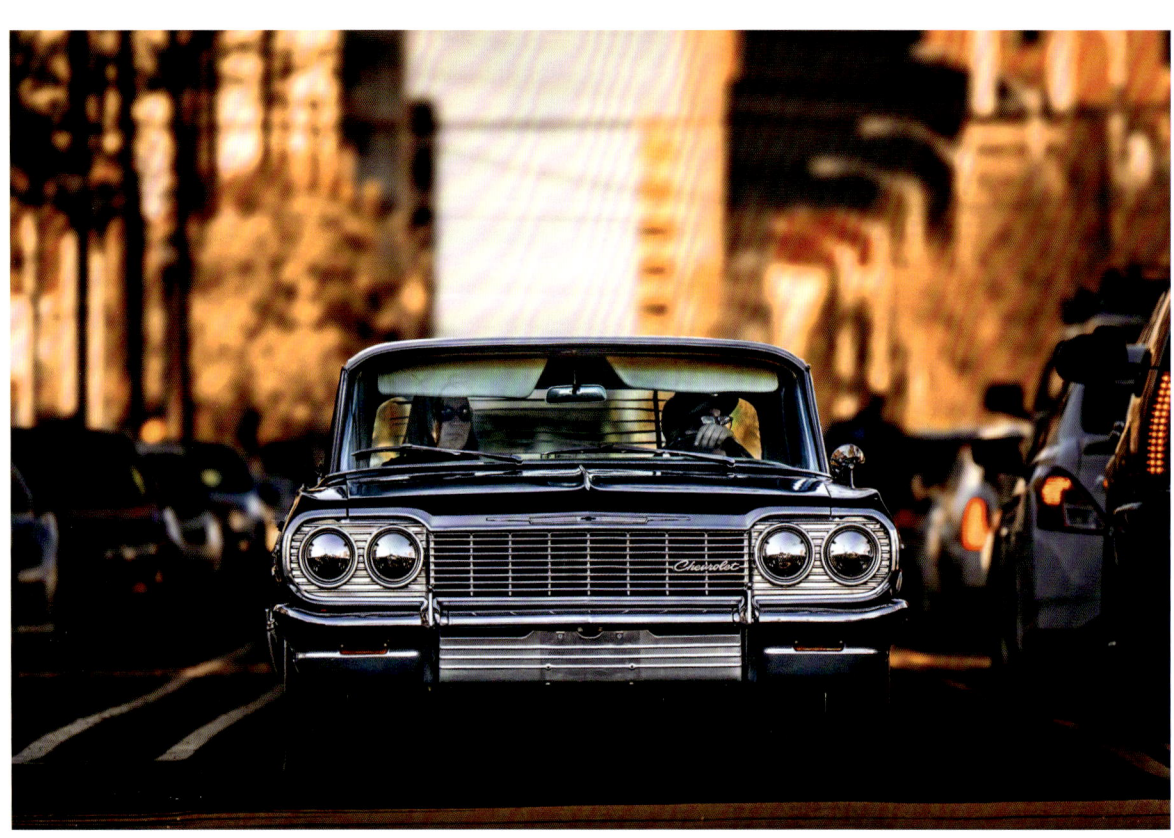

Cruising on Fourth Street, Barelas, Albuquerque, 2024.

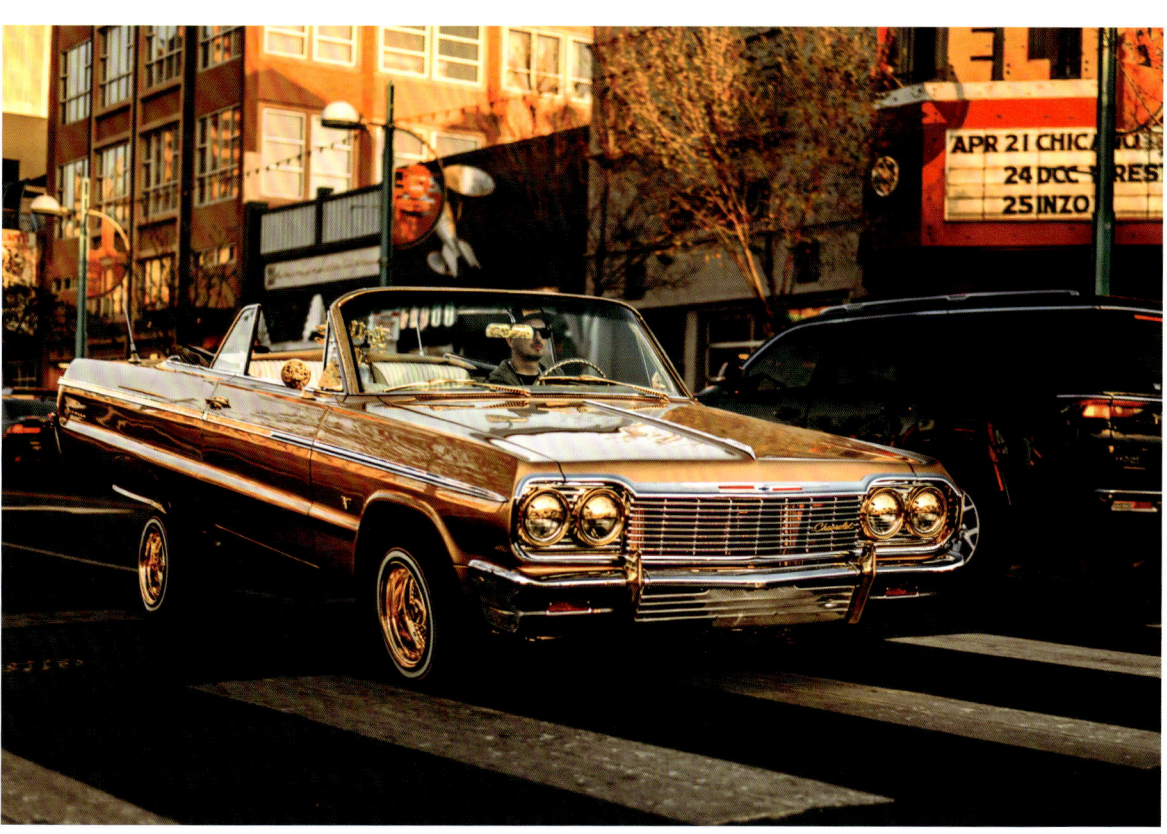

Sunset on Central Avenue, Downtown Albuquerque, 2024.

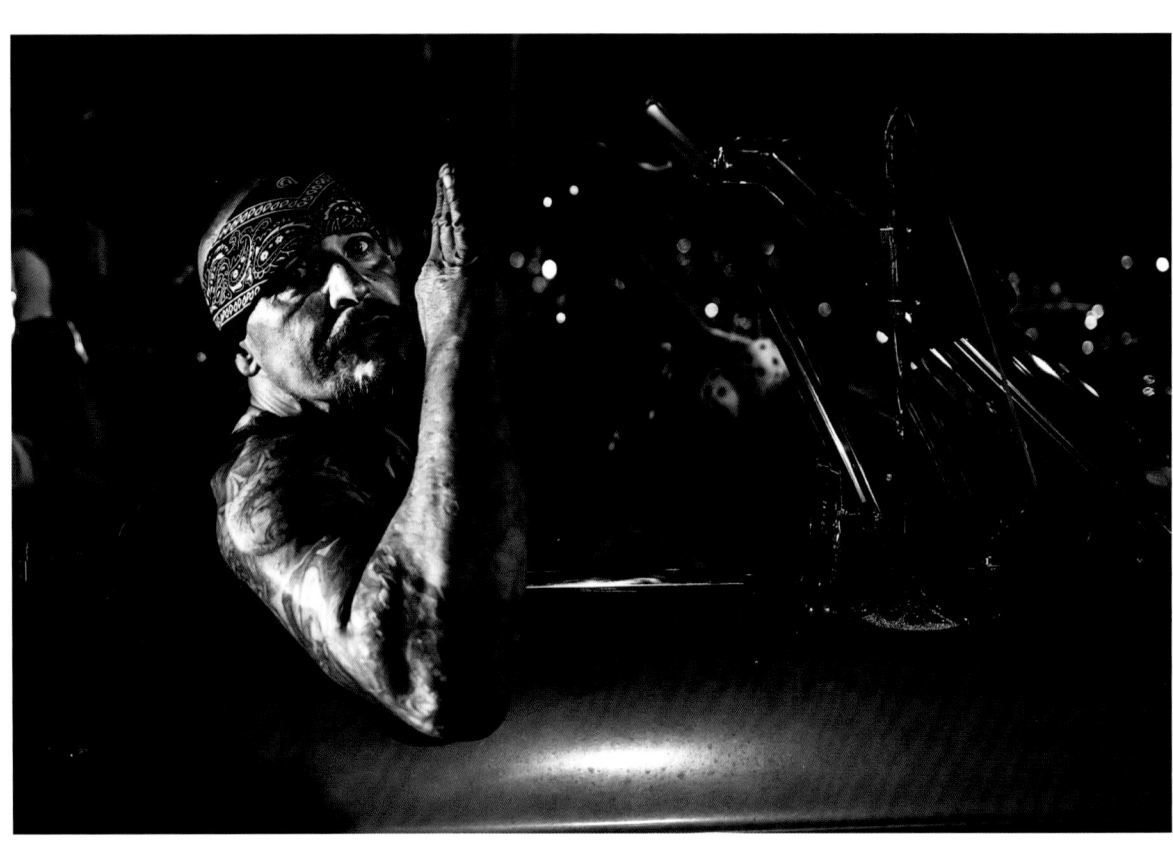

Cruising on a Sunday, Barelas, Albuquerque, 2024.

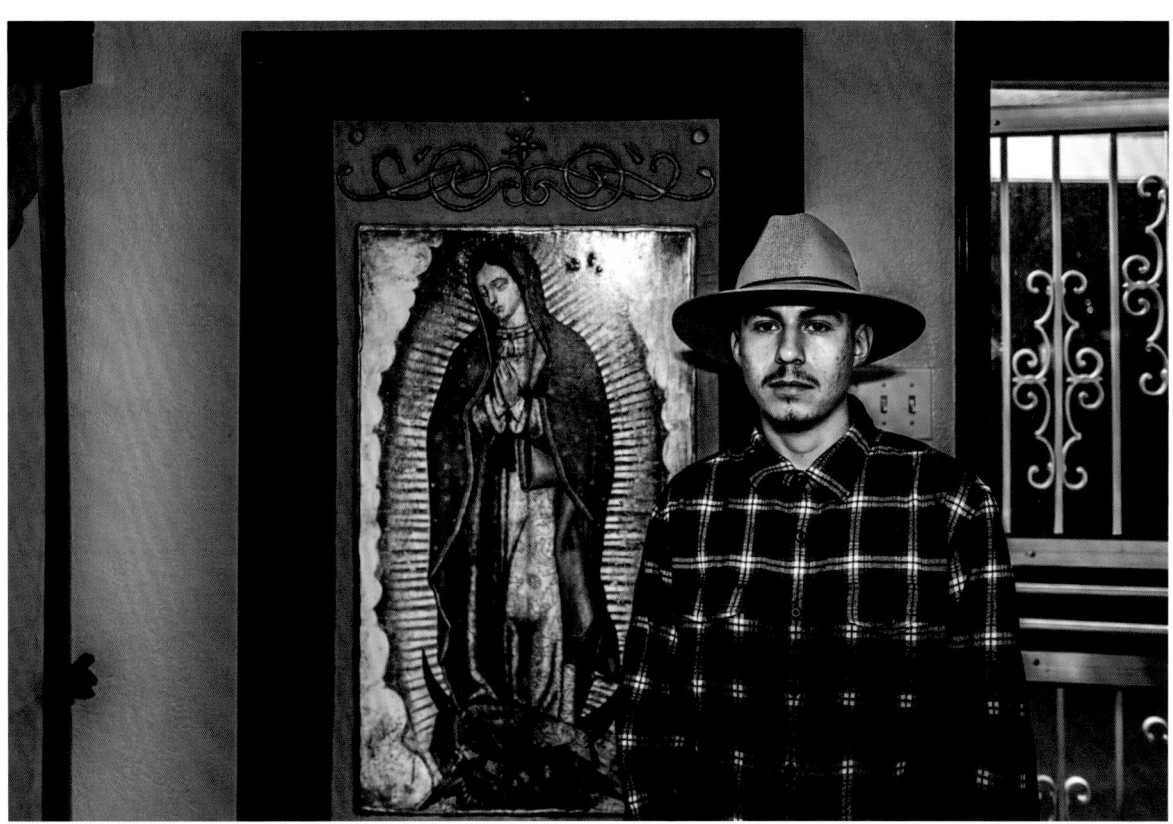

Fabian Gonzalez at home, South Valley, Albuquerque, 2024.

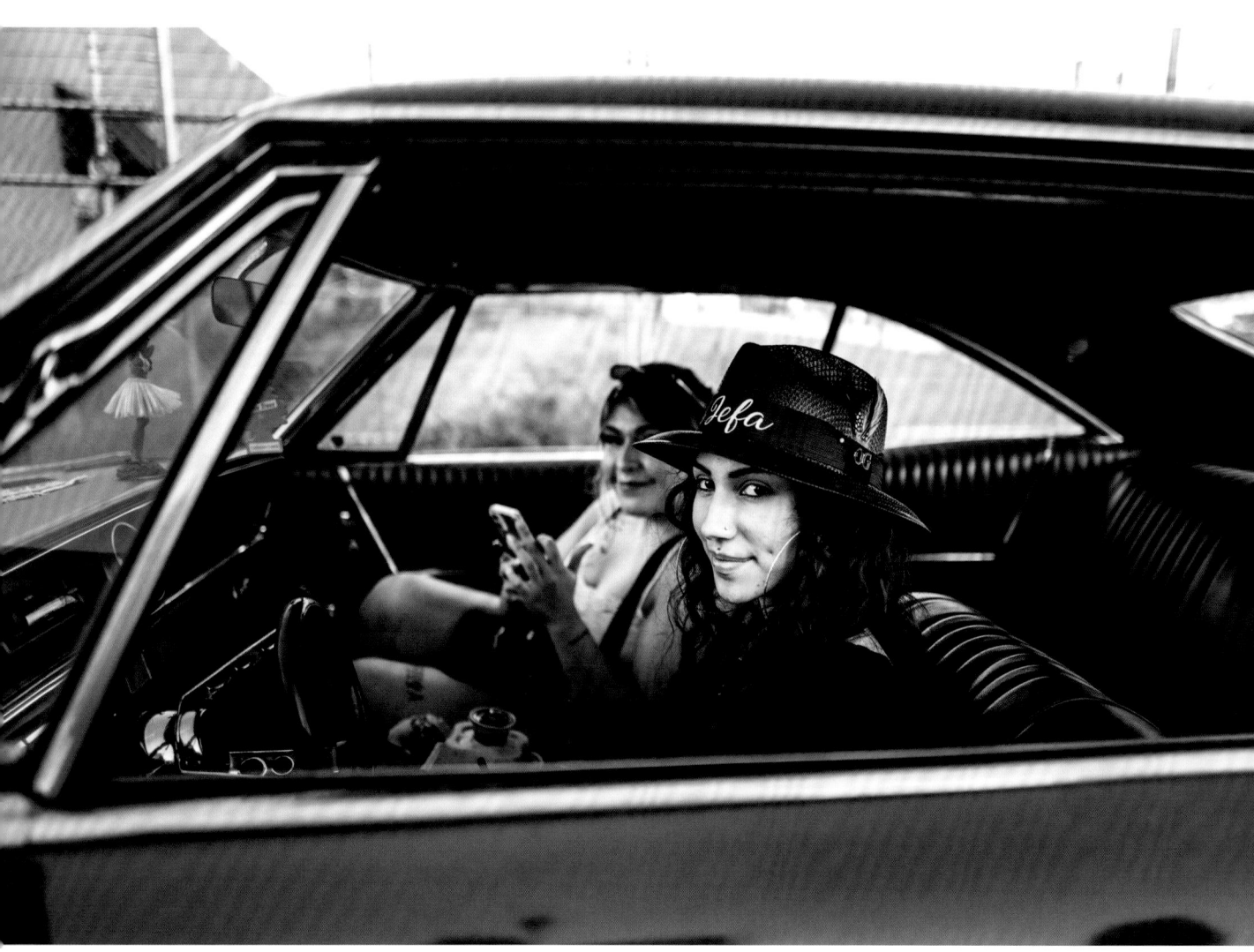

Two friends out for a cruise, Downtown Albuquerque, 2021.

(*following pages*) Good Friday, Española, New Mexico, 2024.

Downtown Albuquerque, 2024.

La Princesa de la Calle Séptima y Avenida Central

Jessica Helen Lopez

¡Oye, princesa! Passenger of the peacock-plumed
carriage of the cock-eyed spoke,
air-lifted, fat-tires tripping down Route 66
on this fine, fun-loving Sunday afternoon.

You all lazy-eyed and mid-day dreaming,
creamy eyeliner slick as a knife and gliding
along 7th Street and Central Avenue.

Jefita, where you be going? Gypsy Rose
of the renegade fleet, perfumed in petals
and nothing ain't prettier than you. *Tonantzin*

emblazoned by the seated heat
of your hips, your onyx stare is *puro* idolatry,
quinceañera parade, *ofrenda* on wheels,

queen of the streets. Camera obscura
captures your smirk, your twitch, your wink
flick-arch of the eyebrow as you float, a four-wheeled
beauty boulevard of dreams.

¡Mira a la princesa! She is the low and slow,
glider of the ultimate galactic ride, *cultura*
and the chrome shines like a silver church bell.

She stares down the shuttered lens, sleek
side-eyed mischief maker, trickster at the wheel,
homegirl by her side, cruising deities,
ride-or-die partners in crime.

And *la Bomba*
howls into
the wind.

Lowriding,
and the *ranfla* bounces
like a technicolor
fantasy.

Paint jobs like *paletas!*
Lime greens! Sandia pinks!
Silver-flecked black like
the arch of a witchy cat
or the chola's
wing-tipped eye,

lining our way to heaven.

And heaven is a place
on earth. Right here,
at the cross roads of
Central Avenue and
Seventh Street.

Downtown, around
town, up and down,
riding the sweet, sweet
Burque streets.

slow

    slow

       slow

      cruising

    cruising

cruising

'til the sun
melts a mellow
moon watching

rising

      rising

            rising

watching.

*Los domingos
están hechos
de azúcar.*

Sundays are
made for
sugar.

Oye, princesa.

*Where you
be going?*

*Can I ride
with you?*

*Can I take
a little trip
with you?*

*Can we take
a little trip*

together?

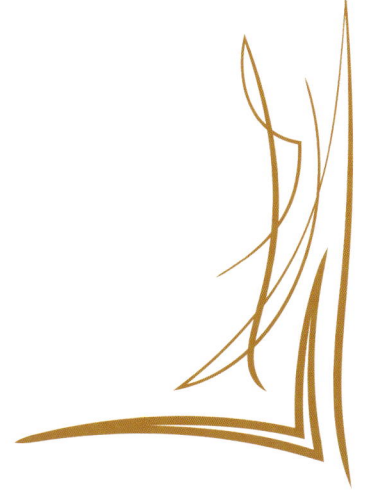

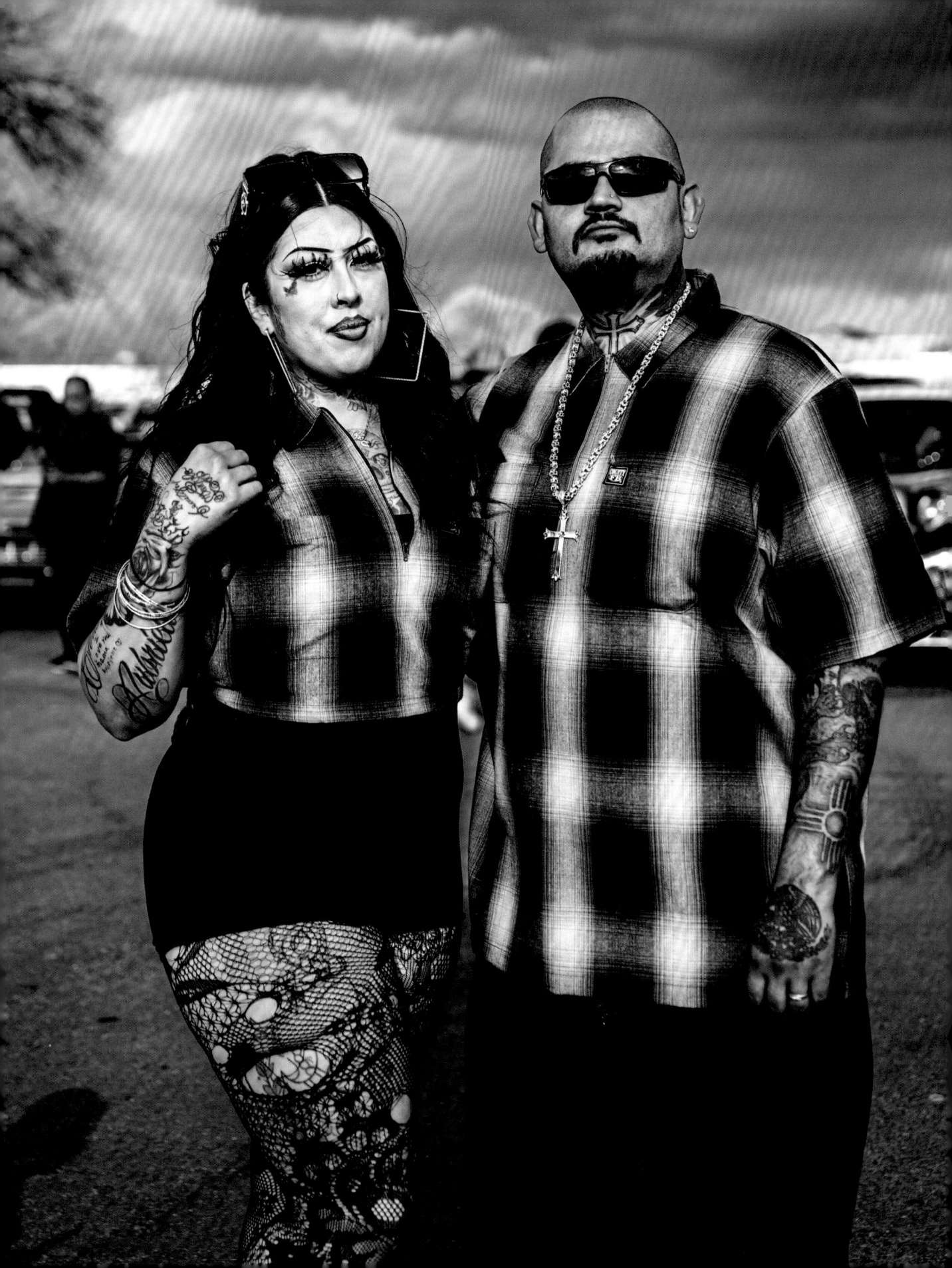

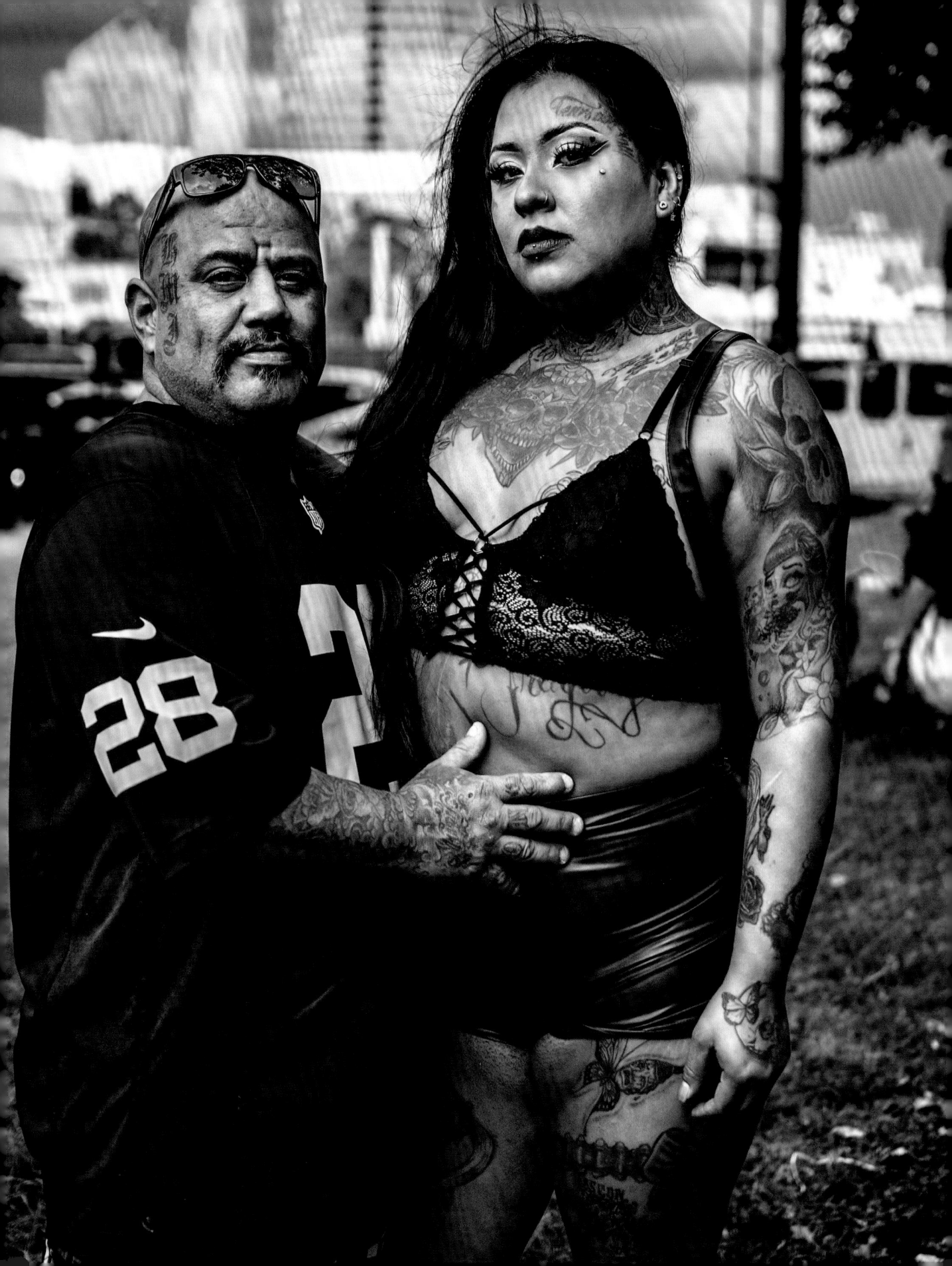

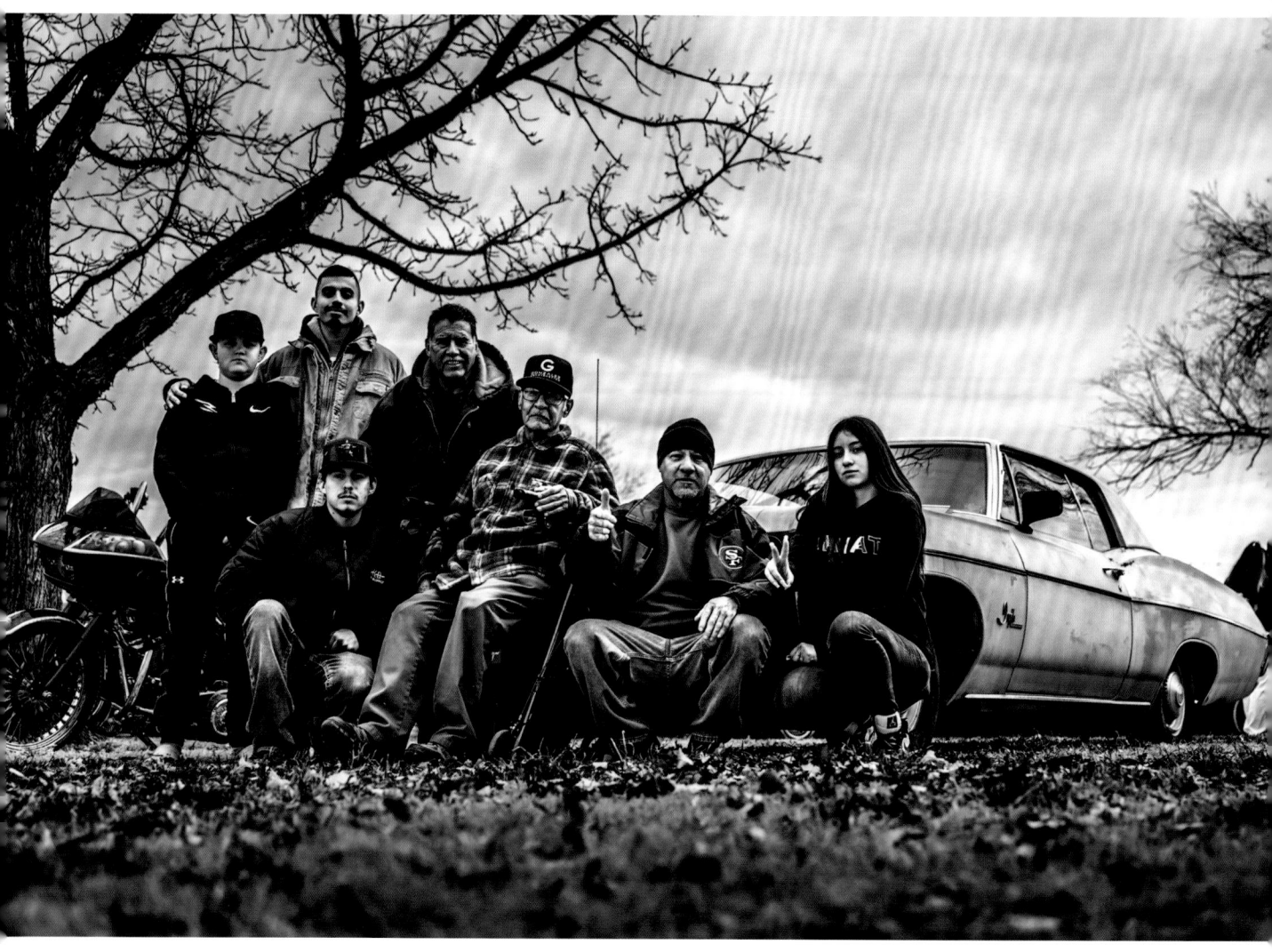

The Gonzalez family, South San Jose Park, Albuquerque, 2024.

(*opposite page*) Isabella stands next to Gilbert Lopez's mini truck, Albuquerque, 2024.

(*following pages*) Lowrider hopper, Albuquerque, 2021.

Raza Unida Bike Club, Albuquerque, 2024.

Taking Over Car Club, Martineztown–Santa Barbara, Albuquerque, 2022.

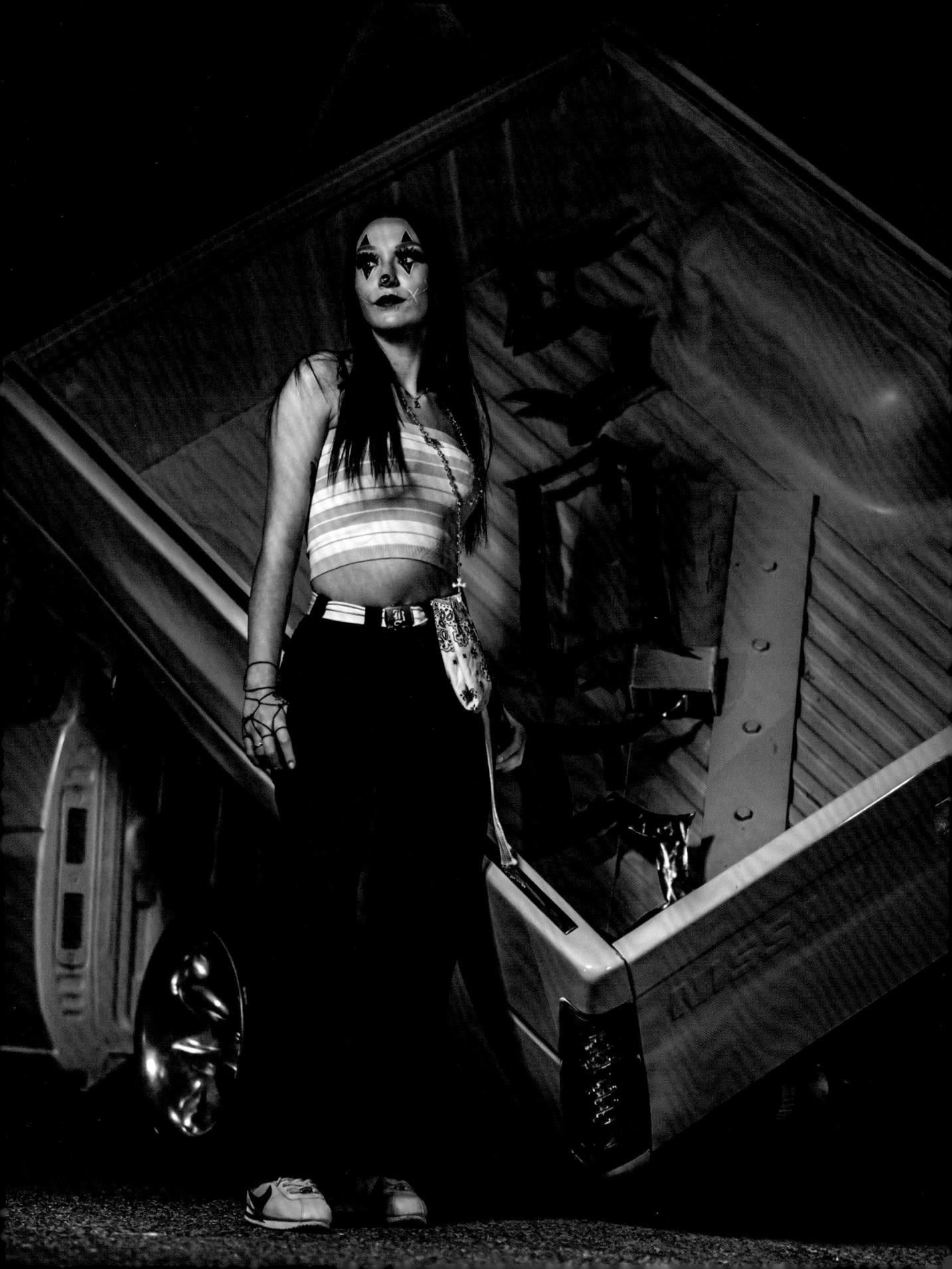

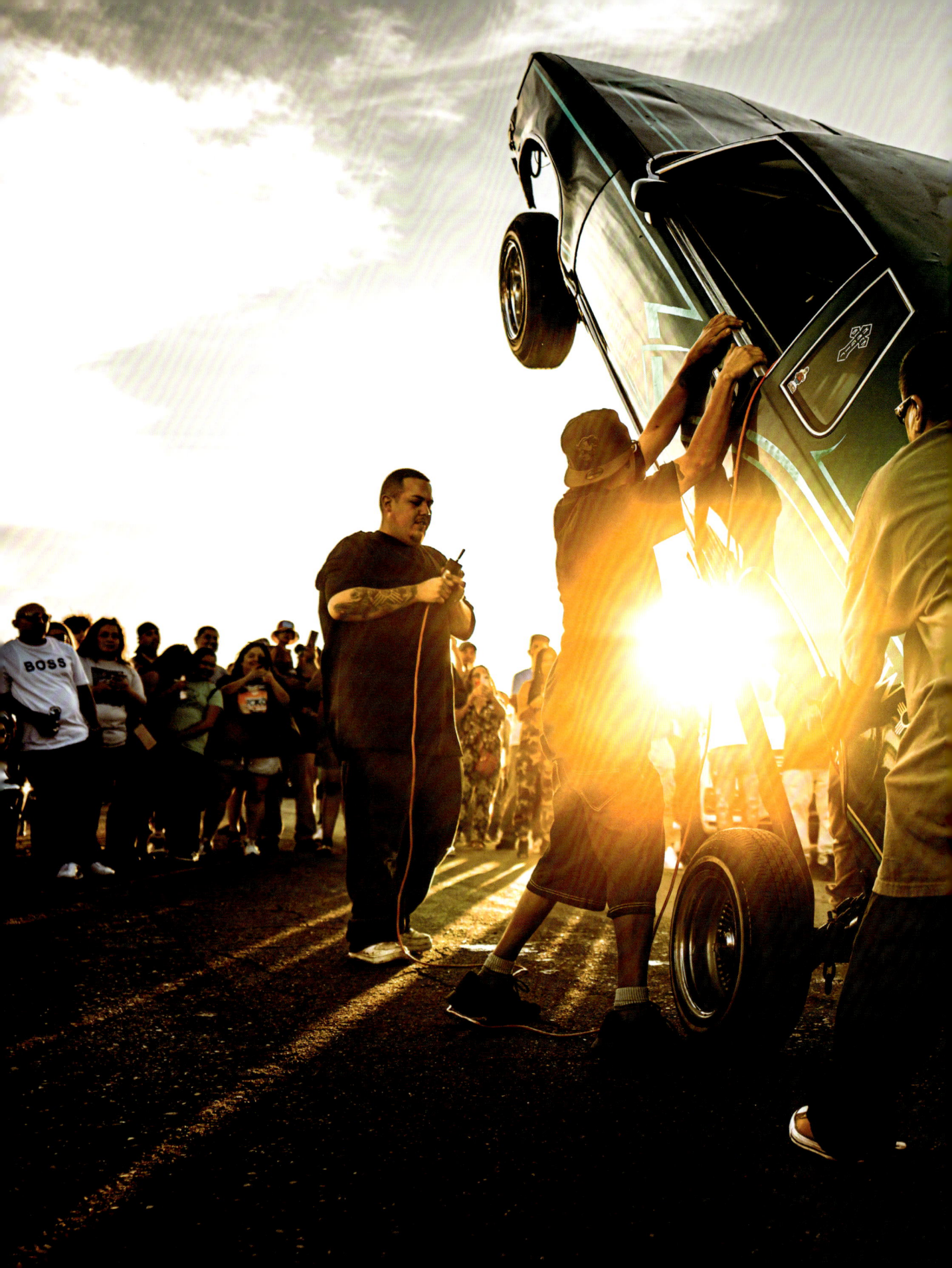

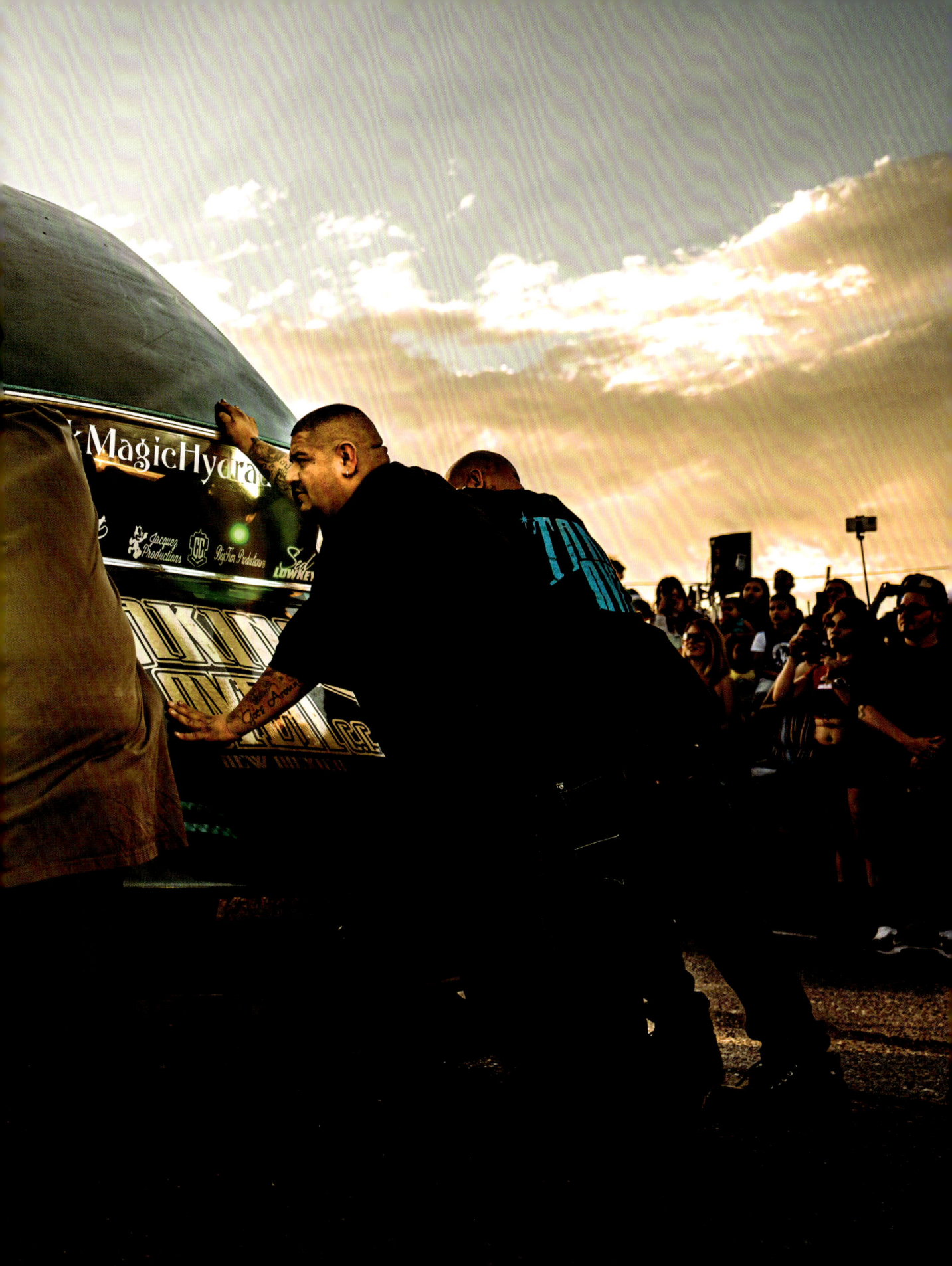

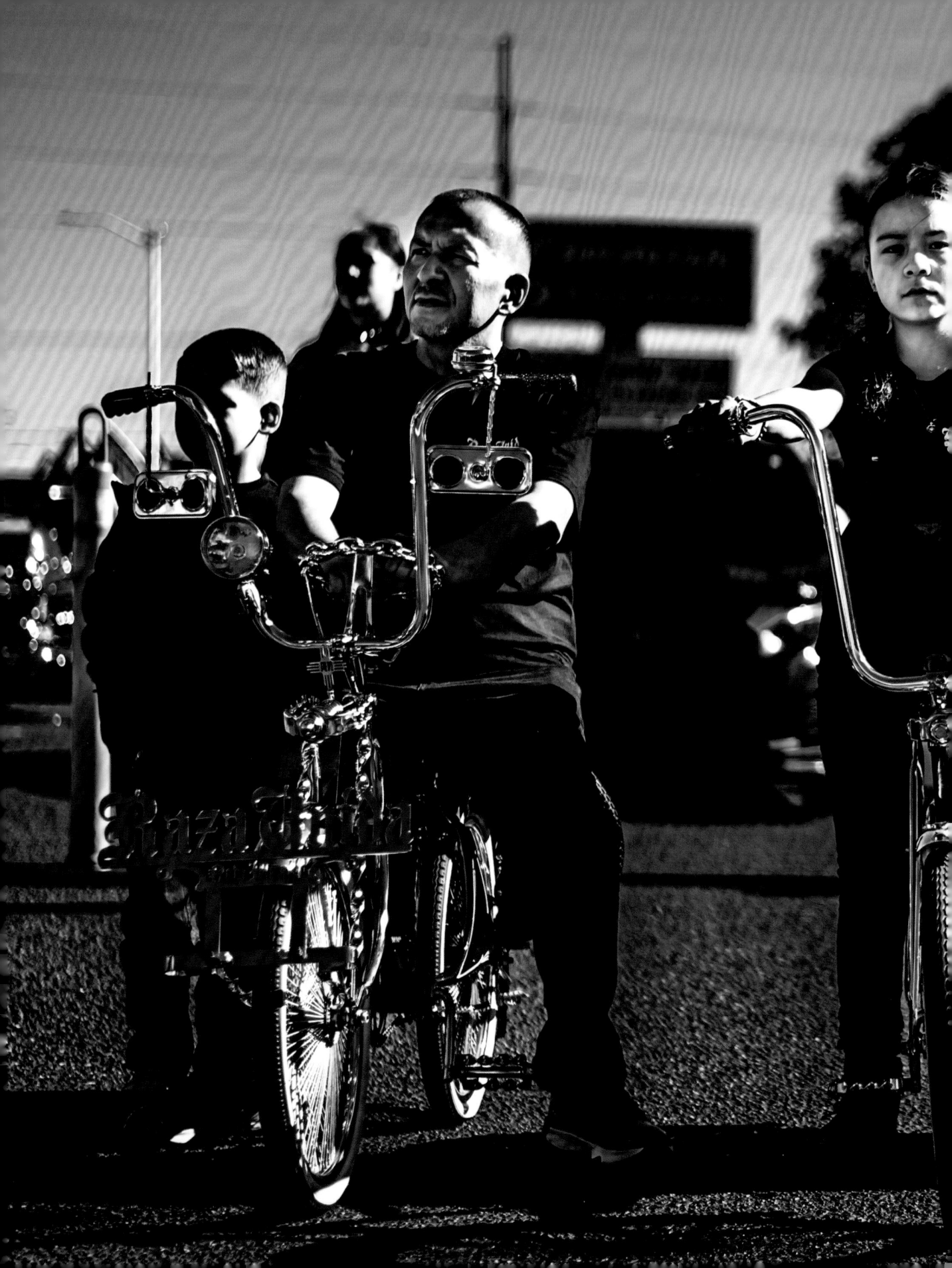

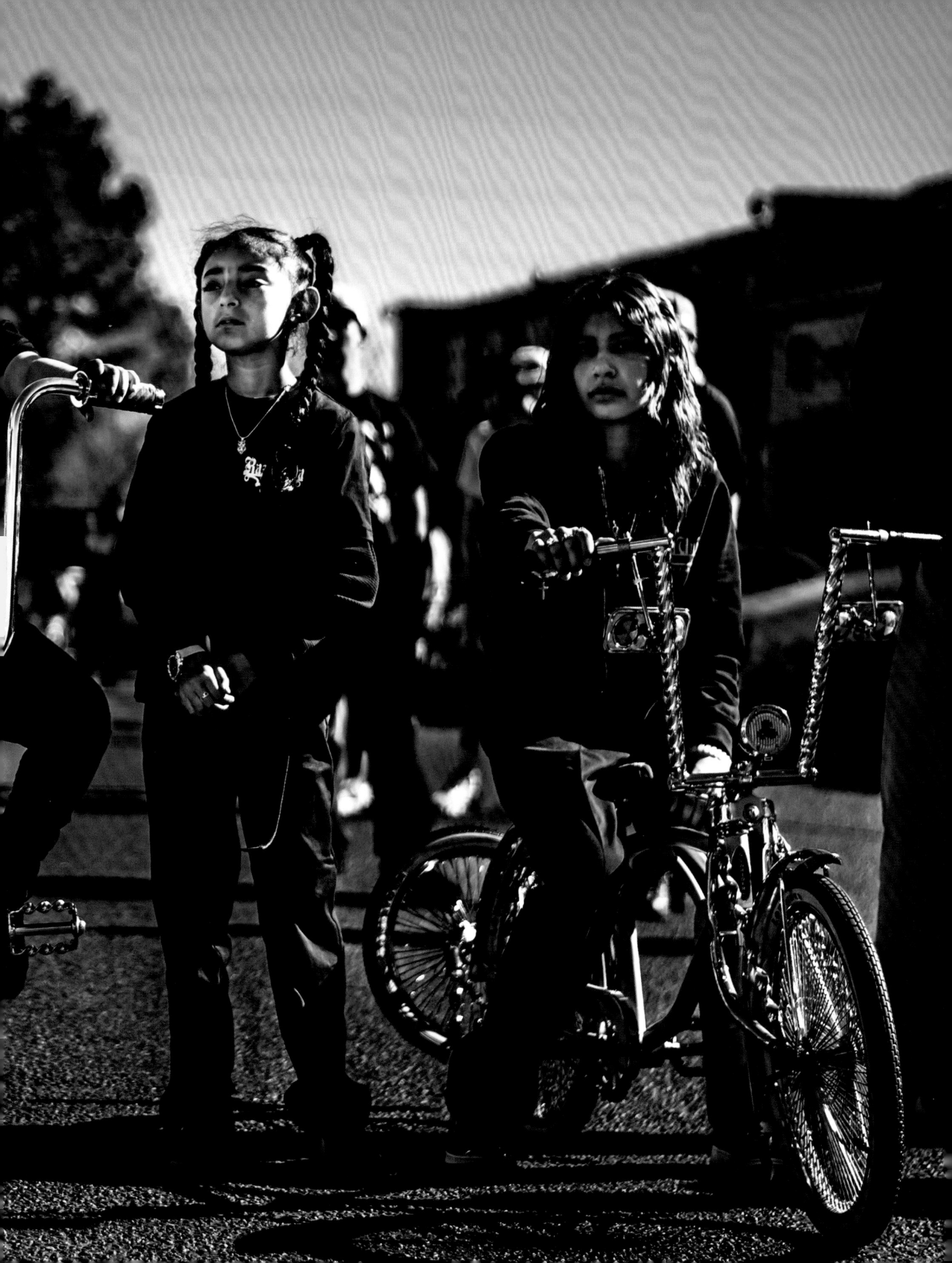

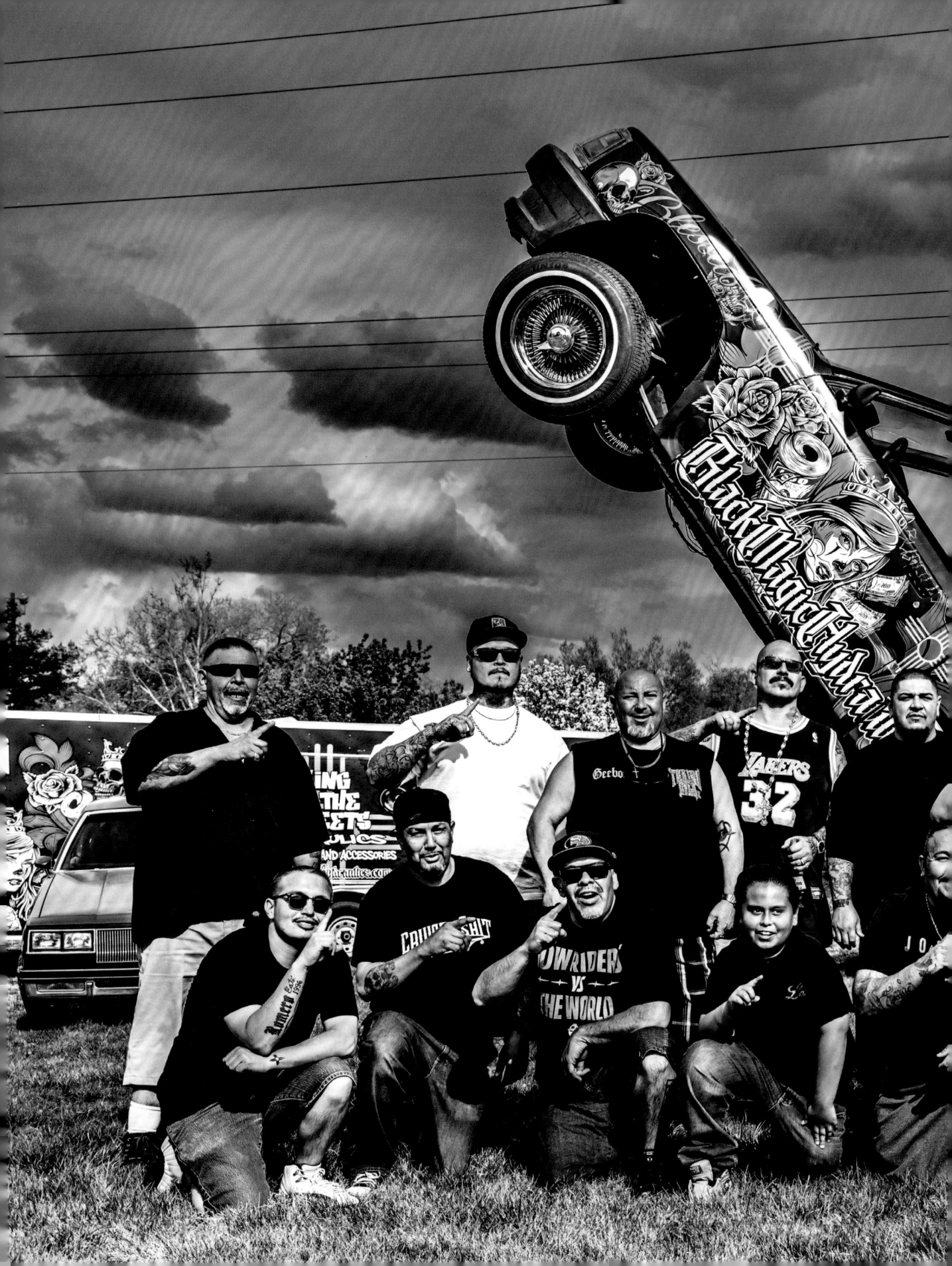

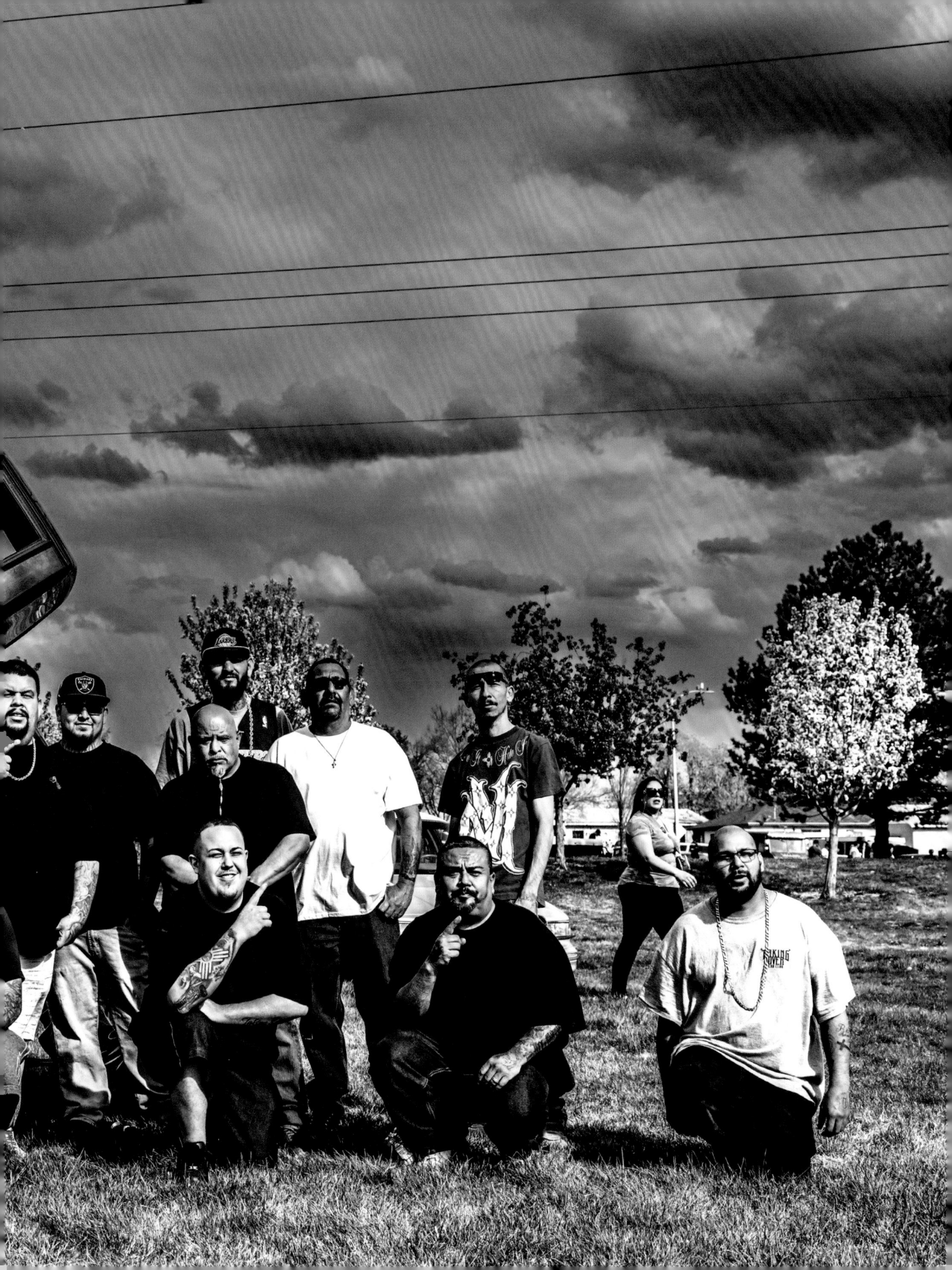

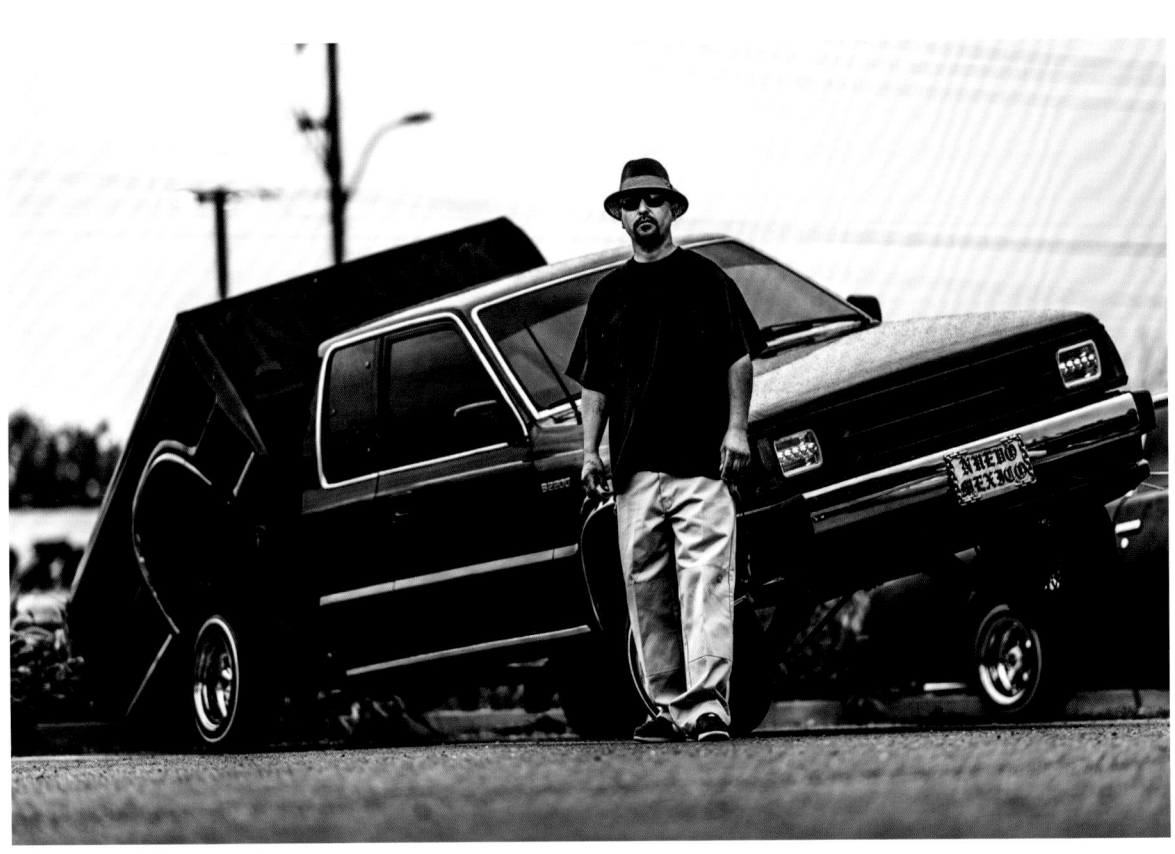

Gilbert Lopez, Barelas, Albuquerque, 2024.

(*opposite page*) Jason Archuleta shows his rosaries, South Valley, Albuquerque, 2024.

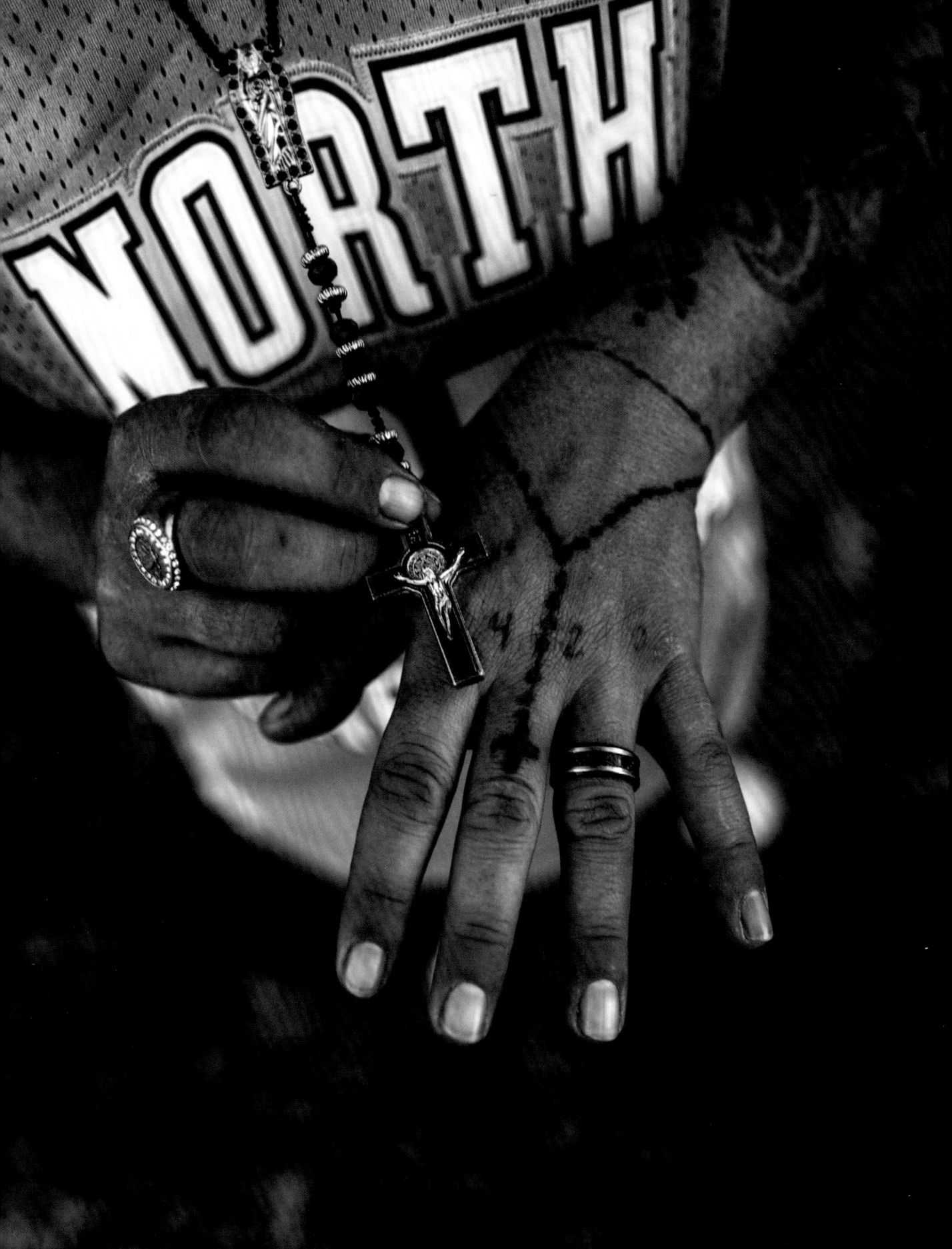

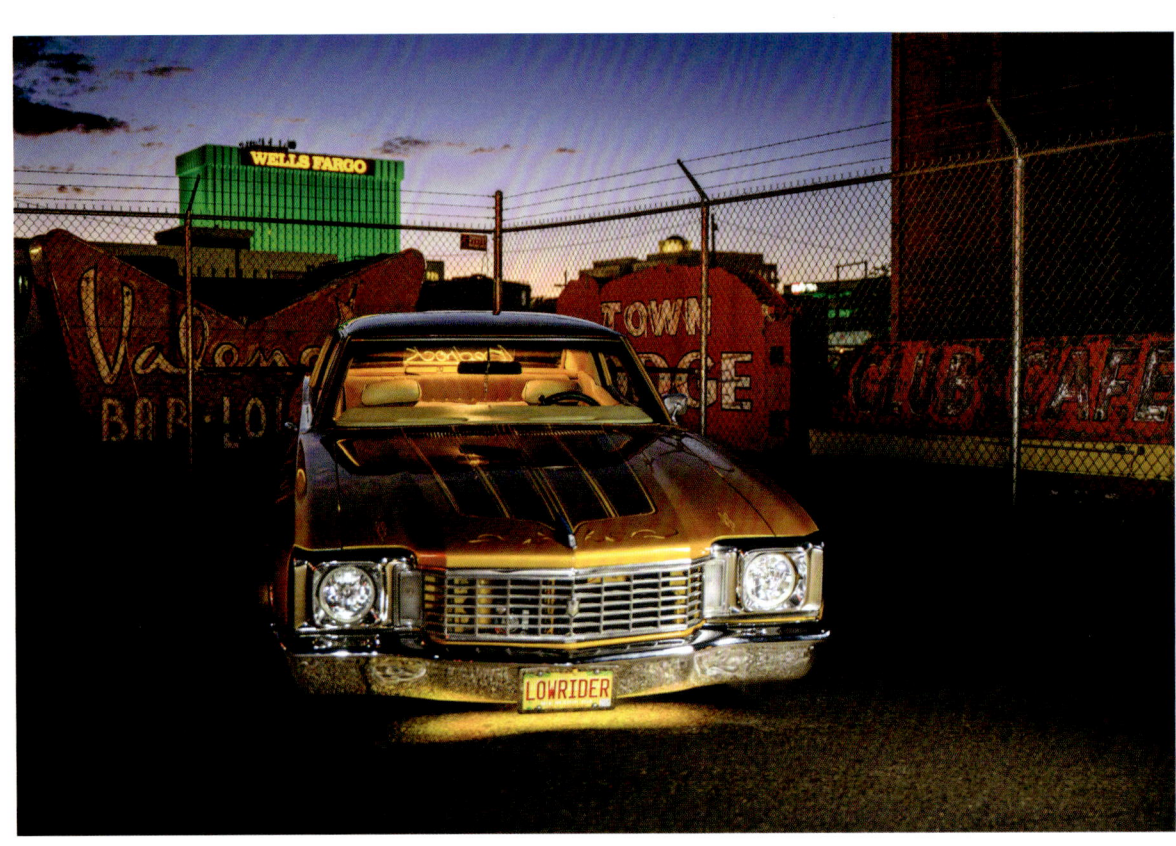

Lawrence Griego's Monte Carlo, Albuquerque, 2024.

(*opposite page*) Unique Lovato, Albuquerque, 2024.

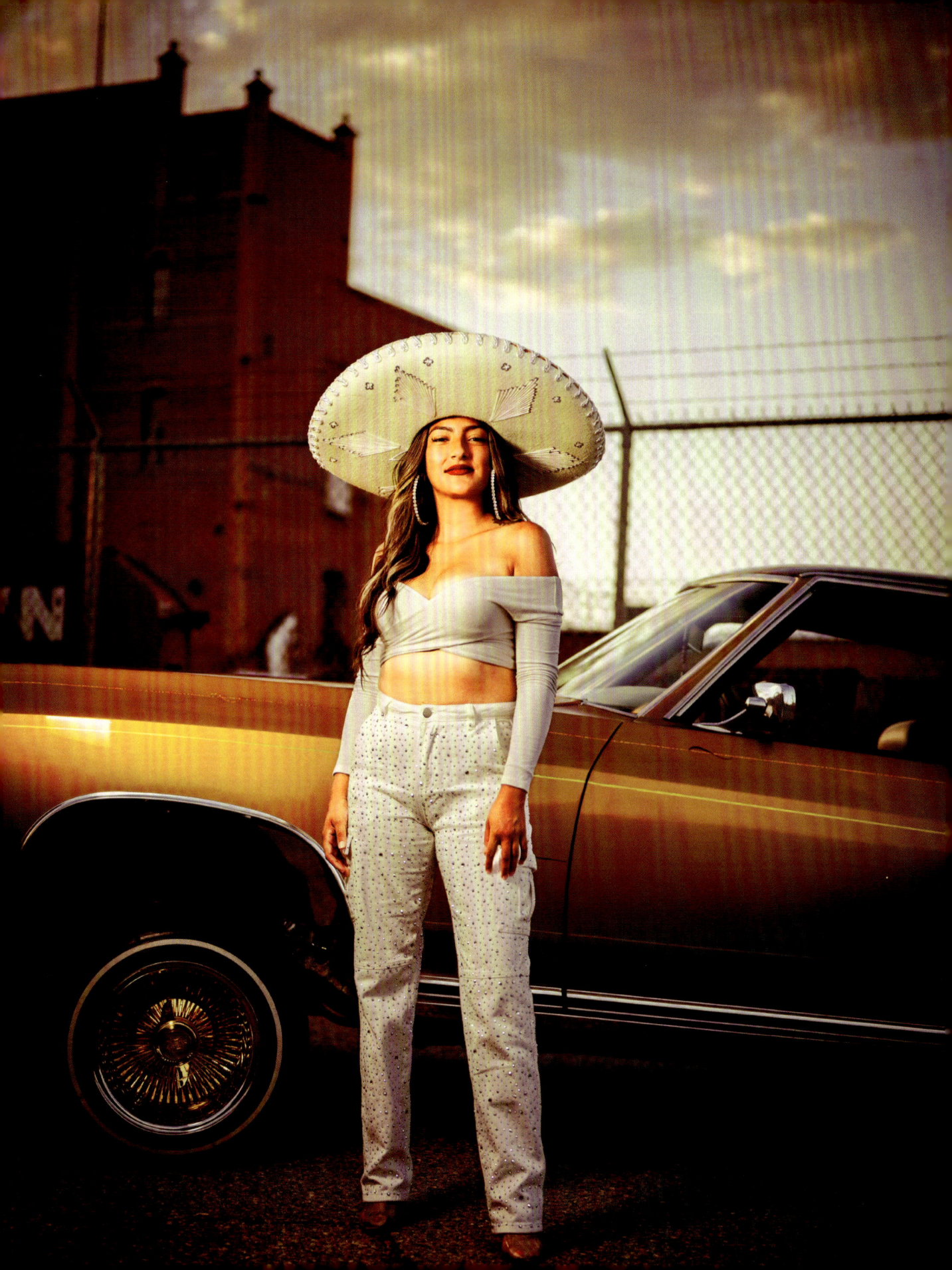

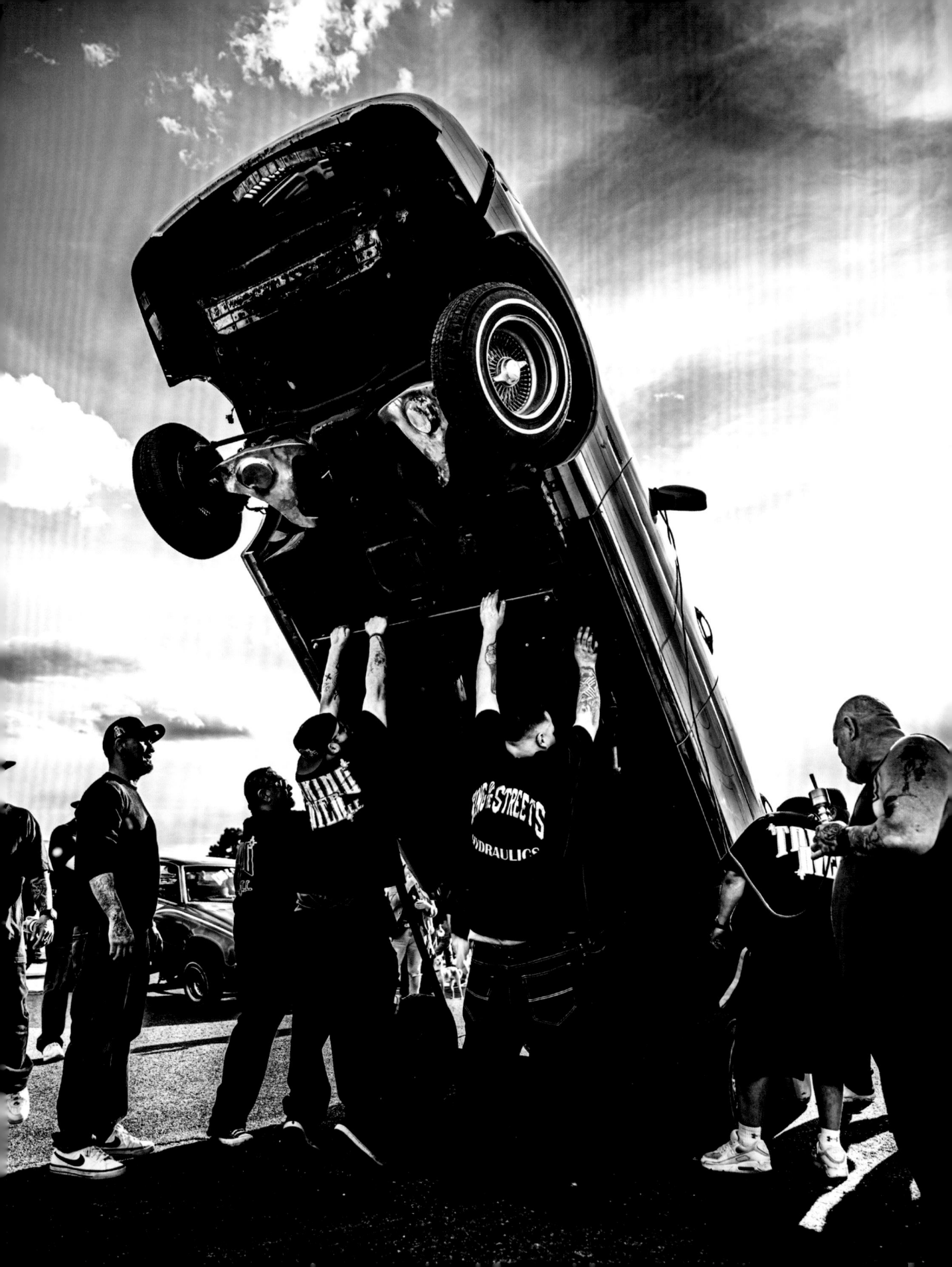

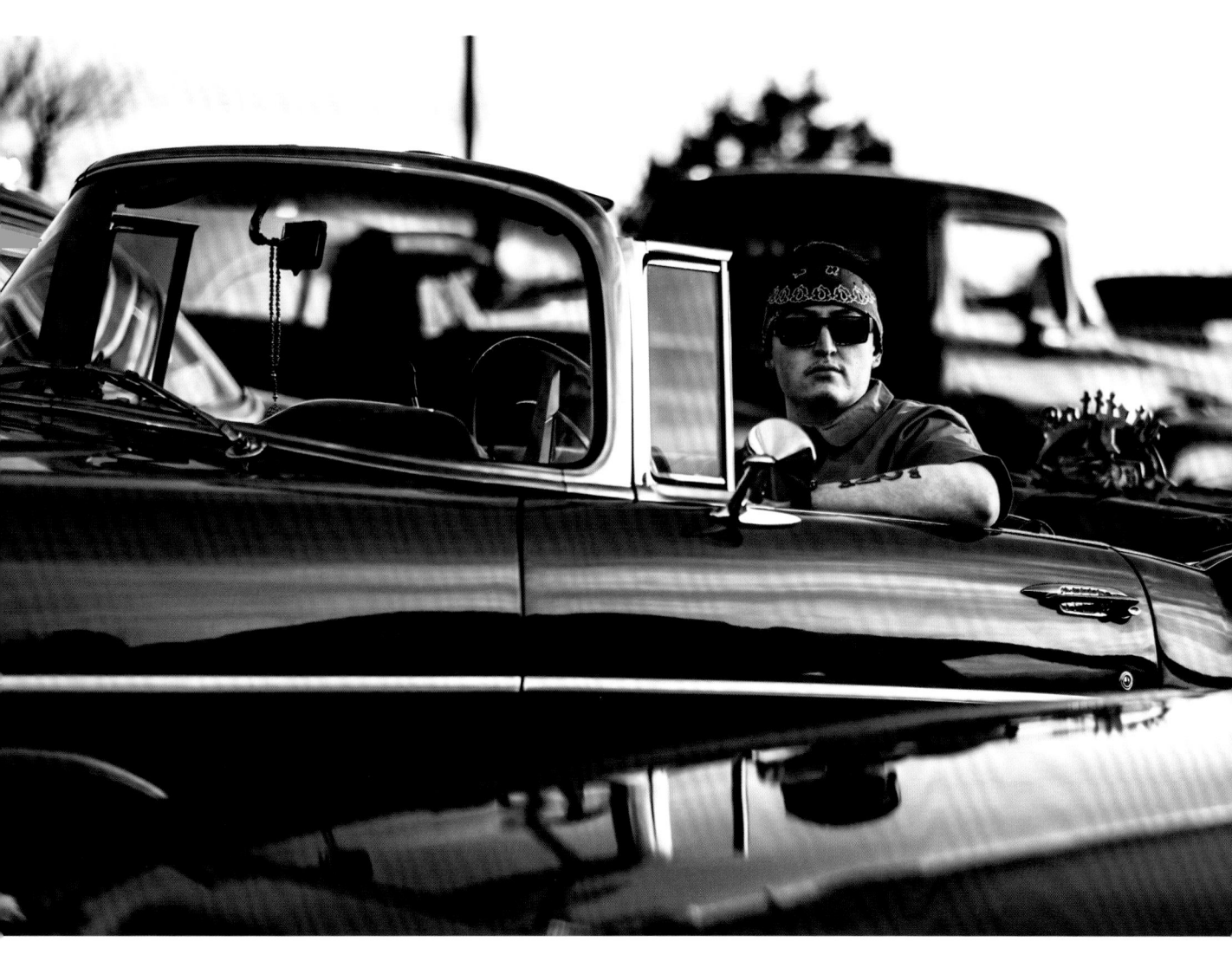

(*opposite page*) People pull down a stuck lowrider hopper, Española, New Mexico, 2024.

Margarito Jose Encarnación, Española, New Mexico, 2024.

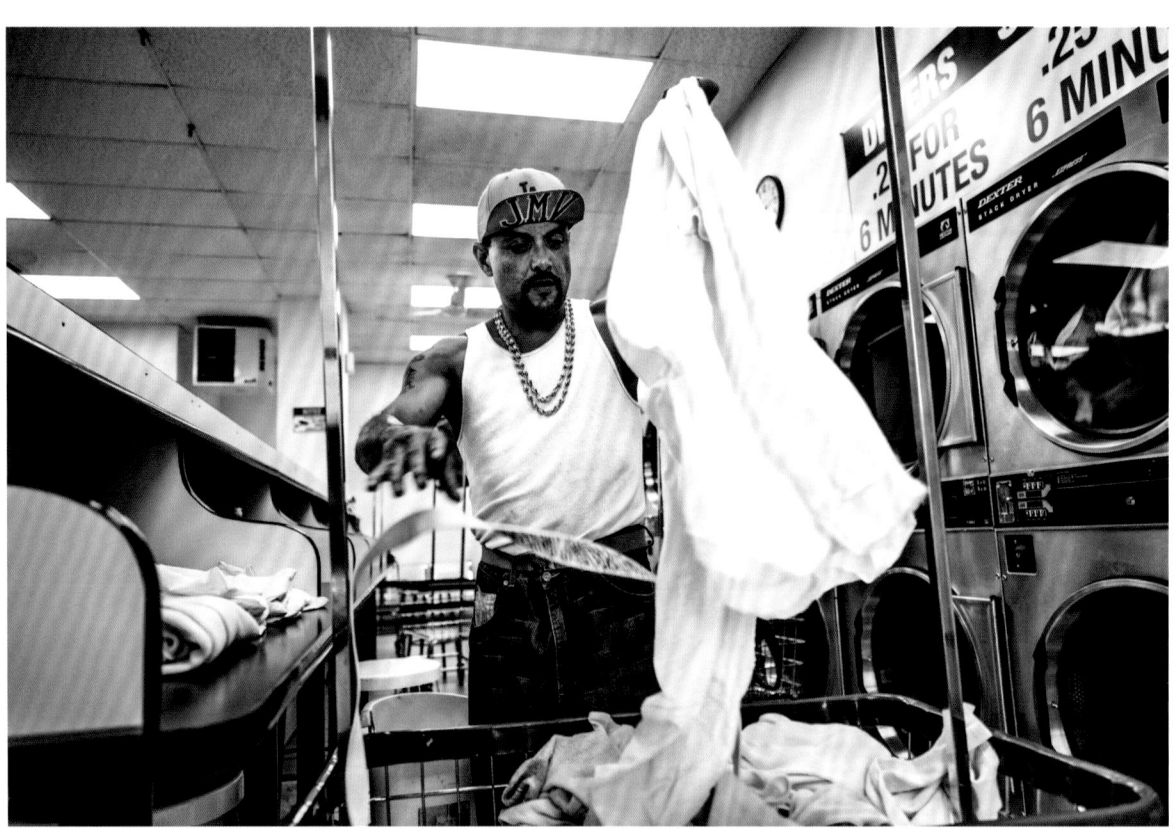

Flaco doing laundry, South Valley Washateria, Albuquerque, 2023.

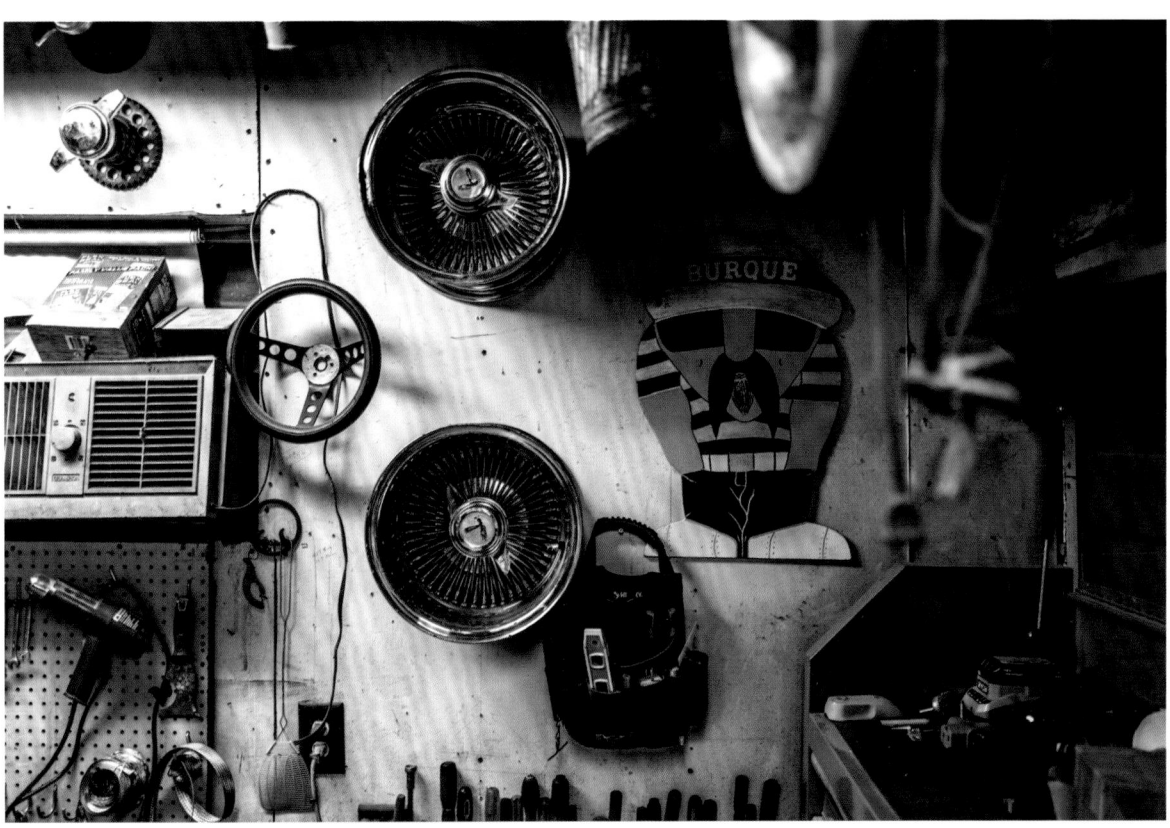

Lowrider workshop, South Valley, Albuquerque, 2024.

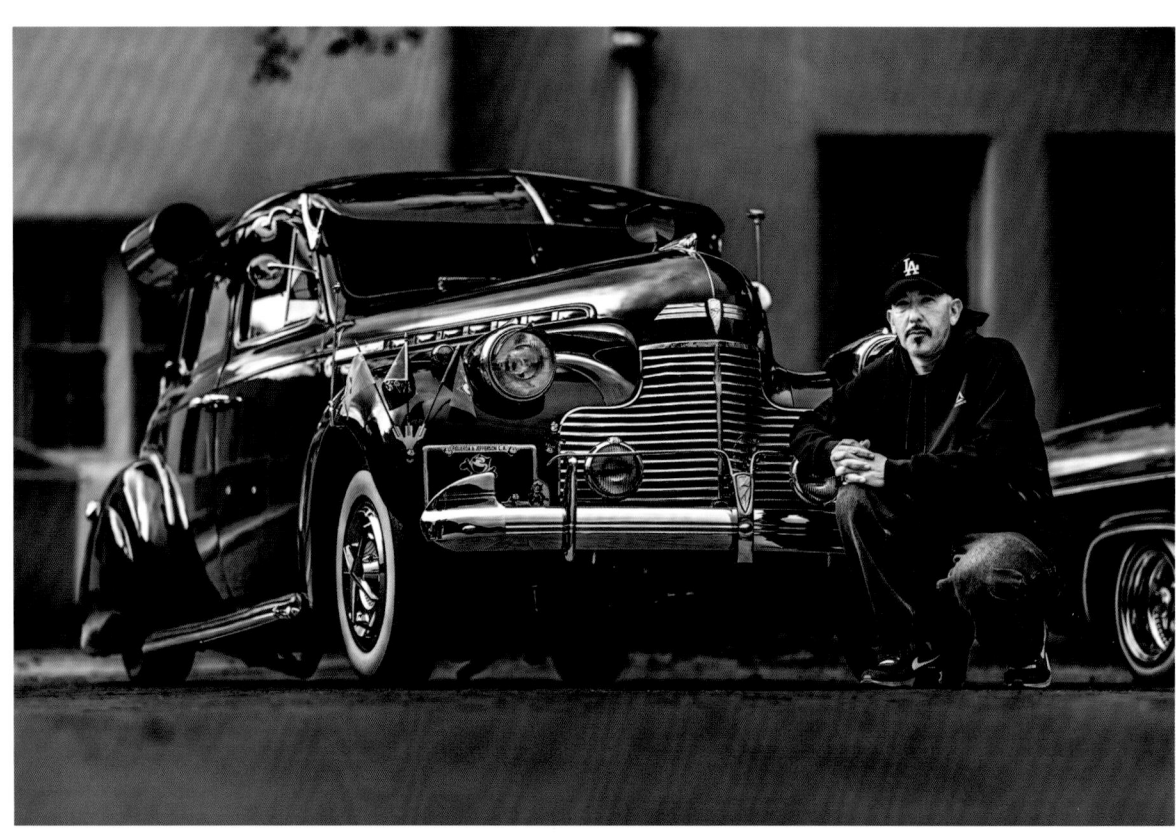

Clarence Valdez with his 1940 Chevrolet Master Deluxe, Barelas, Albuquerque, 2024.

(*opposite page*) Jesus Moralez, San Jose, Albuquerque, 2023.

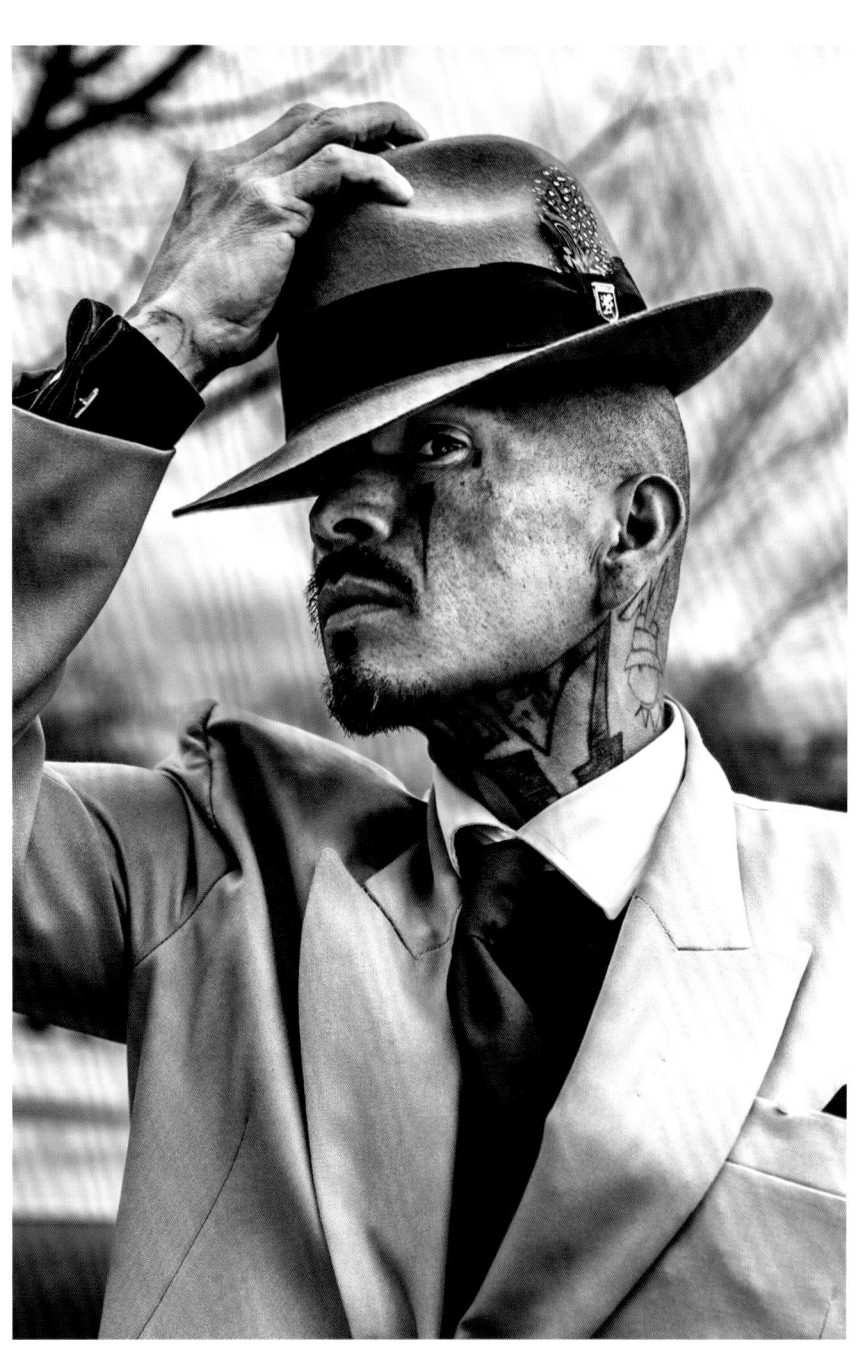

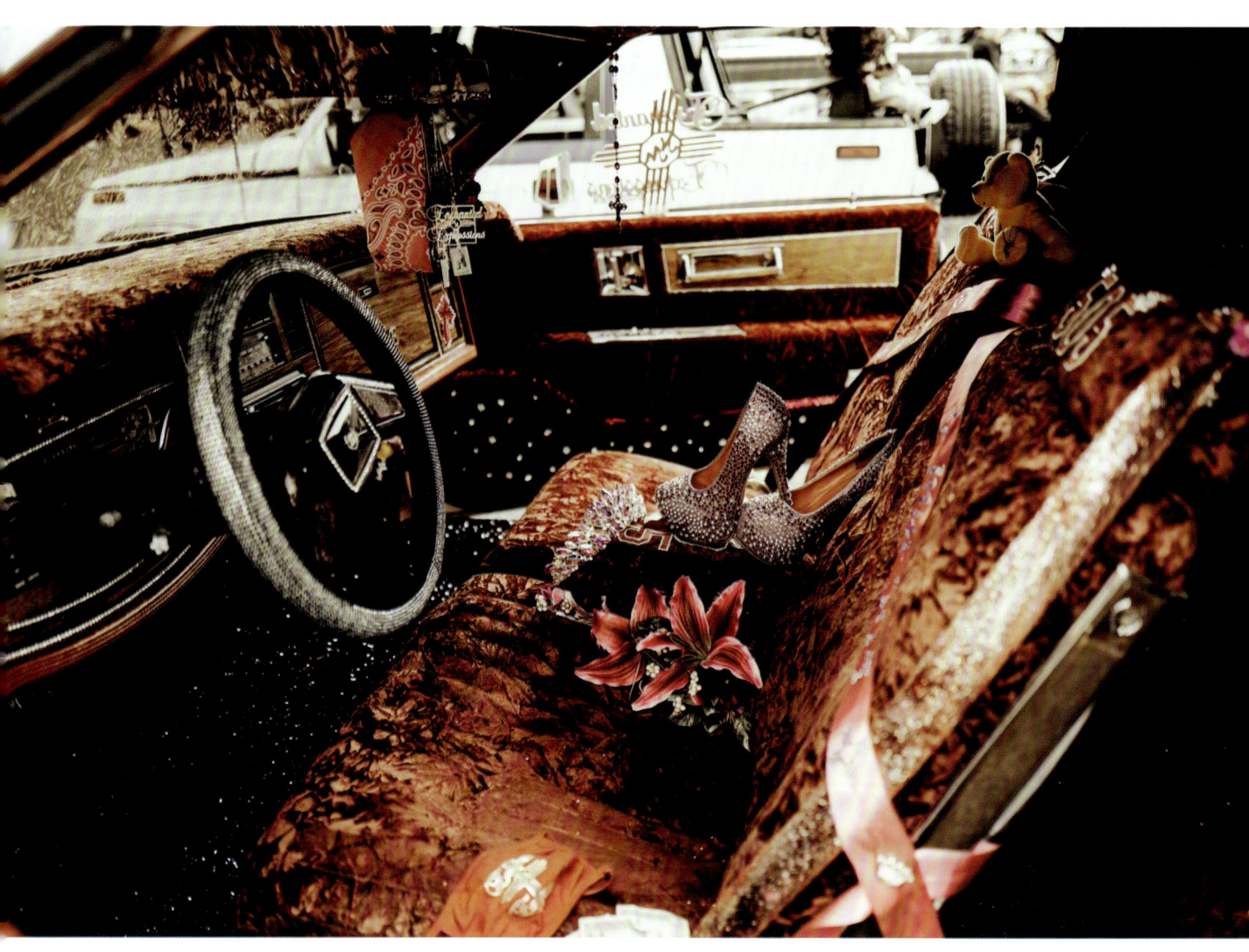

Interior of Justice Lovato's lowrider, Santa Fe, 2021.

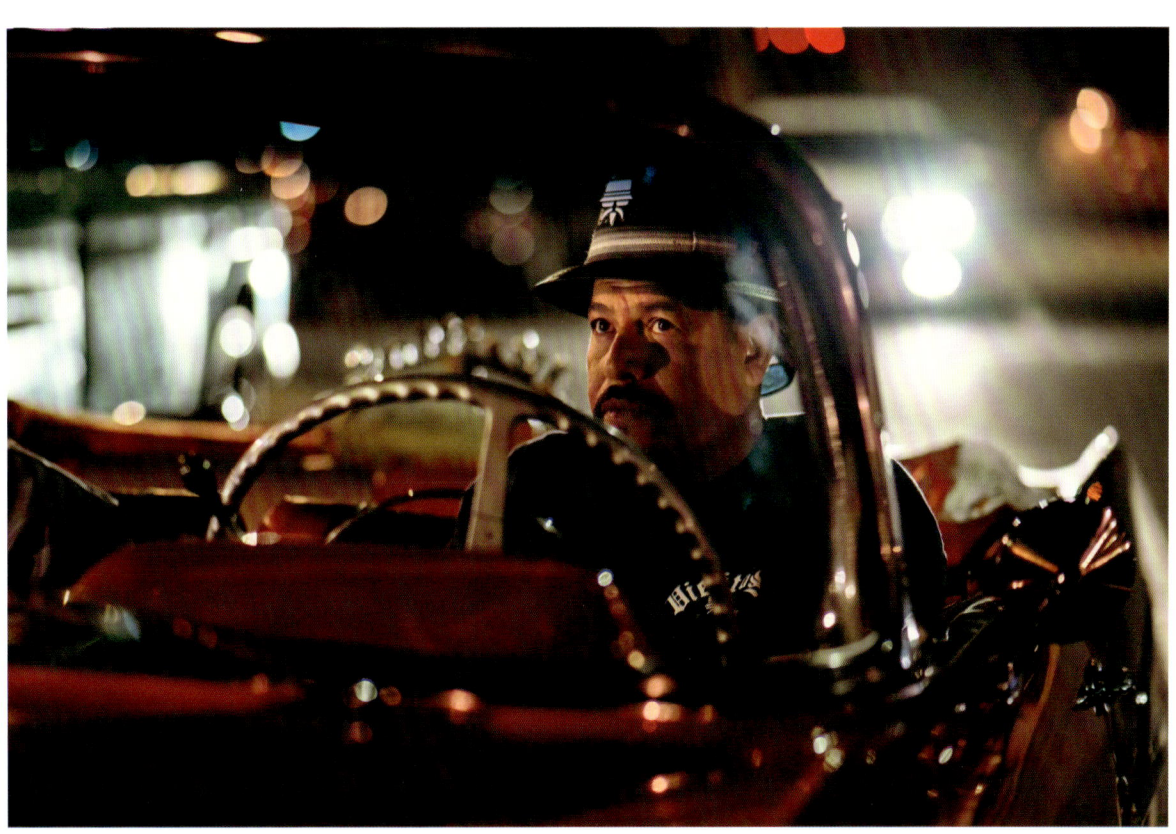

Viejitos cruising the town, Good Friday, Española, New Mexico, 2024.

(*following pages*) Downtown Albuquerque, 2021.

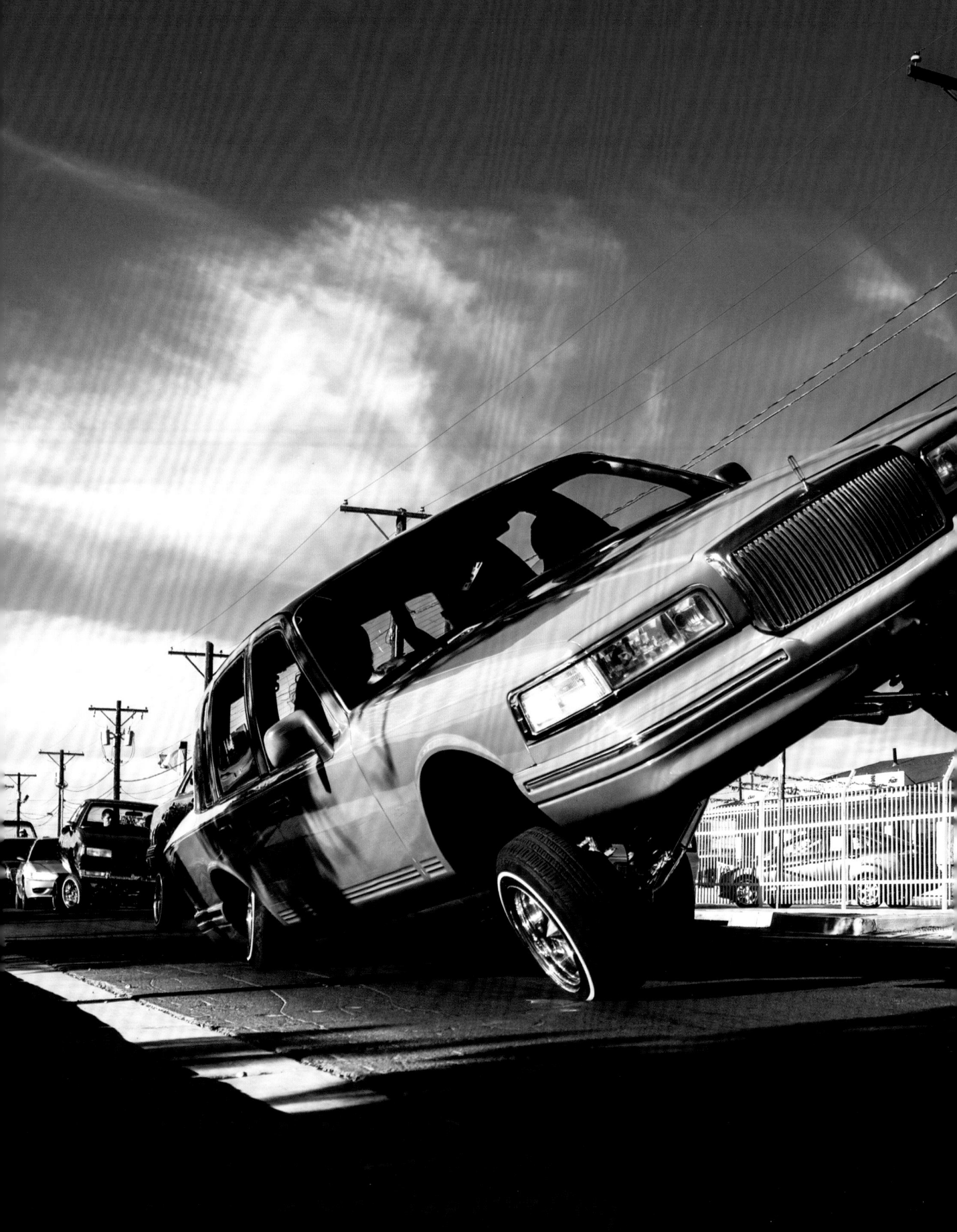

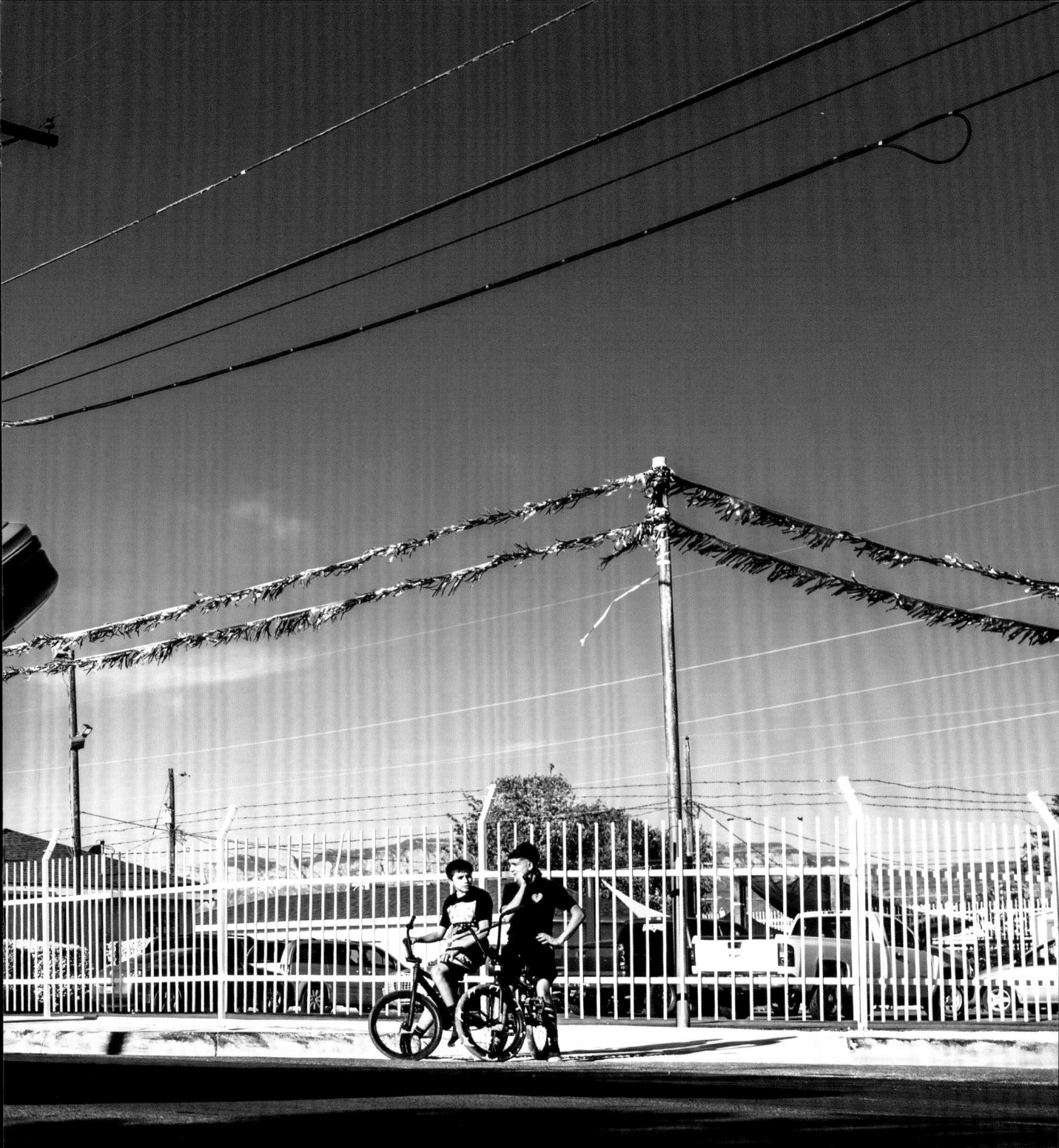

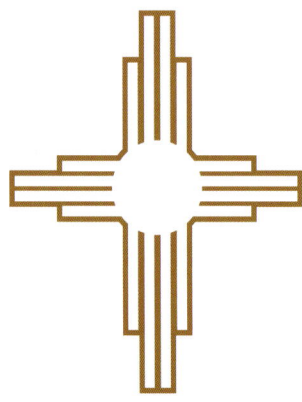